FOREVER FOREST

The Official
150th Anniversary
History of the
Original Reds

Don Wright

AMBERLEY

For David and Stephen, sons and good companions

First published 2015
This edition published 2016

Amberley Publishing
The Hill, Stroud
Gloucestershire, GL5 4EP

www.amberley-books.com

British Library Cataloguing in Publication Data.
A catalogue record for this book is available from the British Library.

ISBN 978 1 4456 6131 5 (paperback)
ISBN 978 1 4456 3517 0 (ebook)

Typeset in 10pt on 12pt Sabon.
Typesetting and origination by Amberley Publishing.
Printed in the UK.

Contents

PROLOGUE

The Game's Afoot

My first journey into real life was the discovery of football.
Gabriel Garcia Marquez, Columbian-born author and journalist,
winner of the 1982 Nobel Prize for Literature

The World Cup in 1966 wasn't won on the playing fields of England.
It was won on the streets.
Sir Bobby Charlton, World Cup winner

There's a boy in the street with a ball at his feet; a game in his mind, his mind on the game.

He plays a one-two off the kerbstones and volleys right-footed at the wall. Back the ball bounces. He plays a one-two off the kerbstones and volleys left-footed at the wall. First one foot, then the other. Again and again. First the inside of the foot, then the outside, then the instep for power. Repetition. Like a piano pupil practising scales. Finding a rhythm, speeding it up, slowing it down. Aiming at a block of bricks. Back the ball bounces. Bringing it down, he turns to dribble across the street. Left foot to right, right to left, left to right, right to left, left to right ... ten touches to the other side.

He plays a one-two off the kerbstones and volleys left-footed at the wall. Back the ball bounces. He plays a one-two off the kerbstones and volleys right-footed at the wall. First one foot, then the other. Again and again. First the inside of the foot, then the outside, then the instep for power. Repetition. Enjoying experimenting. Making the ball swerve and spin. Trying tricks. A sapling aiming to become a Tricky Tree. Back the ball bounces. Bringing it down, he turns to dribble across the street. Right foot to left, left to right, right to left, left to right, right to left ... ten touches to the other side.

He plays a one-two off the kerbstones. The game goes on ... in the mind ... on the street...

Uninterrupted.

In a back-street of terraced and semi-detached houses for miners, ironworkers, factory hands and their families, there is next to no traffic. No cars to disrupt the action. The gaps between the semis provide ideal goal spaces for shooting-in and three-a-side games when all the local lads come out to play. But all you need is a ball and you can play by yourself. That's the beauty of football.

Mr Grundy brings his pony-led milk cart to the street every morning. From a churn on the cart, he ladles the milk into the jugs brought to him by queuing housewives. On summer afternoons, he returns with home-made ice cream. He scoops it into the basins brought to him by queuing housewives, each one looking forward to ice cream with tinned fruit for tea.

Otherwise undisturbed, the boy is allowed to play his game. Except when the coal lorry arrives to empty its load: partly on the pavement and partly on the street. Nathan, a convalescent miner, brings his wheelbarrow and shovel. He shovels the coal into his wheelbarrow and wheels it round the back to the coalhouses to earn a few bob.

One day, to everyone's surprise, a car arrives and stops outside No. 37. What's more, emblazoned on both near and road sides is the legend 'Belle Vue Aces Speedway.' A man in a leather flying jacket gets out of the driver's seat and is welcomed at the front door. He goes inside and after a while comes out with June Isam on his arm. The boys on the street think she looks like a film star with her shoulder-length waves of blonde hair, a stray lock almost covering her right eye in the peek-a-boo style of Hollywood actress Veronica Lake. Now she is going out with a speedway star. Wow. For a brief interlude the ball is put away and the bikes are brought out. The boys race along Milton Road, turn left down Ash Street, left again along Cotmanhay Road, where the trackless electric bus runs, linked by two poles to overhead wires, then left up Milton Street to finish back on Milton Road. Ace. It's an exciting but short-lived diversion. Then, the bikes are returned to their sheds and the serious business of football is resumed.

Most of the boys are Derby fans, the Rams having won the first post-war FA Cup Final in 1946. One of them, Harry, has a season ticket and goes to matches with his parents. He reels off results, teams and goalscorers without hesitation. At school, a teacher overhears him and admonishes him: 'Coe, if only you could remember dates and events in history like that you'd be top of my class.' Harry is never top. In fact, he gets relegated to a lower form. Derby had beaten Charlton Athletic 4-1 after extra time at Wembley and *Children's Hour* on the BBC had been delayed so that the radio commentary could continue. R. A. J. 'Sailor' Brown, an England international inside-forward, played in the Charlton team but fell out with manager Jimmy Seed and was snapped up by Nottingham Forest. He is our boy's hero.

The year is 1947. There are ration books and shortages, which, oddly, help to keep bodies lean and fit, and Prime Minister Clement Attlee's reforming Labour Government is primed to introduce the National Health Service. If you'd said then that, in future years, the NHS would spend millions trying to combat obesity, the reply might have been, 'You must be joking.' On the wireless there's *Music While You Work* from the BBC's Light Programme with its signature tune 'Calling All Workers' composed by Hucknall-born Eric Coates – who was later to find fame with 'The Dam Busters' march. He also wrote 'By the Sleepy Lagoon' which still introduces *Desert Island Discs* on BBC Radio 4.

Stanley Matthews is famous worldwide, but two-footed Tom Finney is the boy's favourite footballer. Nottingham Forest are a struggling Second Division club. Star inside-right 'Sailor' Brown is soon to join Aston Villa for £10,000. Notts County are in the Third Division South but pull off arguably the most sensational transfer in the history of football. Tommy Lawton, the current England centre-forward, moves to Nottingham from First Division Chelsea for £17,000 plus promising wing-half Bill Dickson in part exchange. Players' wages are capped at a maximum of £12 a week, but Lawton gets a club house and a job with a typewriter firm. The papers are full of it. Everybody is talking about his transfer; the housewives with Mr Grundy, the coal merchant and Nathan leaning on his shovel.

It's like a story from *Boys' Own*. A fiction. Come to think of it, like Arnold Bennett's 1909 novel *The Card*. Denry Machin wants to be the youngest ever mayor. His rival is Councillor Barlow, chairman of the struggling local football club. Machin saves the club and becomes the most popular man in the Potteries by personally signing Callear, the greatest centre-forward in England. 'I don't see what football has got to do with being mayor,' protests Nellie, his wife. 'You're nothing but a cuckoo,' Denry pleasantly informs her. 'Football has got to do with everything.'

On the street the game goes on...

By himself, but not alone. First the boy is Forest, then he's Notts. And he's the referee, deciding which volley is worth a goal.

Lawton puts Notts in front. Brown equalizes for the Reds. Who will win?

Relegation lies ahead for Forest. In the 1949/50 season, both Nottingham clubs are in the Third Division South. Lawton will score thirty-one goals in thirty-seven games and Notts will be promoted. Forest will finish fourth with new centre-forward Wally Ardron announcing his arrival with twenty-five league goals.

Ardron will hit a club record thirty-six goals as Forest are crowned champions in the 1950/51 season. But the Lawton era – during which gates at Meadow Lane jump from an average of 7,500 spectators to 37,500 – makes Notts County the top team in Nottingham. Everyone wants to see the superstar, who scores ninety goals in 151 games for Notts before leaving for Brentford in March 1952.

The 1950s prove to be a fabulous period for Forest and change everything. The decade begins with promotion to Division Two and ends with triumph in the FA Cup Final on 2 May 1959. At Wembley, the 'Tricky Trees' defeat Luton Town 2-1 despite having to play the last hour with only ten men after goalscorer Roy Dwight breaks his leg. There are no substitutes allowed.

Ten Years On

1956/57 proved to be a defining season for the team, at the end of which Billy Walker's Reds returned to the First Division after fifty years outside the top flight. Forest began the campaign with away victories at Leyton Orient by 4-1 and at Bristol City 5-1. In his new season's message for the first home match on 25 August 1956 Chairman G. S. Oscroft wrote:

> As you know, we are a club with limited resources. However, with a 100 per cent effort by our players and, more important still, your whole-hearted support, we may all feel confident and hopeful that the arduous campaign ahead will bring us to our ambition – First Division football for Nottingham.

The Fulham side they played against that day included Roy Dwight at centre-forward and Tony Barton – who would later join Forest himself, in December, 1959 – on the right wing. Eddie Lowe – who later managed Notts County – was at inside-left. The winning start continued with Jim Barrett hitting the hat-trick that would take his goal tally to seven from three games.

Forest then led the division on goal average from Sheffield United and Swansea. Bristol City held us to a 2-2 draw at the City Ground at the end of August, but we began September in spectacular style, outplaying Swansea at the Vetch Field to triumph 4-1. It was our biggest win at Swansea for twenty-eight years. The national press raved about the quality of our football: the passing and movement, players supporting each other, keeping the ball, keeping it down, on the ground – 'the Walker Way.'

Doug Lishman scored two of Forest's goals against Swansea and went on to hit the target in four successive games. He had been a Football League championship winner with Arsenal in 1953, and a prolific scorer for the Gunners with 137 goals in 244 games. An astute signing by Walker for £8,000, the England B international had scored on his debut against Middlesbrough at the City Ground in March, 1956.

A crowd of 18,699 watched Forest beat Port Vale 4-2 at the City Ground on 22 September. They witnessed a match of greater significance than the result, important though that was. It had been highlighted in the newspapers as a clash between two former North London idols: Lishman against Eddie Baily – an England international inside-forward signed by

Vale from Tottenham Hotspur nine months earlier.

Billy Walker saw enough to know that if he could pair these two Forest would have a goal-scoring force of true promotion potential. His bid of £7,000 was accepted and Baily, wearing borrowed boots because of the speed of the transaction, made his debut at Huddersfield on 6 October. The Reds lost 1-0. The following week, at home to Bury, nearly 22,000 saw the Cockney 'cheeky chappie' Baily score twice with ex-Commando Lishman also on the scoresheet in a 5-1 win.

Lishman and Baily again got the goals, when a week, later Forest beat Notts County 2-1 before a 31,585-strong crowd at Meadow Lane. The two linked up well together and with strike partners Barrett and Tommy Wilson. The former push-and-run Spurs' star also brought the best out of speedy left-winger Stewart Imlach who produced some immaculate passing.

Alas, Forest had to run out of steam some time and guess who ended our impressive form? Who else but Brian Clough. A promising young man, he gave our great centre-half Bob McKinlay a November nightmare afternoon and stunned 20,000 fans (including me) at the City Ground with his first-ever league hat-trick as Middlesbrough crushed the Garibaldi Reds 4-0. Peter Taylor, incidentally, was in the visitors' goal.

An eleven-match unbeaten run in the league from the end of December was broken on 30 March by a 2-1 home defeat to Leicester City, who were now home and dry in the promotion race. We were left to battle with Blackburn Rovers and Liverpool for second place. Forest had beaten Liverpool at the City Ground in December with a goal by Baily but on 20 April during a visit at Anfield, 47,621 saw them gain revenge in a 3-1 defeat for the Tricky Trees.

So, to the dramatic finale. Sheffield United came to the City Ground on 22 April hoping to get back into the hunt, but they were seen off 2-1; Peter Higham and Wilson scoring our goals to the delight of 29,000 fans. Many Forest supporters (again including me) were at Bramall Lane five days later for the return match, which we needed to win to ensure promotion. There were 28,000 fans occupying three sides of the ground – in those days one length of the pitch was open to the cricket field.

Even the most optimistic of us could not have imagined such a masterly performance as Forest blunted a Blades' team that included goalkeeper Alan Hodgkinson; centre-half Joe Shaw; wing-half Jim Iley (who would later join Forest from Spurs) and, England international, inside-forward Jimmy Hagan.

Dynamic and deadly, Lishman crowned a brilliant performance with a never-to-be-forgotten hat-trick, with Wilson the other scorer, in a 4-0 triumph. It was Lishman's swan-song. He retired aged thirty-four at the season's end to manage the family furniture business.

A crowd of 32,000 went to the City Ground on 1 May to celebrate promotion at the final Division Two match of the season and saw Imlach and Wilson score Forest's goals. But Notts County scored four. Typical Forest. Defeat did not stop the celebrations as thousands of fans swarmed on to the pitch to cheer as the players appeared in front of them waving from the committee/directors' box.

Most thought Notts would follow the Reds to Division One. Instead, County went into decline and descended first into the Third Division and then Division Four. Billy Walker had taken the club from pit to pinnacle and made Forest king of the castle in Nottingham.

PART ONE

The First 50 Years

Nottingham is one of the most pleasant and beautiful towns in England.
Daniel Defoe, *A Tour Through the Whole Island of Great Britain* (1724–26)

Even football's not what it was, not by a long chalk.
D. H. Lawrence, *Lady Chatterley's Lover* (1929)

I

Redshirts and Lace

Wherever you may be in the world mention you're from Nottingham and the response will almost certainly be: ah yes, Robin Hood. Or else: Brian Clough, ah yes.

They are the two characters – legends even – most associated abroad with the city. Anti-establishment figures and radicals with social consciences, both are commemorated by city centre statues. Robin Hood's stands beneath the castle wall; Brian Clough's, appropriately, at Speakers' Corner overlooking the Old Market Square – known locally as Slab Square.

Cloughie's retirement in 1993, after eighteen years as Forest manager, was prematurely announced to the Press by the then chairman Fred Reacher. The mishandling of the great man's departure soured relations with the Clough family, much to the dismay of supporters. But, at least, at the last Premiership home game of the season, a 2-0 defeat by Sheffield United on 1 May, a crowd of nearly 27,000 gave him the send-off he deserved. We were relegated, but our fans and Sheffield's stayed behind to chant Brian Clough's name. Cloughie acknowledged them with his famous thumbs-up gesture.

Fifteen years later, on Thursday 6 November 2008, the Clough family gathered at the City Ground to meet fund-raisers and former players and travel with them in specially chartered coaches to the city centre where a magnificent nine-foot high bronze statue of Brian Clough stood under a green drape ready to be revealed to thousands of supporters who had come to the Old Market Square. Many more watched on regional television as Brian's widow, Mrs Barbara Clough, carefully released the drape and there was the great man, lifelike in his sweatshirt and tracksuit bottoms, hands clasped above his head, seemingly sharing the celebration with the fans.

Mrs Clough said that, when she first saw the statue, it took her breath away. The sculptor, Les Johnson, had achieved perfection. Local radio journalist Marcus Alton, who brought together the statue fund and volunteers, tells their story in his book *Young Man, You've Made My Day*.

He commented, 'Not only was the statue impressive, so were its surroundings.' Three of Cloughie's famous quotes had been engraved in the granite paving around the sculpture. They were: 'I wouldn't say I was the best manager in the business but I was in the top one'; 'If God had wanted us to play football in the clouds, he'd have put grass up there' and 'We talk about it for twenty minutes and then we decide that I was right.'

The quotes had been voted his best three in an online poll by visitors to the website www.brianclough.com, which was initially created by Marcus to campaign for a knighthood for Brian Clough and then to promote the statue fund. Though Clough never did receive a knighthood, he was made a Freeman of the City of Nottingham and received an honorary degree from Nottingham University.

The Clough statue has become a favourite meeting place for local people and visitors alike. It's a good departure point for a short journey to where the Forest story began 150 years ago. Parliament Street is the base of a triangle formed with King Street and Queen Street at the apex of which is Speakers' Corner and the bronze Brian.

We are heading for The Forest. It's an easy walk of about a mile but, just for fun, let's go by tram. We cross Slab Square in front of the Council House, Nottingham's seat of local government, about which Ken Dodd once joked, 'If that's what you call a council house put me down for one.' The Little John hour bell which hangs in the great dome of the Council House weighs 10 ½ tons. The famous bell's clock mechanism was manufactured and installed by Nottingham clockmaker William Cope in the 1920s. He combined the movement of the clock with the striking of the bell. At the time, it was the largest most accurate electric chiming clock in the world and, being the deepest toned clock bell in the country, could be heard for a distance of seven miles.

We catch the supertram at South Parade and travel along Angel Row, across Long Row and up Market Street to the next stop at Theatre Square. To our right is the Theatre Royal, which opened in September 1865 with a production of Richard Brinsley Sheridan's *The School for Scandal*. At almost the same time, just down the road from the theatre, the inaugural meeting of Nottingham Forest Football Club was taking place at the Clinton Arms in Sherwood Street. The classic facade and Corinthian columns make the theatre, now part of the Royal Centre, a major city landmark. Designed by Charles J. Phipps, it was built for £15,000 after being commissioned by lace manufacturers John and William Lambert. Restoration in the 1970s cost the City Council £4 million. The lace connection is another link with Forest.

Now the tram takes us along Goldsmith Street and Waverley Street between the impressive colleges of Nottingham Trent University. We pass the Arboretum on the way to the High School stop and then we arrive at our destination The Forest. An urban public recreational space, it is bounded by the neighbourhoods of Forest Fields to the north, Mapperley

Park to the east, Arboretum to the south and Hyson Green to the west. The Forest name derives from medieval times, when the land was the southern-most part of the legendary Robin Hood's Sherwood Forest that extended from the city to the north of the county. It is protected in perpetuity by the 1845 Nottingham Inclosure Act commemorated by the 'Inclosure Oak' still to be seen at the Mansfield Road entrance. It occupies around eighty acres which were previously part of a vast open area once known as the Lings and covered by gorse and scrubs that extended into the parishes of Lenton, Radford and Basford.

The Forest is a huge natural amphitheatre and in the nineteenth century a line of thirteen windmills stood at the top overlooking a racecourse below. They were removed after the Inclosure Act but there are markers along the path where they once stood. The criss-cross formation of pathways on The Forest that today form part of a city-wide network of walks linking recreation grounds, parks and open spaces were designed by Sir Joseph Paxton, creator of the Crystal Palace – the huge glass structure that housed the Great Exhibition of 1851 in London's Hyde Park. Paxton was the Duke of Devonshire's head gardener at Chatsworth House, Derbyshire, where he designed gardens, fountains and an arboretum. He also built a conservatory – known as the Great Conservatory – and a lily house, specially made for a giant lily, with a design based on the leaves of the plant.

Fame came with Prince Albert's Great Exhibition. Paxton, visiting London, heard that more than 200 plans for the main exhibition hall had been rejected. Within days he delivered his own design – a vastly magnified version of the lily house at Chatsworth. It was comparatively cheap, easy to erect, simple to dismantle and remove; further to this, it was revolutionary, being modular, prefabricated and extensively glass. Two thousand men were drafted to erect the Palace in Hyde Park and it was an enormous success. Six million people visited the exhibition that ran from 1 May to 15 October, and Paxton was later knighted by a grateful Queen Victoria. After the event, the magnificent structure was dismantled and re-erected at the top of Sydenham Hill in South London, where the National Sports Centre now stands. Its name was adopted by Crystal Palace Football Club. Paxton died in 1865.

Flora and fauna are abundant at The Forest. Mature trees include oaks, elms, rowan, silver birch, lime and horse chestnut and there have been recent plantings of London plane, beech and various maples. Perennials include autumn and spring crocus, bluebell and primrose. Unsurprisingly, The Forest attracts many birds including the tawny owl, song thrush, woodpecker and chaffinch. Above the recreation ground the caves of the Victorian Rock Cemetery are a Geological County Wildlife Site. The sandstone caves are known as Robin Hood's Caves. They are reputed to have been the regular hiding place of Robin Hood and his band when they ventured into Nottingham. One can easily imagine Robin, the champion archer, winning the tournament for the Sheriff's Silver Arrow and stopping at the caves to shed his disguise before vanishing with his men into the safety and shelter of Sherwood.

Still the club's spiritual home, today The Forest provides football pitches, and is also well-known to visitors as the site of the annual and ancient Goose Fair. It has recently undergone a £5.2 million restoration with £3.2 million from the Heritage Lottery and £2 million from the City Council, the Cavendish Foundation and other donors. The refurbished pavilion, at the centre of the recreation ground, includes the park ranger's office and a function room as well as changing rooms. Forest football followers might consider supporting the Friends of The Forest, a voluntary group that seeks to protect and maintain The Forest as an accessible, open, green space of historic importance for the city of Nottingham and the football club.

∞

Many of the young men who became the first Forest footballers lived within half-a-mile of the recreation ground where they played, and most were engaged in Nottingham's world famous lace industry. They had begun by playing shinney (or shinty) – a rough form of hockey that seems to have had Celtic origins. But, according to an early historian, by 1864 football had become the more favoured game. That was also the year Nottinghamshire Football Club (Notts County) had been formally established although the Notts men had played the game informally since 1862.

So, in 1865, the Foresters decided to formalize their change of principal sport from shinney to football by establishing the Forest Football Club and a meeting was held at the Clinton Arms in Sherwood Street, which then was little more than a country lane, about half-a-mile away. The hostelry faced Nottingham Cattle Market, which then stood on the site now occupied by the Guildhall. The convenor was J.S. Scrimshaw and fourteen others attended. They were: A. Barks, W. Brown, W. P. Brown, C. E. Daft, T. Gamble, R. P. Hawksley, T. G. Howitt, W. L. Hussey, W. R. Lymbery, J. S. Milford, J. H. Rastall, W. H. Revis, J. G. Richardson and J. Tomlinson. Nottingham was added to the club's title in 1867, when shinney was dropped as an activity altogether.

The founders instructed William Brown to purchase a dozen red caps, complete with tassels, for the players. In those days a team was identified by its headgear and this custom survives to the present day with the awarding of international caps. Forest thus became the original Reds of world football. It was stipulated that the Forest colour would be 'Garibaldi Red'; Giuseppe Garibaldi was the great popular hero of Italian unification and leader of a volunteer army, the Redshirts, who in the spring of 1860 conquered Sicily and then crossed to the mainland and made a victorious march through Italy. He stood for nationalism, freedom and romance and was one of the first celebrities of the new age of mass media. In 1864 Garibaldi came to England on a brief visit and was received with astonishing enthusiasm by populace and princes alike. But he was an inspiration for English radicalism, alarming Queen Victoria who urged her prime minister, Lord Palmerston, to persuade him to cut short his stay. Garibaldi departed these shores but the English paid him the tribute of immortalising his name in blouses and biscuits.

Forest's 'Garibaldi red' caps were bought from another of the original members Charles Daft, a shopkeeper and member of an illustrious sporting family in Nottingham. Cricketer Richard Daft was reckoned to be England's best professional batsman in the early 1870s. Four of the Daft family played cricket for Notts and Richard's son, Harry, also played football for both Notts County and Forest. Charles was in the Forest team for its first match on 22 March 1866, when the opponents were, of course, Notts County.

The challenge match was played at home on the old racecourse on The Forest. According to the club's nineteenth-century historian neither side scored until close upon time when:

> After a sort of steeplechase race across the goal-line and over the railings nearest the grandstand between Hugh Browne and W. H. Revis, the ball was touched down by the latter and the place kick, fifteen yards at right angles from the goal-line, taken by the same player. Thus the first of many interesting games between the two clubs in after years, ended in a win of one goal to nothing for the Forest.

To score, the ball had to be kicked between the goalposts, but there was no crossbar at that time. Revis converted. But the next day the *Nottingham Daily Guardian* reported that 'It was a well-contested match throughout' but 'neither club succeeded in winning a goal.' Eleven of Notts had played seventeen of Forest, said the paper, naming the Notts side but admitting: 'We were unable to ascertain the names of the Forest club.'

The *Guardian* added: 'The Forest men were too strong for any club to allow them such odds.' The game had been seen by 'a considerable number of ladies and gentlemen'. Given the detailed description provided by our man, the historian, and the lack of information in the newspaper report, the evidence supports his version. Clearly the paper did not have a representative present and probably picked up its information from someone after the game's conclusion – possibly connected with the Notts club since no Forest names were known. A contemporary account quoted by Dr Percy M. Young in his *A History of British Football* (1968), upholds the historian's conclusion:

> After a long, negative, scoreless, afternoon, there was a sort of steeplechase between a player named Hugh Browne, of Notts, and

W. H. Revis, of the Forest. The latter touched down the ball, and the place kick, which was taken fifteen yards at right angles to the goal-line, being successful, the Forest were proclaimed winners of the first great match between the rivals.

This report appeared in *The Tourist's Picturesque Guide to Nottingham*, published in Nottingham in 1871.

A return match away to Notts on 19 April was goalless. The two clubs met again on Thursday 13 December in the Meadows, Nottingham, and produced another draw. It was a bright but windy Thursday afternoon and, according to the *Nottingham Review*, when the players 'spread out, the field looked exceedingly picturesque with the orange and black stripes of Notts and the red and white of the Foresters.' The Reds scored first when 'W. Lymbery, by a very fine kick, sent the ball flying through the Notts goalposts.' The equalizer came with thirty-five minutes left to play. Lymbery, reported the *Review* 'was very prominent in the field.' It was at The Forest that Notts finally avenged their first 'derby' defeat when, on Thursday 28 February 1867, according to the Nottingham Journal, W. A. Hodges scored the only goal after 'a smart piece of dribbling.'

Notts County, founded in 1862 (though not formally constituted until December 1864) and Nottingham Forest (1865) are the oldest of the clubs in the Football League or the Premier League. Stoke City celebrated their 'centenary' in 1963, claiming to have been founded by a group of Old Carthusians who had taken engineering jobs at North Staffordshire Railway Company. In fact, according to historians John Ballard and Paul Suff in *World Soccer's Dictionary of Football*, published in 1999, they were formed in 1868 by railway workers as Stoke Ramblers. Stoke went into liquidation and resigned from the League in 1907. A new limited company football club was established but had to wait until 1919/20 to gain League status. The Marshall Cavendish six-volume *Book of Football*, published in seventy-five weekly parts in 1971 and 1972, stated of Stoke City, 'There is no record of the club existing before 1867, which makes it the League's fourth oldest member (after Notts County, Forest and Chesterfield) rather than the second, as they like to suggest.' Forest first met Stoke in the Potteries on 14 December, 1872, when neither side scored. The return match at The Forest was won by the home side 3-0.

No matter, the world's first football club was none of those but Sheffield FC, formed on 24 October 1857, and now members of the Northern Premier League. They were early lawmakers. The *Sheffield Rulebook* had been written in 1859 by Nathaniel Creswick and William Prest, founder members of the club. Sheffield played Forest in both friendlies and the FA Cup competition. The first Nottingham 'derby' was as strongly influenced by the Sheffield rules as by those of the Football Association in London, adopted on 1 December 1863, and published in pamphlet form. Just as influential were the ten rules of *The Simplest Game* issued in June 1862 by John Charles Thring, a master at Uppingham School in Rutland, not a great distance from Nottingham. Certainly, the FA took into account the earlier laws formulated at Sheffield and Uppingham as well as those of Cambridge University.

Creswick, Prest and Thring were firm in the conviction that the kicking game was superior. Handling should not be allowed and nor should hacking, defined as 'kicking an opponent on the front of the leg below the knee.' Handling and hacking were 'rugbeian ideas' complained Thring according to N. L. Jackson in his classic *Association Football*, published in 1899. It took half-a-dozen meetings to classify and codify The Football Association Laws of 1863, which, as Thring wanted, disallowed carrying and throwing the ball, together with hacking. So football took its first step towards becoming 'the beautiful game' – much to the disgust of the Blackheath club, whose representative denounced these exclusions as so 'unmanly' that 'Frenchmen' would beat us. Quite a perceptive remark really.

In Melvyn Bragg's *12 Books that Changed the World*, published in 2006, *The Rule Book of The Football Association* (1863) is listed alongside Isaac Newton's *Principia Mathematica* (1687), *Magna Carta* (1215), *On the Origin of Species'* by Charles Darwin (1859), *On the Abolition of the Slave Trade* by William Wilberforce (1789), and *The First Folio* of William Shakespeare's plays (1623). It would seem to be an extravagant claim, such an inclusion, until one considers that soccer is spread further than any of the world's religions and that there are more countries in membership of FIFA than belong to the United Nations. Lord Bragg, who is an Arsenal supporter, attributed the authorship of the Laws of Association Football to a few 'Oxbridge' graduates. An East Midlands teacher and a silver plate manufacturer and a wine merchant, both from Sheffield, made their contributions, too. Forest made a bulk purchase of 120 copies of the FA Laws in 1873 at a cost of 12 *s* and 8 *p*.

The Reds played a goalless draw against Sheffield Norfolk at The Forest on Boxing Day 1867 and, interestingly, the return match was at Bramall Lane, now Sheffield United's ground, on Shrove Tuesday 1868, when the home side won 1-0. Some idea of the varied rules by which the games were still being played can be gained from a report in the *Nottingham Review* of Forest's visit to Newark on 16 January that same season. The match took place on Newark's London Road ground and the *Review* commented, 'The Nottingham team was all abroad at first on account of the Newark rules being totally dissimilar to their own.' However, 'some first-rate play was shown on both sides and, altogether, the match was a very enjoyable one.' Unsurprisingly, neither side scored.

Few goals were scored in the early games involving Notts and the Reds but that changed on 9 February 1875, when 'a large number of spectators' at The Forest saw a 5-1 home victory. 'The previous match this season was a tie and this, coupled with the fact that the Notts team had been showing good form having as late as Saturday last beaten the formidable

Sheffield club, made the present issue doubly interesting,' it was reported. 'The Foresters were never seen to play better than yesterday, the result being the signal defeat of the Notts club,' the local press commented. Sam Widdowson captained the Reds and the side included Lymbery and Revis.

Notts wore amber and black hooped shirts until 1880, then chocolate and Cambridge blue halves before, in 1890, black and white stripes were adopted, bringing them the nickname 'Magpies' by which they are still known. The Notts club also became a limited company. Red has always been the Forest colour and they are commonly known as the Garibaldi Reds or just the Reds. They are also called the Foresters, the Tricky Trees or, simply, the Trickies, conjuring, with their passing, patterns on the pitch as intricate as Nottingham's famous lace. 'Trickies' may sound like a modern appellation but, in fact, it dates back to the late nineteenth century when it was said, 'The Redshirts play the trickiest game in the country.'

2

Father Figure

Known as 'the Grand Old Man of Nottingham Sport', Walter Roe Lymbery played football until he was thirty-three, cricket until seventy-three and golf until eighty. By then he was also called 'a young man grown white'. He was a striking figure with white hair, moustache and beard, and he bore a passing resemblance to King Edward VII.

Most importantly, he was one of the young shinney players on the Forest recreation ground who cast aside their sticks to take up football. Except that Walter didn't totally discard his shinney stick. He handed it down through the family as an heirloom. His grandson, the late Ian Lymbery, carried it to bed with him as a useful weapon should burglars break into the house. Now, thanks to a generous loan by Ian's nephew Nick Clifford and other members of the Lymbery family, Walter's shinney stick has pride of place in the Forest collection, pre-dating all other artefacts and, indeed, the club itself.

It's possible that shinney, shinny or shinty – it's known by all three names – was introduced to the young men of Nottingham by Walter, whose family had Irish connections. When in the seventeenth century Oliver Cromwell subjugated the whole of Ireland many large estates, taken from Catholic overlords, were given to his forces in lieu of payment. Kilcup House and lands in County Waterford were part of these forfeited properties and Gregory Lymbery became its new owner. Lymberys were to reside there for generations. One of Gregory's descendants, John Lymbery, came to Nottingham in 1806 and built the first house in Hyson Green. He founded a dynasty of lace manufacturers. Walter was his grandson.

Yet there is no doubt that Walter was influential in the switch from shinney to football. Not only was he one of the fifteen young men who met at the Clinton Arms in Sherwood Street in the autumn of 1865 to establish the Forest Football Club but he became the first chairman. Scrimshaw, the convenor, was never elected chairman. Lymbery held that office from 1866 to 1868, when he took over from J. S. Milford as secretary and carried out that role until 1886. He was also club captain and, in 1869, effectively became secretary/treasurer determined to put the accounts in order.

He and (first goal scorer) W. H. Revis were both stewards of the Forest Football Club Athletic Sports held for the first time on 23rd April, 1870, at Trent Bridge. It was reported that thousands of spectators ringed the field, among them many 'fashionably costumed ladies.' Revis won the prize for kicking a football furthest with a kick of 161 feet 8 inches. A cycle race over a mile was won by J. Cumberland with a time of 4 minutes 45 seconds. S. Jackson won the high jump with a leap of 4 feet 8 inches and Lymbery tied for second place with a competitor named Crisp at 4 feet 6 inches. The sports were so successful that they were held at Trent Bridge on the first Saturday of May up to and including 1911. Sam Widdowson became a star performer over the hurdles, as a sprinter, in the half-mile and mile races and in the steeple-chase.

William Henry Revis was educated at Nottingham High School and worked in the lace industry before spending fifteen years in the United States as an import merchant. He returned to Nottingham in 1914, becoming a hosiery manufacturer. On his death in 1923, he left a bequest totalling £48,000 to University College, Nottingham, to fund scholarships for poor students. The W. H. Revis Bequest Fund is still active supporting students at Nottingham University. Next to Lord Trent (Jesse Boot founder of Boots the chemists), Revis remains the university's most generous benefactor: Forest's first goal scorer, what a man he was.

Lymbery's first book-keeping entry upon taking charge of the club's accounts was: 'Cash in hand ... ten pence'. By 1872 the kitty had risen to nearly £9. It fluctuated above and below the £10 mark until £20 was topped in 1880.

Since there was no 'gate' money, funds came chiefly from the players' pockets. They each paid a match fee of 1 *s*. That went up to 5 *s* a month and, in 1875, an additional membership fee of 10 *s* was introduced. Two years later that had gone up to one guinea. The club bought the kit but charged players 1*s* 6*d* for a cap, 3*s* 2*d* or 4*s* 3*d* for a shirt (depending upon quality) and 2*s* 6*d* for a pair of socks.

Lymbery records paying one shilling to the groundsman, F. Moore, for cleaning four balls and threepence for 'ball mending'. Postcards notifying players of their selection were delivered by an errand girl, who received sixpence.

In December 1872 there was a charge probably significant in the history of football. The sum of five pence was found for an umpire's whistle. This is the earliest record of the umpire (referee) having a whistle to control the game.

In December 1879 Forest paid Midland Railway 12 *s* for damage to a saloon carriage. Victory high spirits or early Christmas revelry, who knows? Shortly after this the club had to reimburse a Mrs Bates the sum of 27s for damage to a perambulator caused by a visiting Sheffield Wednesday team.

Lymbery's meticulous book-keeping records that when Glasgow Rangers came to Nottingham they shared equally with Forest 'gate' money totalling £25 9s 3d and the Scots also got expenses of £5 10s 1d. Forest threw for them a dinner costing £24 2s 4d so the club was well out of pocket on the visit. By the beginning of 1880 the club's administrators had finally grasped the difference between gross and net takings so a visiting Scottish-Canadian touring team, who attracted the first three-figure income (£108), got their half-share after expenses.

The Scottish FA had organized a tour to the United States and Canada and, to help meet the expense, arranged a series of exhibition matches against England's leading clubs. The game against Forest was played at Trent Bridge on 10 February 1880, and attracted a gate of 5,000. Forest planned to turn out their full FA Cup side, which had reached the semi-final stage, but, because of injury, had to call upon a youngster named Ernest Jardine. The team was: J. Sands (goal); C. J. Caborn (back); W. Luntley, E. Luntley (three-quarters); M. Holroyd, E. Jardine (half-backs); A. H. Smith, A. C. Goodyer (right wing); F. W. Earp, J. T. Turner (left wing) and S. W. Widdowson (centre). The Scots included three players from Rangers and four from Queen's Park. They had beaten Darwen 7-3 and Manchester 8-0 in previous matches, so Forest did well to hold them to 2-0. Young Jardine subsequently became Sir Ernest Jardine and president of the club. A lace machine manufacturer, he ran a works football team, Jardine FC, and was a long serving president of Nottinghamshire Football Association. He was also High Sheriff of Nottingham and Member of Parliament for East Somerset. Created a baronet in 1919, he lived in the Park, Nottingham, and died in 1947, aged eighty-seven. His sister, Agnes, married into the Lymbery family.

As a young man Walter Roe Lymbery had spent eighty to 100 days a year travelling the world's markets promoting Nottingham lace. He then established a successful business in St Mary's Gate in the Lace Market. A Sunday school teacher for ten years, he was a chorister for fifty-one years and a trustee and active singing member of Nottingham Sacred Harmonic Society for fifty-two years.

The 'grand old man' died at his home in Sherwood Rise, Nottingham, on 14 October 1925, aged eighty-one. It was said that as a full-back there was none superior in his day and to the end there was no finer sportsman. His wife, Alice, survived her husband by only a fortnight. She was seventy-four.

One of Walter's sons, Harold Robert Lymbery, married a Miss Phyllis Luntley, uniting two Forest families. Her father Edwin Luntley and uncle Walter Luntley were half-backs for the Reds in the 1870s.

∞

Harold kept a Lymbery family journal of historical interest including a dispute over the origin of The Forest Football Club conducted in the correspondence columns of a local newspaper. The *Nottingham Evening Post* on Saturday 29 February 1936, ran a report headed 'Memories of a Nottingham Octogenarian' today celebrating his nineteenth birthday. It was about John William Whitby of 13 Clarendon Street, Nottingham, born in the city on 29 February 1856, and a cousin of former Lord Mayor, H. S. Whitby.

John Whitby recounted to a *Post* reporter how he understood Nottingham Forest FC to have adopted red as its colour.

> As a boy, I was in the Robin Hood Rifles Cadet Corps and I remember that a few of us bought a ball and used to play on the old Castle Green … We wore red garibaldis (battledress blouses) and a club was formed and called the Castle Club … Later we moved to The Meadows and the Castle Club shortly afterwards became Nottingham Forest, the garibaldis being retained.

Harold Lymbery wrote to the newspaper to refute this claim. 'The Forest FC was formed in 1865, when Whitby would have been only nine years of age,' he pointed out. His father, the late W. R. Lymbery, was one of the founders and, after captaining the side for a year or two, had held the office of honorary secretary from 1868 to 1881.

> I have examined the lists of members from 1868 to 1873 and do not find Mr Whitby's name amongst them. Such well-remembered athletes as C. F. Daft, C. J. Spencer, C. S. Wardle and S. W. Widdowson were members in those early dates,

he added.

In his reply, Whitby admitted as much but added to our knowledge of the cadets.

> I was a young member of the cadet corps, composed of the sons of leading tradesmen of the town – a kind of 'swagger' corps … We drilled at the Castle and the uniform was a red garibaldi, military cap, green gloves and black trousers. The drill was the usual 'form fours', 'stand at ease', and 'quick march', with lectures upon the art of using the sword-stick fashionable at that period. After drill we played what we called football. In those days anything was good enough to kick, from a sheep's bladder to a bundle of rags, with five to twenty on a side, without any rules or regulations. At this time football was becoming a favourite game and, finally, we obtained a ball and formed a club, calling ourselves The Castle Football Club and always playing in our red garibaldis.

Whitby went on to say that sometime later, when he was not a member, the Castle Club rented a field off Queen's Walk, The Meadows, which was bounded by a dyke that was crossed by a wooden bridge – though some tried to jump it.

> These players amalgamated with some other club, playing shinney or hockey or perhaps football on The Forest, and the name was then changed from the Castle Club to Nottingham Forest FC, the only club in the country, I believe, who played in garibaldi blouses. Other clubs wore shirts or pullovers.

Some of the confusion may be accounted for by the fact, that after fourteen years at The Forest, the club left in 1879 to play some matches on the Castle ground in the Meadows, where, in early spring, thousands of crocuses bloomed. But, in 1845, when the railway wanted land for expansion and Nottingham needed space to grow, an Act of Parliament allowed development on former common land. Industrial buildings, terraced houses, shops and pubs began to be built. The Meadows, an area of some 300 acres stretching down to the River Trent, was being transformed leaving just the memory preserved by the naming of Crocus Street.

It is recorded that the Notts Castle Football Club disbanded in 1878 and its players joined Forest en bloc, considerably strengthening the club even though not all of the newcomers could gain a place in the side. One who did was Charles John Caborn. Born in Nottingham on 25 October 1856, he was educated at Nottingham High School and became a lace manufacturer and member of the firm of Redgate and Caborn. He played cricket and football for the High School and was a fine athlete. He joined Nottingham Castle FC on leaving school and was its captain from 1876 to 1878. Between 1878 and 1889, Caborn played in nearly all Forest's important matches and Cup-ties and he captained the Reds from 1885 until he retired in January 1889, becoming a vice president.

Forest's first match at the Castle Ground was against a representative side numbering thirteen players selected from other Nottingham area clubs. The Reds won 6-0 with England international Arthur Goodyer scoring a hat-trick. Then a prestigious five-a-side tournament was held there on Saturday 11 October with £10 prize money for the winner and £5 for the runner-up. It attracted 'the best men in the Midlands,' according to the *Nottingham Guardian*. Two teams came from Sheffield, and one each from Derby, Ashbourne and Cromford. Nottingham Wanderers, Nottingham Trent, Hucknall and Basford Park also took part. Forest chose five of their best: Charles Caborn, England international Edwin Luntley, Walter Luntley and Fred Earp with another international Sam Widdowson as captain. The Reds, with a goal by Earp, won the final against Sheffield Hallam to take the 'tenner' prize.

A Widdowson hat-trick gave Forest a 3-0 victory against Clapham Rovers on the Castle ground on 27 February 1881, and a crowd of 3,000 was there on 11 February 1882, for a clash with Notts, which the Reds won 2-1 with goals from Salathiel Norman and Earp. The most important matches, however, were played at Trent Bridge cricket ground, where, from 1880 to 1882, Forest made their home until, to quote a phrase used in a newspaper of the time, they were 'supplanted by Notts County.'

When the Nottinghamshire Football Association was founded in 1882, Walter Roe Lymbery was appointed its first honorary secretary and he held the office for five years. The inaugural meeting took place at Forest's committee rooms at No. 3 Maypole Yard, Nottingham, on Saturday 12 November. Forest, Notts County, Notts Wanderers, Notts Rangers, Nottingham Swifts, Notts Olympic, Vernon Rangers, United Amateurs, Basford Rovers and Sneinton Rovers were founder members with Trent, Banks, Beeston Wanderers and Kimberley elected at the next gathering on 7 December. Walter was joined on the county FA committee by Sam Weller Widdowson, who can be ranked as one of the greatest of all Foresters.

So who truly was 'The Father of Forest'? Arthur Turner, a Nottingham sports journalist who compiled the club's centenary book in 1965 bestowed the accolade on Sam Weller Widdowson. Sam was an international player, an innovator without parallel in the national game, an England selector, a referee, an administrator and an all-round sportsman. He was not, however, one of the founders and I've championed Walter Roe Lymbery, captain of both shinney players and footballers, the first elected chairman and, as secretary/treasurer, the man who exercised paternal control when he put the club's accounts in order and ensured its survival.

It's interesting to read what others have said about the two stalwarts. Both are credited with contributing hugely to the club's success by Alfred Gibson and William Pickford in their definitive four-volume *Association Football and the Men Who made It*, published in 1906 – so highly valued you have to pay £500 to £800, depending on condition, to get the set today. They describe Lymbery as 'that splendid friend of the Reds' and 'an enthusiastic worker' after whose appointment as secretary in 1868 'the club went ahead rapidly' to become the strongest in the provinces. About Widdowson they commented: 'There have been few greater footballers.' Further evidence comes from distinguished football writer James Catton. In his book *Wickets and Goals*, published in 1926, Catton labels Sam 'a hefty athlete, game as a cock, quite a 'card' in his way, and one of the finest forwards of his day.'

3

The Great Innovator

In his whimsical volume *Pickles the World Cup Dog and Other Unusual Football Obituaries*, Peter Seddon notes that Sam Weller Widdowson was

> a fine swimmer, oarsman, cricketer and quarter-miler, and served Forest as both player (1866–85) and long-term committee member. He won one cap for England (1889) and at cricket was selected once for Nottinghamshire (1878). He was an innovator besides. In 1874 he invented, wore and patented the first shin guard. Adapted from a cricket pad, it comprised strips of bamboo cane encased in fabric, strapped to the bare leg or worn outside the stockings. Although initially derided, the protectors were first mentioned in Association Laws in 1880, and shin guards are now officially designated a compulsory item of equipment and manufactured in their millions.

Like Lymbery and many early Foresters, Sam was engaged in Nottingham's thriving lace trade. The Widdowsons were an enterprising family involved in a variety of businesses. They were victuallers, hosiers, butchers, bakers, millers and farriers. Sam was born on 16 April 1851, in Hucknall Torkard on the outskirts of Nottingham, the sixth of ten children of Levi and Ann Widdowson. Levi was a butcher who much admired Charles Dickens' successful and joyful first novel *The Pickwick Papers*, published in 1836.

He was not alone, for *Pickwick* appealed to all classes and each monthly instalment was awaited as eagerly as the most popular television 'soaps' like *Coronation Street* and *Eastenders* are today. There were Pickwick hats and Pickwick canes; Pickwick coats and 'Penny Pickwick' cigars. There were corduroys named after Mr Pickwick's witty and trustworthy Cockney manservant, Sam Weller, for the relationship between Pickwick and Sam is at the heart of the book. And Levi named his son after Sam Weller, too.

Sam began work as a book-keeper but soon moved into the mainstream of Nottingham lace manufacture. He started as a warehouseman probably to gain experience because in his early thirties he became a director of a celebrated lace firm, Thomas Adams and Co. Thomas Adams was a notable Quaker and committed philanthropist. His warehouse and showroom at Stoney Street remains the largest building in this historic quarter-mile square area of the city. Designed in Anglo-Italian style by Thomas Chambers Hine, the Adams Building included a chapel, washrooms and tea-rooms for 500 workers, who also had a sick fund, savings bank and book club. In 1999, after a £16.5 million restoration, it was reopened by Prince Charles as New College.

The Lace Market and adjoining Hockley Village form a vibrant city district with theatres, arts and film centres, bars and restaurants. Nearly all of the old warehouses, impressive examples of Victorian industrial architecture, have found new uses as luxury apartments and high-specification offices as well as academic buildings. There's also Bolero Square in front of the National Ice Stadium where there ought to be, but isn't, a statue of Jayne Torvill and Christopher Dean in full flow. Both from Nottingham and working class backgrounds, they charmed the world with their ice dance to Ravel's 'Bolero', an orchestral piece originally composed as a ballet, that the pair had specially adapted for the 1984 Winter Olympics in Sarajevo. Ravel's most famous work, Bolero has a constant percussion rhythm rising in a continuous crescendo. Their gold-winning performance was awarded perfect scores by the judges – appropriately, on Valentine's night.

Widdowson played his first games for Forest early in 1869, probably the home and away victories against Sawley in March under the captaincy of Walter Lymbery. It is possible that the debut came a little earlier. The *Nottingham Review* records that a J. Widdowson played in a drawn game at Newark's London Road ground on 16 January 1869. Former secretary Ken Smales lists a J. Widdowson as a Forest player in his official statistical record of the club but could find no other information about him. Could the J have been a misprinted S? It seems likely.

∞

The Forest passing game favoured by Widdowson was indirectly influenced by a military man. He was Brigade Major Francis Marindin, who made the Royal Engineers a formidable force in early English football with a distinctive style that hugely impressed Sam when the two sides met at Trent Bridge on 23 December 1873. The major and he were the two captains.

Marindin was Bde Mjr at Chatham where the Royal Engineers Establishment – now the Royal School of Military Engineering – had been set up for instruction in the duties of 'sapping, mining and other field works.' He was one of the leading movers in the development of the game and of the FA Cup competition. Royal Engineers were finalists in the inaugural 1871/72 season. At that time the Engineers' activities ranged from designing the Royal Albert Hall to the development of the 'steam sapper', a traction engine that pulled a train of vehicles across the country and was the forerunner of the Army's mechanical transport.

With enthusiasm and resourcefulness, the major drilled his young officers at Chatham into a fine football team and in 1869 the Royal Engineers joined the Football Association. Marindin held office as FA president from 1874 to 1879. Not only did he play in the first FA Cup Final, he refereed seven of them.

Before Widdowson invented shin guards, bruises and more serious injuries were commonplace. Marindin, as an Old Etonian, had been a team-mate of the ebullient red-bearded Hon. A. E. Kinnaird (the future Lord Kinnaird and for thirty-three years FA president), football's first superstar. On one occasion, so it is said, when they were watching a match together Lady Kinnaird commented to Marindin, 'I do worry that one day Arthur will come home with a broken leg.' Her companion replied, 'Have no fear ma'am, if he does, it will certainly not be his own.'

The Royal Engineers under Marindin introduced formation into football tactics. Before the 1870s most teams had relied on rudimentary playing positions with the emphasis on individual dribbling and forward rushes – you might say 'kick and rush'. Marindin introduced a 1-2-4-3 line-up with a three-quarter back (in front of the goalkeeper), two half-backs, four wingers and three centres. The Engineers adopted a strategy of short passes with combination the key to their success. And so successful were they that over four seasons from 1871 to 1875 the team lost only three games (two of these being the FA Cup finals of 1872 and 1874) in eighty-six played. They won seventy-four and drew nine, conceding only 21 goals while scoring 244. Royal Engineers appeared in four of the first seven FA Cup finals, winning the trophy in 1875 after beating Old Etonians 2-0 in a replay.

The Trent Bridge clash between Forest and the Engineers was eagerly awaited in Nottingham. It was a raw day with a strong, chilly wind blowing across the ground but, according to a contemporary report, the 3,000 hardy spectators witnessed one of the most exciting football matches ever played in Nottingham. The Engineers wore their usual strip: jerseys, bobble caps and stockings, all horizontally hooped in regimental red and blue, with dark blue serge knickerbockers. A fine and stirring sight it must have been. Forest, of course, were in red. The visitors went ahead after just ten minutes and, as was then the custom, the sides changed ends. Play was end to end and even for a long spell before Forest equalized through C. J. Spencer. The Engineers, however, got a late winner. Congratulating Forest on a good game, the major said the Reds were the best team the Sappers had played in their tour of the north.

Widely known simply as 'the Major', Marindin retired from the Royal Engineers in 1879 and, some years later, became senior inspector of the railways. He then helped to develop London's new electric lighting system and was knighted in 1897. He died three years later, aged sixty-one.

Sam Weller Widdowson took on board the effectiveness of the short-passing game and devised his own line-up: 2-3-5, two full-backs, three half-backs and five forwards. Soon this became the standard formation adopted in England and throughout the world. It was amended to W-M when Herbert Chapman, then manager of Arsenal, withdrew the centre-half to become a centre-back or stopper but 2-3-5 continued unchanged until well after the Second World War in some countries and into the 1950s for team-numbering and naming in programmes.

∞

Widdowson was also at the forefront when technological help for referees began with the introduction of a whistle. It was used for the first time in a match on The Forest against Sheffield Norfolk in 1878. The idea came from the Forest committee who agreed there must be a better way of calling attention to a breach of the laws than by the then practice of an umpire waving a white flag. The FA was interested in the experiment and sought the opinion of Forest's Sam. He gave it the 'thumps up' and soon the whistle became part of every referee's equipment. An article in the Gibson and Pickford *Association Football and the Men Who Made It* confirms Forest's pioneering role. Referees themselves were fairly new. In the early 1870s clubs had provided umpires just as in minor football today the teams often provide individuals to run the line. When referees were appointed at first their role was simply to decide disputes between the umpires, making judgments if referred to – thus the title referee. They say modern goal-line technology with cameras pointed at each goal, all operated from a control room in the stand, will prove the game's most significant change in 150 years. Football though is not about justice. It's about conflict, passion, beauty and art. Leave fans with the drama – and something to argue about.

In that same year, 1878, the Reds played a game under lights. There were twelve of them, dim by modern standards, but lighting up the scene just the same as, on 28 October, Forest were beaten 2-1 by Aston Villa in Birmingham. Eighty years later the first Football League match to be played under floodlights took place at Villa Park between Aston Villa and Portsmouth. In the very first FA Cup Final the Royal Engineers had lost by the only goal to The Wanderers despite being firm 7/4 favourites. But they had a player injured with a broken collarbone after only a few minutes' play. The Wanderers took part in another early lighting experiment when four lamps were installed behind each of the goals for a match against Clapham Rovers on 5 November 1878. A match between

Forest and Notts Rangers on 25 March 1889 was the first to be played under electric lights. A battery of fourteen Wells lamps, each of 4,000 candle power, at a cost of just £25 lit the Gregory ground, Lenton, which was the Reds' home from 1885 to 1890. The novelty attracted 5,000 spectators but Forest didn't shine. Rangers won 2-0.

Widdowson was the referee when goal-nets were used for the first time. This was at the Forest ground in a match between the North and the South in 1891. Neither Sam nor Forest could claim the credit for this innovation, however, for the nets were the product of a Liverpool man, James Brodie.

Widdowson's Reds were beaten 2-1 by Old Etonians in the semi-final of the FA Cup at Kennington Oval on 22 March 1879, having reached the penultimate stage at first time of asking, a unique distinction. Notts County were beaten 3-1 in the first round at Beeston cricket ground. Sheffield were overcome 2-0 in three inches of snow in Nottingham in round two on 21 December. There were four inches of snow on the ground when Edinburgh University came for a friendly interlude on 18 January but, even so, 1,500 spectators came, too. The Reds won 4-1 and Widdowson scored twice. The Cup competition resumed ten days' later when Forest became the first provincial club to appear in London. They gained a third round 2-0 victory over Old Harrovians at Kennington Oval. Widdowson scored again and there was an own goal. The fourth round was also played at the Oval and Oxford University were despatched 2-1. Forest were beaten home and away by Glasgow Rangers that same season. Revenge for the Reds came at Trent Bridge on 30 October 1880, when Rangers were beaten by an English club for the first time. Fred Earp scored both goals for Forest in a 2-1 victory in front of a crowd of 2,000.

Forest were FA Cup semi-finalists for the second successive season but this time lost by the only goal to Oxford University at the Oval on 27 March 1880. First round opponents were once more Notts County who were beaten 4-0, 2,000 spectators seeing Widdowson score twice. He got another brace in the snow in Lancashire on 13 December when Turton were beaten 6-0 in round two. Third round opponents Blackburn Rovers were also thrashed 6-0 watched by a Nottingham crowd of 2,500. Widdowson and Goodyer each scored twice. Sheffield FC came on 18 February for a fourth round tie that ended controversially. The visitors were leading 2-1 with only two minutes remaining, but Widdowson scored the equalizer after a dazzling dribble. The referee ordered extra time but the disappointed visitors refused to continue and walked off. It was claimed that Widdowson lined up his team and kicked the ball into an empty Sheffield net for the winner. In fact, Sheffield were disqualified. Sam Widdowson scored seven of Forest's eighteen goals in that Cup run.

In March 1880 Widdowson played in his usual position at centre-forward for England against Scotland at Hampden Park and scored in a 5-4 defeat. Forest team-mate Edwin Luntley was also in the England team. Sam re-appeared in a top-class match at the ripe old age of forty. He had been elected to the national ruling body, the FA Council, and, to fulfil his duties as a selector, left his sick-bed to attend an international trial at Kennington Oval. Just before kick-off it was learned that one player had failed to turn up. So Sam, despite being unwell, turned out in borrowed kit and boots and played a blinder.

Sam was chairman of Forest between 1879 and 1884 and, in 1888, was the club's representative at a meeting of the newly-formed Football League, when an application to join was turned down. It was decided that only twenty-two dates were available for League fixtures and, therefore, only twelve members could be accommodated. Sheffield Wednesday were also rejected but Notts County succeeded in their application and so became one of the League's founder members. At the end of the first Football League season Forest tried again but received only one vote. The four bottom clubs, including both Notts and Derby County, successfully sought re-election.

Having established himself as a lace manufacturer, Sam married Harriet Laslett of Margate, Kent, a Roman Catholic, at St Barnabas RC cathedral, Nottingham, in 1879. The couple lived in style, with servants, and providing private education for their nine children. Widdowson lived in the Nottingham area all his life. In 1912 he and his brother, Edwin, became controlling directors of the Beeston Picture Palace Ltd. Sam died of pneumonia aged seventy-six in May 1927, his widow living until October 1945. Both are buried in Beeston cemetery.

4

Corinthian and Forester

Famous Forester and Corinthian Dr Tinsley Lindley was born in Nottingham in 1865, the year of Forest's formation, and died in his seventy-fifth year in 1940. He is buried at Wilford Hill Cemetery overlooking the Trent Valley and the city. The club's 150th anniversary comes seventy-five years after his death. There is a certain harmony in the concurrence of these events.

When Forest supporter Ron Clarke discovered the grave was unmarked, he decided to do something about it and in October 2013, led a campaign to raise funds for a permanent and fitting headstone. The target was reached before Christmas. 'I think he was the George Best of his day,' Ron commented. 'Brian Clough got his statue in the city centre and I thought Tinsley deserves something, too.' Forest players and supporters attended the unveiling ceremony at Wilford Hill on 31 March 2014. Forest stars included club captain Chris Cohen and vice captain Andy Reid. Long-lost members of the Lindley family, including a great grandson who had arrived from Luxembourg, were also present. Cohen said,

> It has been great to come and show our respect for Dr Tinsley Lindley this afternoon. Players like him helped the club develop the history we all treasure today.

So why a Corinthian and what made his fame?

The Corinthians stood for the highest standards of sportsmanship, skill and a style of play with all the emphasis on attack. The club was founded on 26 October 1882, at a meeting, called by N. L. 'Pa' Jackson, then honorary assistant secretary of the FA, in a small gas-lit room in Paternoster Row, London.

It was decided that the Corinthians colours would be dark blue and white striped cap, white shirt with the blue monogram CFC on the left breast, dark knickerbockers and stockings. It was agreed that the Corinthians should bring together the best amateur players in England. Importantly, clause seven of the rule book laid down that 'the club shall not compete for a challenge cup or any prizes of any description whatsoever.'

Later an exception was made to allow the Corinthians to compete for the Sheriff of London's Shield, a forerunner of the FA Charity Shield, the best amateur side of the season playing the top professional team. Under 'Pa' Jackson's management, Corinthians drew two games with Sheffield United in 1898, the first year of the tournament, and then became the first winners of the Shield, beating Aston Villa 2-1. Their reputation had been established beyond doubt in 1894 when, with Lindley leading the attack, FA Cup-holders Blackburn Rovers were beaten by eight goals to one. In 1904 they played Bury, who had just enjoyed a 6-0 victory over Derby County in the FA Cup Final, and thrashed the Lancastrians 10-3.

Although no rule defined qualification for membership, there was a tacit understanding that it should be confined to old boys of the leading public schools – Eton, Harrow, Charterhouse, Winchester, Westminster and Repton – or members of a university, though some exceptions were allowed. Membership was limited to fifty.

The Lindleys were involved in the lace trade from its outset and Tinsley Lindley's father, Leonard, was employed as a lace dresser, becoming Mayor of Nottingham in 1882. The family lived in Clipstone Avenue, Nottingham. He first made his name as a footballer at Nottingham High School and went on to play for Cambridge University. Reportedly, one of the fastest sprinters of his generation, he was reputed to wear ordinary walking shoes for games instead of football boots, which he felt slowed his pace. In that sense, he was, like Widdowson, an innovator.

'Pa' Jackson himself described Lindley as 'an almost ideal centre'. In his book *Association Football*, published in 1899, Jackson wrote of the Forester,

No man ever kept his forwards together better than he did. His passing was clever and accurate, he was always at work, and he did not miss many shots at goal.

A few pages later, he added,

G.O. Smith (Old Carthusians) stands alone as the successor to T. Lindley as the best centre-forward.

When *Annals of the Corinthian Football Club* was published in 1906, all-round athlete and scholar C. B. Fry, revered like a Greek god by the Edwardians, described Lindley as 'one of the greatest centre-forwards ever known'. Fry contributed to the 'Annals' a number of character sketches of famous Corinthians. Of the Nottingham man he wrote that Lindley, lightly built, had the 'wonderful facility of evading the heaviest charges' and defenders 'often found themselves chasing a shadow.'

'Moreover,' wrote Fry, 'was he not weaned to football at the hard Nottingham school, where every trick was thoroughly known and taught? Even the Scotchman – clever as he was – could teach him nothing.' Truly a Tricky Tree, Lindley was 'a regular Cinquevalli with his feet, he would juggle the ball through from anywhere.' He had a dislike of heading and 'preferred dribbling to taking long shots' but, above all, 'he was very good at taking the ball on the full volley from a centre.' Fry, a great England cricketer as well as a football international, added, 'It was just eye and timing, like a Ranji glance to leg.' Paul Cinquevalli, incidentally, was a Polish-born music hall and circus juggler, who was one of the acts in the first Royal Command Performance.

Lindley was picked out as a star of the Corinthians by Gibson and Pickford in their 1906 four-volume football classic. A ball-playing centre-forward, he scored fourteen goals in thirteen appearances for England between 1886 and 1891. He scored on his international debut on 13 March 1886, against Ireland in Belfast. Nottingham Forest teammate and fellow Corinthian Teddy Leighton was also capped for the game which England won 6-1.

Leighton, known as 'Kipper', had a stationery business in Clinton Street, across the way from Forest's Maypole Yard headquarters. Lindley went on to captain England on four occasions. And he was honoured as a Life Member of the Corinthians. Only Frank Forman in 1902 and Stuart Pearce ten times in the 1990s have led England as Forest players. Goalkeeper Peter Shilton, who was the England captain fifteen times was given the honour for the first time on 25 May 1982, a week after he had left Nottingham for Southampton.

But it was as a Forest player and later committee member that we remember Lindley, who scored a hat-trick on his debut in a 6-1 home win over Wolverhampton on 17 February 1883. He was the Reds' centre-forward over nine seasons and scored 62 goals in ninety-two games, including 14 goals in twenty-four FA Cup-ties. He played his last match against Walsall Town Swifts at Walsall on 2 April 1892, when he was at outside-right having lost his place at centre-forward to another legendary Forest marksman Alex 'Sandy' Higgins. He also played cricket for Cambridge University and Nottinghamshire.

Dr Tinsley Lindley, who lived at 14 Park Terrace, Nottingham, was a doctor of law, not a medical man. He was a lecturer at Nottingham University and a county court judge. During the First World War, he served as the chief officer of the Nottingham Special Constabulary and as deputy director of the Nottinghamshire Territorial Association. He was awarded the OBE in 1918 for these services.

He once fell foul of Football League rules. The League was concerned about the poaching of players between clubs. So when Lindley accepted an invitation to play a match for Notts County, the League reacted by issuing the club with a £5 fine and a point deduction. Notts called a meeting of League clubs and urged that the punishment should be a fine only. Barrister Lindley argued that, in effect, two punishments had been handed out for one offence. He won. By six votes to five (Preston were not represented) the clubs agreed with him and the point was restored to Notts but the fine was increased to £25.

Both Tinsley and his elder brother, Leonard, who had played for the Reds in 1880, became Forest committee members. And he had not finished making headlines. A front page story in the *Athletic News* on 17 March 1930, caused quite a stir in English football. It was headlined, 'Players worth £40 a week'. This was at a time when the maximum wage was capped at £8. What caused a fuss was the byline, 'Football reforms by Tinsley Lindley, the famous Corinthians' international'. Thus the Forester was one of the first campaigners against restrictions on players' earnings. The maximum wage wasn't abolished until 1961, when the £20 cap was swept away. Fulham chairman, the film and radio comedian Tommy Trinder, had earlier boasted that his star inside-forward Johnny Haynes was worth £100 a week. Now his word was tested and, with a wry smile, he paid up. His catchline was, 'You lucky people.'

The Corinthians were famed 'missionaries' taking the game far and wide with tours throughout Europe and to North America and South Africa. It was on their second tour to South Africa that the Corinthians played the Orange River Colony on Monday 13 July 1903. There were 5,000 spectators and the home side included at centre-half Forest's 1898 FA Cup-winning captain, John McPherson. Corinthians won by the only goal but, according to the *Annals*,

> The old Scottish international and captain of the Notts (sic) Forest team when they won the English Cup still retained much of his old skill.

Forest played Corinthians for the first time on 17 November 1887, and won 2-1. Corinthians won by the same score in London on 26 January 1889. At Queen's Club, London, on 2 November 1895, Forest won 2-0 and on 4 January, 1896, were the victors at home by 5-1. A game at Queen's Club on 10 March 1900, was drawn 2-2 and at the same venue on 6 April 1901, Corinthians were the winners 2-1.

∞

Born at Ilkeston on Christmas Day 1856, Fred Beardsley was a frequent Forest team-mate of Tinsley Lindley's and became one of the finest goalkeepers in England despite being just 5 feet 7 inches in height. What he lacked in inches, he made up for in agility and character. And he was a key figure in the stories of both Nottingham Forest and Arsenal. One of his team-mates was later to say of Fred: 'He would have been bumped out of the ground had he not been agile as a cat. Good old Fred, a sturdy little chap, used to pitch opposing forwards over his back. He took it all.'

Fred made his Forest debut in a 3-0 home win against Darwen on 29 January 1881, and was in the side against Sheffield and Blackburn Rovers during that season. He took part in all seven FA Cup games during the 1884/85 season when Forest played a semi-final and replay against Scotland's famous Queen's Park. First they beat Rotherham Town 5-0 on 8 November at one of their last matches at the Parkside Ground, Lenton, their home since 1882. Sam Widdowson hit a hat-trick. Rotherham had conceded ground advantage and there was a crowd of 1,000 spectators. Next Sheffield Heeley were defeated 4-1 on a wet 6 December in Nottingham that was brightened by a Freddie Fox hat-trick. The third round was at Bramall Lane against Sheffield Wednesday who were knocked out of the Cup by 2-1, Widdowson and Lindley scoring for the Reds. Then Old Etonians were beaten 2-0 away, Lindley again and Sherwood-born Tom Danks, another of Forest's early internationals, getting the goals. Danks was just twenty-one when he played at inside-right for England against Scotland on 21 March 1885, in a one-all draw at Kennington Oval.

Forest went to Derby cricket ground to play the semi-final against Queen's Park and 10,000 supporters were there, too. It finished 1-1, Danks scoring again. The only FA Cup semi-final to be played north of the border, the replay at Merchiston Castle School ground, Edinburgh, attracted another 10,000 gate and Queen's Park won 3-0.

An unusual experience befell Fred Beardsley when Forest were playing Glasgow Rangers in a friendly in front of a crowd of 4,000 at Cathkin Park on 9 April 1887. With ten minutes to go and the Reds trailing 1-0, the goalkeeper attempted to catch a high ball but fell clumsily and sprained his ankle. Almost at the same time Forest full-back W. McLeod suffered a leg injury. Both were accidental, not fouls, and the ball remained in play as they lay on the ground. Rangers got the ball in the net and then the two injured were carried off. The gentlemanly Glaswegians declined to count the second goal and the score remained 1-0.

Widdowson, Lindley, Leighton, Fox and Danks all played for the Reds in the 1887/88 season when quick and tricky inside-right Frank Burton made his debut at Stoke-on-Trent in a 2-1 Birmingham Cup second round defeat on 29 October, Danks scoring the Forest goal. A twenty-two-year-old who had been persuaded to quit after just one season with Notts and join the Reds, Burton learned his football at Nottingham High School and also played on The Forest for the Banks club. He played for the north against the south and was in the England side that beat Ireland 6-1 in a British Championship match at Anfield, Liverpool, in 1889. After retiring from Forest, he became managing director of Joseph Burton and Sons, founded as a grocery in 1858 by his father, a miner's son, in Smithy Row, Nottingham. It became an upmarket food emporium similar to London's Fortnum and Mason and occupied most of the Exchange mall within the

Council House building that was opened by the Prince of Wales (later Edward VIII) in 1929. It became known locally as Burton's Arcade.

An 1887/88 fixture card lists matches for reserve and colts teams as well as the Forest first team. While the seniors met Preston North End, Sheffield Wednesday, Blackburn Rovers, Bolton Wanderers, Notts County, Derby County, Burnley and Stoke-on-Trent, the reserves were matched with Leicester, Boston, Grantham, Newark, Retford, Matlock and Long Eaton. The Gregory ground, Lenton, staged most of the home games but the colts played at The Forest against local sides such as Nottingham University College, Southwell St Mary's, Notts Athletic, Basford Rovers, Mansfield Woodhouse and Long Eaton Victoria. Clearly, the Reds, with Widdowson and Lindley as vice presidents and Caborn and Edwin Luntley on the committee, were planning for the future. Widdowson was also honorary treasurer.

Forest were drawn at home against an Irish club, Linfield Athletic, in the first round of the FA Cup on 2 February 1889. It was 2-2 after extra time and arrangements were made for the replay in Belfast a week later. Forest made the trip across the Irish Sea only to find that Linfield had scratched from the competition. It was a wasted journey except that their hosts hastily arranged a friendly. This Athletic won 3-1. When the Reds went to Ninian Park for a fifth round tie against Cardiff City on 18 February 1922, they became the only side to have travelled for cup games in all four home countries. Because of the Irish withdrawal, the operative word is travelled, of course, not played. Burton scored at Ninian Park but Forest lost 4-1 in front of 50,470 spectators.

Fred Beardsley's last game for Forest was on 25 February 1889, when the Reds were beaten 3-2 by Chatham in a FA Cup second round third replay on a neutral ground, the Kennington Oval. Yet three years earlier he had moved to London after being sacked by Chilwell Ordnance Depot for taking time off to play football. He found work at the Royal Arsenal's factory at Dial Square, Woolwich, and became one of the founding fathers of Arsenal Football Club. Coincidentally, Mjr Marindin worked at the Woolwich Arsenal before being awarded his commission in the Royal Engineers.

Beardsley played in a total of fifteen FA Cup-ties for Forest and the committee honoured Fred with the presentation of an inscribed and ornately engraved silver cigarette case. A miniature painting of the player himself decorated the lid and an inscription recognised his 'valuable services as the Forest goalkeeper'. Sir Ernest Jardine said he was 'one of the cleverest goalkeepers' he had ever seen.

∞

Royal Arsenal FC was formed at a meeting of players at the Royal Oak Hotel, Woolwich, in December 1886. A number of them had played for

Nottingham Forest. As well as Beardsley, there were Joseph 'Morris' Bates, Charlie Bates and Bill Parr, who later became the team manager. But it was Beardsley who agreed to approach his former club for assistance in finding some kit. Forest responded with a full set of red shirts and a football. In return, they requested that the new club allow Fred to rejoin them for FA Cup-ties.

Minutes of the December meeting recorded that 'the lads from Nottingham' were very experienced in training, especially in the use of weights, which helped to build up leg muscles. They were to organize the team's training programme.

Royal Arsenal wore the kit given them by Forest in the first match played on Plumstead Common on 8th January, 1887. The modern Arsenal marked Forest's centenary in 1965 with the reciprocal presentation of a set of red shirts and these were worn in the centenary match against Valencia at the City Ground on 28 September that year.

Morris Bates was one of the earliest headers of a ball and was nicknamed 'Iron Head.' Two more Nottingham men became Arsenal team members: full-back Arthur Brown and outside-left William Scott joined from Notts Rangers.

When Arsenal became a limited company in 1893, Beardsley became vice-chairman and served for the next two decades. Brown was also a director and served as assistant secretary. Parr was a notable shareholder as was Ellen 'Nellie' Beardsley, Fred's wife.

The Woolwich Reds and the Nottingham Reds met for the first time on Easter Tuesday 1891. Fred had been replaced in the Arsenal goal by another Nottingham man, Edmund Bee. Forest dominated the game and, it was reported, only brilliant saves by Bee kept the score down to 5-0.

Arsenal went into a downward spiral ending in liquidation. When a new company was formed and Arsenal moved north of the Thames to Highbury the Nottingham men, including Beardsley, did not subscribe. Fred joined the committee at Charlton but became disillusioned and decided to concentrate on his tobacconist's shop. He died in 1939, aged eighty-two. In 1940 a German bomb demolished his former shop.

5

Forging an Alliance

Forest were fortunate in the quality of their early leaders; outstanding characters such as Walter Roe Lymbery, Sam Weller Widdowson and Tinsley Lindley. And the club's good luck (or good judgment) continued with the appointment as secretary of Harry Radford in 1889. A forward-thinking administrator, Radford had been a dedicated public servant who came to office after being a Nottingham Corporation officer.

Notts County were invited by William McGregor of Aston Villa to the inaugural meeting of his proposed Football League at Anderton's Hotel, London, in March 1888. Even the great Sam Weller Widdowson was unable to secure the Reds admission at a second meeting, held in Manchester, where the original twelve invited clubs, including Notts and Derby County, were confirmed as members.

At the end of the League's first season the bottom four clubs, including both Notts and Derby, were obliged to seek re-election. Forest were encouraged to try again but received only one vote against seven for Notts, the weakest of the bottom four who were all readmitted. Having been excluded, Radford, enterprising and ambitious for the club, concluded there was only one thing for it. Competitive football was essential if the Reds were not to fall far behind their rivals. Forest must organize a league of their own. Mainly through his efforts, the Football Alliance was formed in the autumn of 1889. Joining Forest in this competition were Newton Heath (now Manchester United), Small Heath (now Birmingham City), the Wednesday (Sheffield), Sunderland Albion, Crewe Alexandra, Bootle, Darwen, Grimsby Town, Walsall Town Swifts, Long Eaton Rangers and Birmingham St George. The clubs of the Alliance demonstrated their strength by drawing 1-1 with the Football League in a representative match at Olive Grove, Sheffield, on 20 April 1891.

Forest made a promising start to the first Football Alliance season, beating the Town Swifts at Walsall by three goals to one. Centre-forward Bill Hodder scored two goals in what proved to be his only game in the

Garibaldi shirt. He had joined Forest from Notts County, for whom he scored three goals in twenty matches in their first season in the Football League. After quitting Forest, he joined Notts Rangers and went on to play for Sheffield Wednesday and Lincoln City. There were 3,000 spectators at Walsall, who gifted their visitors an own goal. Birmingham St George were beaten 3-1 away and there were home victories against Sunderland Albion (3-1), Darwen (3-1), and the 'double' was achieved over Walsall Town Swifts (3-0) but there were also heavy defeats: 12-0 to Small Heath in Birmingham, where Forest were reduced to ten men through injury, and Darwen's 9-0 revenge. When they went down 2-0 at Bootle on 2 April, Forest ended the season next to the bottom club, Long Eaton Rangers, who dropped out. Champions were the Wednesday with Bootle runners-up. The Wednesday also reached the FA Cup Final but were beaten 6-1 by Blackburn Rovers.

Clearly, drastic action needed to be taken to restore the club's reputation. Again, thought Radford, there was only one thing for it. The days of the gifted amateur were ending. Forest must embrace professionalism. And look north. Notts County had shown the way a year earlier. Scottish players were the key to success. They had signed Sandy Ferguson, Davy Calderhead, James Macmillan, and their star bustling centre-forward Jimmy Oswald, already an international, from Third Lanark.

The role of football club manager has evolved over the years and is changing still. Today some top clubs employ directors of football and head coaches leaving the job description 'manager' to the past. Have we seen the last of great leaders such as Matt Busby, Bill Shankly, Don Revie, Brian Clough and Alex Ferguson? One can only hope not. Before 1889, the Nottingham Forest team was selected by committee. The selectors may have numbered seven or more members, including the captain, vice captain, secretary and, possibly, the trainer. When Harry Radford was appointed secretary, he was given more responsibility and exercized greater influence than his predecessors. His title, perhaps, should have been secretary/manager; certainly, the League Managers' Association, which lists thirty managers of Forest to date (including 'caretakers'), counts Radford as the first. Arthur Turner, editor of the centenary book (1965) accepts him as secretary only with Bob Marsters (1912–25) the first secretary/manager, Harold Wightman (1936–39) team manager and Billy Walker (1939–60) the first club manager.

However you look at it, Radford proved to be an astute talent-spotter and brought a number of fine players to Forest. He had worn the red shirt with distinction in the early years under the captaincy of Lymbery and alongside Widdowson. Gibson and Pickford in their 1906 classic wrote of him,

He was an amateur of the best type and left a record behind him of sterling honest play on the football field. And it is a matter of infinite credit to his character that he is today a prominent member still of his old club and may be seen, and pardoned, as excited and anxious as the most fever-smitten latter-day enthusiastic supporter of the historic Reds. He is a Forester to the backbone.

Radford discovered left-back Adam Scott playing for Albion Rovers at Coatbridge in North Lanarkshire, and snapped him up in August, 1890. Only 5 feet 5 inches tall, the twenty-three-year-old Dumfries-born youngster was as keen as mustard and a tenacious tackler. He went on to make 265 appearances for the Reds and develop a reliable partnership with right-back Andy Ritchie, who came from East Stirling, aged nineteen a year later, and was only an inch taller than Scott. They played together in the 1898 FA Cup Final and formed, perhaps, the smallest full-back partnership in the professional game. Ritchie, who played more than 200 matches for Forest, retired in 1899 through injury and Scott in 1900; the same month as Scott, twenty-six-year-old centre-half Dave Russell joined the Reds from 'the Invincibles' Preston North End, with whom he had won the League and Cup double in 1888/89.

Signed from Derby County in August 1890, Alexander 'Sandy' Higgins, born in Ayrshire in the year of Forest's formation, was Radford's major capture. An excellent dribbler and one of the most feared marksmen of his time, he had also been one of the unluckiest of international players being awarded only one Scottish cap despite scoring four goals in an 8-2 win over Ireland in 1885. 'Sandy' was one of the most consistent of all players and, for Forest, scored 84 times in 105 appearances – a goal every 112 minutes of play. He was seen as an ideal replacement for one of the last of the great amateurs, Dr Tinsley Lindley. In fact, they were paired as centre-forward and inside-left in five FA Cup-ties and a prestigious friendly against Scotland's Queen's Park.

∞

Having been based at the Castle ground in the Meadows for less than a year, Forest had spent two years at Trent Bridge cricket ground before relocating to the Lenton area, first to Parkside and then the Gregory ground. Now they returned to the Meadows, acquiring Woodward's Field, near the junction of the Embankment and Arkwright Street, adjacent to the Town Arms and near the tram terminus at Trent Bridge. There the club built its grandest home yet and gave it the name the Town Ground.

The *Nottingham Evening News* told its readers on 27 September 1890, that the Town Ground would have 'a very nice playing piece and it will also be an excellent ground for seeing the game.'

Its reporter went on,

The club officials must have gone to great expense in levelling and re-turfing for, as far as I could judge, at least 1,500 square yards of ground have been operated on. The field sloped considerably towards the Trent on the south side but that side has now been brought up to the level of the other and the field has a capital appearance. The new ground, however, will want a lot of rolling and working before it is fit to play on in wet weather. Along the bank side, a tier of six rows has been erected for spectators, which down its 120 yards of length should accommodate 2,000 people and the top of the bank will be a splendid coign for several hundred more. At the Wilford End there is also a similar high bank and at both ends there are seats and wooden gratings for the feet. The adoption of the concave form for the end seats will be a great advantage to spectators as, without craning their necks, they will be able to see well what takes place at each corner from any position, which is not often possible with a straight row of seats.

The reserve stand for members and others is on the south side, fifty yards in length and with eight tiers of seats and should accommodate about a thousand spectators. It is of sufficient height to permit the seated spectators in the front row seeing well over the heads of those standing down below. It will be roofed and places bang in front, well under cover, are reserved for the football reporters.

This last point was a matter of some significance for the gentlemen of the Press, who had harboured a grudge over earlier provision. Dealing with the first match played at the Gregory Ground in 1885 a newspaper commented,

There were about 2,000 spectators, everyone seemed pleased with the new enclosure and its appointments [...] capital provision was made for spectators and players but there is room for improvement in one direction. Neither at Parkside nor at the Gregory Ground have the Forest committee ever afforded any accommodation for the members of the Press whose duty it is to report the matches. They have, as usual, been forgotten [...] we hope a desk or table will be supplied as on most grounds in the country.

The aggrieved critic added,

Notts have not finished laying out Trent Bridge but it is their intention to erect a covered desk.

Harry Radford's influence can be detected in all this. Curving the corners of the stands to allow an unimpeded view was quite visionary at the time. Clearly he saw the importance of valuing supporters and developing good relations with journalists. His is an approach that certain Cyclopean later chiefs might gainfully have employed.

Forest had spent £300 on Parkside and £500 on the move to the Gregory ground. A far greater sum, £1,000, had been invested in their splendid new ground and the club sought to show it off with a prestigious opening fixture. At the beginning of the season a charity match had been played at Wolverhampton Wanderers and it was decided to invite Wolves, a Football League club, to come to Nottingham for this special occasion. Unfortunately, on the arranged date, Goose Fair Thursday 2 October, Notts County had a League fixture against Bolton Wanderers at nearby Trent Bridge. Notts complained to the League that their gate would be affected. As a result, Forest were warned that unless they altered the date of the opening all League clubs who had fixtures with the Reds would be ordered to cancel them.

Wolves, therefore, were ruled out as opponents. Instead, Forest fixed up to play former FA Cup rivals Queen's Park of Glasgow. Dave Russell captained the Reds who had both Higgins and Lindley up front.

According to a local newspaper report, the route from the centre of town along Arkwright Street to Trent Bridge was thronged with Forest and County supporters going to the rival matches at grounds either side of the river. Between them they indulged in 'a good deal of badinage.' The attendances were estimated at 6,000 for Notts and between three and four thousand at the Town Ground, where the Mayor of Nottingham for 1889, Alderman Edward Goldschmidt, at the end of his year of office, kicked off. The match was won by Forest 4-2, with two goals from eighteen-year-old inside-right William 'Tich' Smith, and one each from Higgins and Horace Pike, the youngest of three brothers from Keyworth all of whom wore the Garibaldi.

The next day Stoke, who had dropped down from the Football League, came for the first Alliance match at the Town Ground and 3,000 spectators were there, too. They saw Lindley score in his only appearance in the competition that season and Horace Pike get another but the visitors went away with a point from a 2-2 draw. Stoke were to lose only twice and return to the Football League as Alliance champions. The Wednesday not only lost their title they ended at the foot of the table. Forest finished fifth but, oddly, Darwen who were sixth were elected to the League. The Reds beat Darwen 5-2 in their first Alliance home match of the season on 13 September 1890, when, watched by a crowd of 3,000 at the Gregory Ground, William 'Tich' Smith scored twice on his debut. The return match at Darwen on 13 December was an exciting 4-4 draw with Higgins scoring all of the Forest goals.

Winger Teddy May, who had joined from Notts County, scored four goals in only his second match for the Reds as Bootle were trounced 7-0 at the Town Ground. Then Newton Heath were crushed 8-2. Arthur Shaw, another recruit from Notts, and Horace Pike both hit hat-tricks.

Tinsley Lindley was reunited with Sandy Higgins for the FA Cup and the pair shared a goal feast in the first round on 17 January 1891, when Clapton were trounced 14-0 on their Old Spotted Dog ground in east London. It remains the biggest away win ever recorded in English first-class football. Higgins scored five and Lindley four. Tich Smith and Neil McCullum both got two goals and the other was Shaw's. The Reds' team was: William Brown, Jack Earp, Adam Scott, Albert Smith, Dave Russell, Tommy Jeacock, Neil McCullum, William Smith, Alex Higgins, Tinsley Lindley and Arthur Shaw.

There is a mystery about Neil McCullum, a tricky right winger, who has gone down in Scottish football history as the man who scored Glasgow Celtic's first-ever goal in the 5-2 defeat of a Rangers XI on 28 May 1888, the Bhoys inaugural game. He seems to have joined Blackburn Rovers in February, 1890, and Celtic records have him returning to them in 1891. According to a Scottish report, 'he was the subject of interest from Nottingham Forest but the Celtic members made it clear to the English club's representative that he would be lucky to leave Glasgow in one piece should he tempt the popular McCallum to the midlands.'

The report adds, 'McCallum did however eventually move south to Nottingham in August, 1892, after making thirty-three appearances and scoring 17 goals for the Bhoys.' He played for Celtic in the Scottish Cup Final in 1889 and was in their Cup-winning team in 1892.

Yet it would seem the 'representative' got his man for in 1890/91 McCallum scored eight goals in twenty Alliance games for Forest and twice in five FA Cup-ties. The episode bore the stamp of Harry Radford. McCallum missed the 1891/92 season, when he was clearly back in Glasgow, but returned to Nottingham when Forest achieved Football League status. The Scot, whose running style was described as 'rather flat-footed' possessed a vicious shot and liked to cut in from out wide to unleash an angled drive at goal.

The second round tie against Sunderland Albion required a second replay before Forest triumphed 5-0 at Bramall Lane, Sheffield, but in round three the Reds were knocked out 4-0 by Albion's local rivals, Sunderland, newly-elected to the Football League, at Roker Park.

The goals kept coming in the Alliance, however. Higgins hit four and McCallum two as Crewe Alexandra were beaten 7-0 at their Recreation Ground but the title challenge faltered with a double defeat in two days by Small Heath, despite a hat-trick by Horace Pike in the first game at the Town Ground, which the Birmingham side won 5-4.

Even so, it had been an encouraging season especially as the club's reputation had been restored with victories over FA Cup winners Blackburn Rovers, Scottish Cup winners Hearts and Scottish League joint champions Glasgow Rangers. Dumbarton, beaten by Hearts in the cup final, had drawn 2-2 with Rangers in the league play-off to share the title. Forest finished with a 1-1 draw with Football League champions Everton. Hearts had been beaten 8-2 in Nottingham, where Tich Smith got a hat-trick and Higgins scored twice. Blackburn had been despatched 4-0, Horace Pike (2), Smith and McCallum scoring and a crowd of 4,000 at the Town Ground saw a Dave Russell hat-trick see off Rangers.

∞

Keith Warsop and Paul Wain in their history of Notts County *The Magpies* comment that Notts was the club of 'the well-heeled classes' and, for the 1877/78 season, in a trend towards even more exclusivity dropped Forest from its fixture list, considering the Reds to have 'an artisan background'. If that was the perception it was not a lasting one. By the time of its twenty-fifth anniversary the Forest club had become an accepted, respected and established part of the Nottingham social scene. A 'Grand Tyrolean Bazaar' was held by the club in the Mechanics' Hall, Nottingham, on Thursday, Friday and Saturday, October 22, 23 and 24 1891. It was opened by Lord and Lady Belper and the patrons included the Duke and Duchess of Newcastle, the Duke and Duchess of Rutland, Earl and Lady Manvers, Viscount and Lady Newark, and Viscount Galway. Famous Foresters involved included Dr Tinsley Lindley as a vice president, Sam Weller Widdowson treasurer, Harry Radford secretary and Tom Danks on the committee.

A ninety-two-page brochure was published for the event and here's how it set the scene:

> The visitor finds himself amid the charming and sublime scenery of an Alpine village in the Tyrol. Here are Swiss cottages and chalets with balconied fronts and overhanging roofs, the basements being used as bazaar stalls. In front stands the turreted Edelweiss Castle and in the foreground a waterfall with rocks and pine dotted slopes, a timber watermill and a rustic log bridge.

It was all designed and painted under the direction of Mr Bridges, who is described as 'the renowned scenic artist to HRH The Prince of Wales.' Music was by a students' orchestra and other entertainment included a hypnotist, Tyrolean marionettes, a ventriloquist, a magician, a comedian and a fortune teller. A brochure prediction was that Forest would 'make a bold bid for champion honours' and this came true. They won the Football Alliance.

Three thousand folk came to the Town Ground for the opening Alliance game of the season on 3 September 1891. They saw the Reds score seven goals against Burton Swifts without reply and Sandy Higgins hit a hat-trick. They also saw the Forest debut of twenty-three-year-old Scottish international centre-half John McPherson signed from Hearts with whom he had won a Scottish Cup winner's medal that February and gained his only cap, against England, in April. 'Jock' was to serve the Reds for a decade, become club captain and lead the 1898 FA Cup-winning side.

Dave Russell returned at centre-half for the next Alliance home match on 12 September, when McPherson went to inside-left left and scored in a 5-2 win against Walsall. In their first three Alliance games Forest had scored sixteen goals, conceding just three, and the seemingly unstoppable Higgins had got seven of them. The Reds went on to win the next four and did not drop a point until the beginning of November when they were held 1-1 at home by Sheffield Wednesday, the Forest scorer Higgins, of course. It was Wednesday who ended the unbeaten run by 3-1 at Sheffield in game twelve on 28 November. Forest stormed back, literally, as Bootle were swept aside 5-1 in a Nottingham rainstorm on 12 December. Higgins missed this game. Tinsley Lindley came in at centre-forward and scored.

After an absence of five matches, all but one of which were friendlies, Higgins returned to the side for the clash with close rivals Newton Heath in Manchester. He scored in a 1-1 draw. His form never flagged and he hit all the Forest goals in a 4-1 victory on a snow-covered pitch at Lincoln on 20 February. A 3-0 defeat of Newton Heath in Nottingham on 19 March was decisive in the title race. Higgins, McPherson and right-winger Bill Mason were the scorers. There was an attendance of 9,000, of which 2,000 had travelled from Manchester. Forest finished champions, two points ahead of the Manchester side with Small Heath (Birmingham) third and Sheffield Wednesday five points behind in fourth place. The Reds had won fourteen of their twenty-two Alliance matches and drawn five.

Forest played before the biggest crowd in their history so far when 25,000 went to Wolverhampton's Molineux ground on 27 February 1892, and saw a 1-1 draw with West Bromwich Albion in an FA Cup semi-final. A week later 14,000 turned up at the same ground for a replay that also ended one-all. West Brom triumphed 6-2 in the second replay at Derby on 9 March and went on to beat Aston Villa 3-0 in the final at Kennington Oval on 19 March. In their earlier rounds, Forest knocked out Newcastle East End, Sunderland Albion and Preston North End. The Newcastle side had played in a black and white strip instead of their usual crimson to avoid a clash of colours when they came to Nottingham. For the following season they also changed their name to become Newcastle United.

Higgins was superb, scoring 26 times in nineteen Alliance appearances and seven in six FA Cup-ties, including three in the semi-final games. Lindley, who played in all the cup-ties, was the scorer in the first semi-final. He retired from the field at the end of the season and joined the club committee.

6

In Another League

Harry Radford, who had been at the forefront of the founding of the Football Alliance, took the lead in negotiating its dissolution and absorption into the Football League. So far as he was concerned, the Alliance had never been more than a waiting room for the League. And the case for admission was strong. Forest had just taken eventual FA Cup winners West Bromwich Albion to a third match at the semi-final stage as well as becoming Alliance champions. But Notts County had to be won over as the League was protective of its member clubs.

The League's expansion programme was finally agreed at the annual meeting held at the Queen's Hotel, Sunderland, on 13 May 1892. There would be two divisions. Sixteen clubs would form Division One, enlarged from twelve in the original league, and the second division would have twelve members. West Brom, who had finished bottom, were excused from having to apply for re-election in recognition of their FA Cup success. Accrington, Stoke and Darwen had to seek re-election. Forest, Wednesday and Newton Heath from the Alliance along with newly-formed Liverpool FC, Newcastle East End, Middlesbrough and Middlesbrough Ironopolis sought selection. The two Middlesbrough clubs agreed to amalgamate if accepted.

In advance of submitting an application, Radford led a Forest deputation to seek the support of the Notts directors. He was able to announce that an agreement had been reached. County would not stand in Forest's way provided they had home fixtures first against the Reds and five other clubs chosen by them and these games were played before Christmas. A problem, of course, was that Forest would have to persuade the League to compile the season's fixture list taking account of this complication.

Liverpool were less fortunate. They were rejected even before the vote was taken on the grounds that 'they did not comply with regulations'. League champions Everton had been forced to leave their rented ground at Anfield after a dispute and an attempted hijack by another company registered as Everton FC and Athletic Grounds in March 1892. The new company at first sought to replace Everton in the Football League and when that ruse failed formed Liverpool FC and tried again. No doubt Everton's opposition was decisive.

Alliance champions Forest gained First Division status, receiving nine votes – one fewer than the Wednesday and three more than Newton Heath (Manchester United). All but three of the remaining Alliance clubs were admitted to the Second Division. Long Eaton Rangers, just a few miles west of Nottingham, were one of those rejected and disappeared from the football map soon afterwards.

Goodison Park, Everton's new home and the first major stadium in England to be built specifically for football, was opened by Lord Kinnaird and Frederick Wall of the Football Association on 24 August 1892. The first League match at the ground was played on 3 September and 14,000 saw the champions held by newcomers Forest to a 2-2 draw. Inside-left Horace Pike scored the very first competitive goal seen at Goodison (an exhibition match had taken place a week earlier) to give the Reds the lead but Fred Geary equalized. Sandy Higgins for Forest and Alf Milward of Everton were the other scorers.

The Forest team for their first League match was made up of: William Brown; Jack Earp, Adam Scott; Tom Hamilton, Albert Smith, Peter McCracken; Neil McCallum, Tich Smith, Sandy Higgins, Horace Pike and Tom McInnes. Glaswegian McCracken and McInnes, born in Bowling, Dunbartonshire, were making their first appearances for the Reds and both spent seven seasons at the club. A confident and resolute defender, twenty-five-year-old McCracken was signed from Sunderland Albion and had played previously for Third Lanark. He missed only one game in the 1892/93 campaign and went on to play 130 times for Forest before joining Middlesbrough in May 1899, captaining the Teessiders in their first Football League season. McInnes came to be regarded as one of the best forwards of his day and played in international trial matches but never gained a Scottish cap. He joined the Reds as a nineteen-year-old from Clyde and scored fifty-four goals in 193 appearances during his Forest career. He was an ever-present in his first season and averaged a goal every three games. There were two McInnes playing in Nottingham in 1892 confusing some historians. Glasgow-born Tom McInnes had joined Notts County in December 1889 and he did gain an international cap against Ireland in March that year as a Luton player. He left Nottingham in 1893 to join Third Lanark and later played for Everton. Thomas Fair Macaulay McInnes left Forest for Lincoln City. He married Ethel Pearson in Lincoln in 1903 and they had four children.

A crowd of 7,000 saw Scott, McInnes and McCallum score in the first League match at home a week later but the seven-goal thriller ended in a 4-3 defeat to Stoke. Preston North End did the double over Forest in closely-fought matches one after the other. Then came the first League victory and, satisfyingly, it was at Derby. McInnes was on the mark again with Higgins and Smith clinching a 3-2 triumph. This was followed by a first League meeting with Notts County who, as had been agreed, were the home team. The clash on 8 October drew a crowd of 14,000 with receipts of £408. Notts were the winners 3-0. Even more fans, 15,000 of them, saw Forest's revenge in the return match on 25 February. Horace Pike scored first and McInnes got a brace as the Reds were convincing winners 3-1. Unfortunately, ace marksman Sandy Higgins dislocated his shoulder, causing him to miss the remainder of the League programme.

Forest did the double over Derby with a one-nil win at home and also won the return with Everton 2-1. The biggest crowd to watch Forest was 25,000 at Goodison Park in the second round of the FA Cup on 4 February when they were knocked out 4-2 by Everton. Goalkeeper Danny Allsopp, a twenty-two-year-old six-footer weighing 14 stone, was signed from Derby Junction and made his Forest debut on Christmas Eve, when a home crowd of 6,000 saw Wolverhampton Wanderers beaten 3-1. He made 245 appearances during an eight-year association with the club.

With seven home and three away wins, Forest ended the season in tenth place on twenty-eight points. Derby were fourteenth. Notts, third from bottom, had to take part in a 'test match' (equivalent to a modern play-off) to try to preserve their First Division status. The bottom three faced the top three of Division Two. Notts were beaten 3-2 by third-placed Darwen and were relegated. Four seasons went by before the Nottingham rivals met again in a League game but County triumphed in the FA Cup in 1894. A crowd of 15,000 saw Forest held 1-1 at home in the third round on 24 February and there were 12,000 at the replay a week later when Notts delivered a 4-1 knockout blow. County became the first side from outside the top flight to win the FA Cup when they beat Bolton Wanderers 4-1 at Goodison Park. They were also, of course, the first club to bring the Cup to Nottingham.

∞

Aston Villa were Football League champions but Forest had what the Americans describe as a winning season, with fourteen victories and twelve defeats, to finish seventh. It was notable for the debut against Sheffield United on 15 February of twenty-year-old Fred Forman, the eldest by eighteen months of Forest's famous Forman brothers.

Fred and Frank, who made his Reds' debut as a nineteen-year-old in a third round FA Cup-tie at Aston Villa on 2 March 1895, became the only brothers from a Football League club to represent England together until Manchester United's Gary and Phil Neville nearly a hundred years later. Bobby and Jack Charlton were 1966 World Cup-winning brothers but were with different clubs (Manchester United and Leeds

United, respectively). Brothers A. M. and P. M. Walters (nicknamed, unsurprisingly, Morning and Afternoon) had also played together for England in 1889 and 1890 but as amateurs with Old Carthusians.

Frank made his debut for England in a 3-2 victory over Ireland in Belfast on 5 March 1898. It was the first of nine international caps, all won with Forest. He also captained his country, leading England to a 1-0 victory over Ireland in the Home Countries Championship at Balmoral Showgrounds, Belfast, on 22 March 1902. He was described in *Association Football and the Men Who Made It* as 'the famous international, in every sense of the word a great half-back'.

Fred was selected for the 1899 internationals – in those days, three matches with the home countries, Scotland, Wales and Ireland. They were his only caps but he scored three goals. Neither Frank nor Fred were ever on a losing side for England and both were on the scoresheet in England's still record win – the 13-2 defeat of Ireland at Sunderland. Fred also went on an FA tour of Germany and Austria. He scored two goals in England's 13-2 victory over Germany in an unofficial international in Berlin on 23 November 1899. No cap was awarded but he received a commemorative badge.

The brothers were not the only members of their family to serve Forest and England. Their nephew, Harry Linacre made his First Division debut as an eighteen-year-old at Bury on 4 November 1899, He kept goal for the Reds for nearly ten years, playing more than 330 matches, and gained international caps against Wales and Scotland in 1905. Consistent and courageous, he, too, was not on a losing England side. All three were born at Aston-on-Trent and played for the village side.

The Formans both became Forest committee members at the end of their playing days. Frank hung up his boots in 1903 and was on the committee until his death, aged eighty-six, at his home in West Bridgford on 4 December 1961. He had been made a Life Member of the club. Fred was a member of the committee from 1903 until his sad death at Skegness on 14 June 1910, aged thirty-six. A younger brother, Tom Forman, joined the Reds in August 1900. A speedy left-winger, he made two First Division appearances at the end of the 1900/01 season, two in 1901-1902 and one in 1902/03. Although failing to make the grade at Forest, he did very well after leaving the club. He scored 16 goals in 126 League games for Barnsley and was also in their FA Cup Final side in 1910 when they were beaten after a replay by Newcastle United. After the final, he was transferred to Tottenham Hotspur, for whom he scored once in eight appearances in 1910/11.

Forest had to settle for seventh place in the 1893/94 season, notable for the retirement of Sandy Higgins in April. His contribution had been recognized by the club with the award of a testimonial match against Sheffield Wednesday. It was not quite the end of the Higgins story as his son, Alex junior also nicknamed 'Sandy', joined Forest in June 1920 and helped the club preserve its Second Division status with 7 goals in thirty-three League games. Higgins Junior had won the Football League championship and FA Cup winners' medals with Newcastle United as well as four Scottish caps.

A home crowd of 6,000 saw Tommy Rose and John McPherson score the goals that gave the Reds their first League win over Aston Villa and Forest held on to seventh place in 1894/95. The next season they were thirteenth and then eleventh in 1896/97, when on 3 October, Goose Fair Saturday, there was a pitch invasion by unruly members of the crowd at the Town Ground. Police were unable to keep control and referee J. B. Brodie abandoned the match with twenty minutes left. Derby claimed half the gate money of £357. Forest refused the demand but they were fined £20 by the League. The visitors' only satisfaction was victory by two goals to one when the match was replayed before 5,000 well-behaved spectators in November.

The first match of the season had been a friendly at the Town Ground against Burton Wanderers. What made this unusually interesting was the appearance for the Reds of two sets of brothers: the Formans and Adrian and Arthur Capes, both born in Burton-on-Trent. Forest won the game 8-0 with Fred Forman and Adrian Capes among the scorers. Adrian, the elder brother by almost two years, spent a season at Forest but went on to give excellent service to Port Vale, hardly missing a match in five years. He was known as 'Sailor' some fifty years before Bert Brown had that nickname in the 1940s. Neither were seamen but had the rolling gait of those who had ridden the waves. Arthur had six seasons in Nottingham as an all-action winger or centre-forward, scoring 43 goals in 190 appearances.

Supremo Harry Radford retired after eight years as secretary but for a while he continued to work hand-in-hand with his successor Harry Hallam. Elected to the Football League Management Committee in 1898, he became vice-president in 1905 and served in that office until declining health forced him to stand down in 1908. Gibson and Pickford commented:

> He has been an active worker in the Nottinghamshire Football Association, which is one of the largest and best managed in the country, and was a vice president of that also until 1904, when the pressure of his other offices rendered it difficult for him to attend the meetings with not that regularity that his soul desired. For nine years the clubs in his (Midland) division have returned him as their representative on the Football Association Council, where he occupies a prominent position on a number of committees.

Radford's knowledge of the game was, they wrote, 'as extensive as that of almost any other prominent legislator in the world of football.'

Forest made a slow start to the 1897/98 season. A crowd of 15,000 at the Town Ground saw them held to a draw by newly-promoted Notts County, who had been reduced to ten men through injury after 55 minutes. Next they lost 2-0 at West Bromwich and then came draws with Sheffield United and Sunderland at home and Wolverhampton Wanderers away. The sixth First Division match, however, brought a satisfying 3-1 victory at Notts County followed by the defeat of Blackburn Rovers by the same score at home. Liverpool, Preston North End and Stoke were all beaten before Christmas and, on New Year's Day, Len Benbow and Charlie Richards got two goals each in a 6-3 win for the Reds at Sheffield Wednesday.

There was a crowd of 10,000 at the Town Ground for the visit of Bolton Wanderers a week later. Arthur Capes and Benbow scored in a 2-0 league victory that was also a testimonial match for Tom McInnes. Forest were enjoying a rich vein of form in readiness for the challenge of the FA Cup beginning at the end of the month.

7

Against All Odds

First up in the FA Cup were Grimsby Town of Division Two and 6,000 went to the Town Ground to see Forest win comfortably by 4-0. Charlie Richards, who was to join Grimsby a year later, scored twice with one each from Arthur Capes and McInnes. Richards, described as an 'invaluable forager', also had an eye for goal, hitting the target 26 times in eighty-six games for Forest and having a career record of 68 in almost 200 League games. He wrote himself into the history books by scoring the first League goal for Manchester United after their name change from Newton Heath. This came in a 1-0 win at Gainsborough Trinity in 1902.

Trinity were Forest's second round opponents on 12 February. A 10,000 crowd at the Town Ground saw another 4-0 home win over another Second Division side. And Richards repeated his brace, Benbow and McInnes getting the other two. The third round was an altogether tougher assignment away to favourites West Bromwich Albion. A 16,500 crowd at Stoney Lane saw the Throstles 2-0 in front at half-time but three goals in a ten-minute spell midway through the second half left Forest triumphant. Scorers for the Reds were Frank Forman, Richards (his fifth in three cup-ties) and left-winger Alf Spouncer.

Semi-final opposition came from the Southern League. Southampton, however, were not to be taken lightly. Far from being minnows, they were champions for three successive seasons and were to reach the FA Cup Final in 1900 and 1902, when they took Sheffield United to a replay. Another Southern League club, Tottenham Hotspur, became the only non-Football League club since the League's formation to win the Cup when they beat the Sheffield club after a replay in 1901.

It was at Bramall Lane that Forest met Southampton on 19 March. A crowd of 30,000 saw Len Benbow score for Forest in the second minute but an equalizer came twenty minutes later and neither side could get the decider. The replay at Crystal Palace was played five days' later before only 16,800 on a bitterly cold day. A raging blizzard caused a long hold-up and conditions had hardly improved when it was restarted. McInnes and Richards scored late goals to put the Reds through 2-0 and take their FA Cup aggregate to 14-3. Southampton, however, were unhappy and protested that the game should never have been restarted and should be replayed. They were over-ruled by the FA.

Forest were to face in the Final local rivals Derby County who, along a much more arduous route, had beaten holders Aston Villa, Wolverhampton Wanderers, Liverpool and Everton. *The Graphic* captured the popular mood when it stated the Reds 'were to be accounted as one of the luckiest clubs which ever figured in a final tie.' It was a view that seemed to be justified when in a First Division match five days before the Final a crowd of 12,000 at the Baseball Ground saw Steve Bloomer score a hat-trick as Derby hit five without reply against a Forest side that was without skipper McPherson and five other regulars. Derby had fielded their full Cup team.

Both teams set up camp in the spa resort of Matlock at the south-eastern edge of the Peak District to prepare for the big game. There was intense excitement in the East Midlands and, according to a contemporary report, reserved seats were quickly sold and others 'placed on the market at considerably enhanced prices'. Some 5,000 supporters left Nottingham for London in special trains and, it was said, the area around St Pancras and King's Cross stations 'resembled Nottingham Market Place at Goose Fair'.

Cup Final day, Saturday 16 April, dawned brightly and thousands of supporters sporting their club colours hurried by tram and train to the Victorian pleasure ground at Crystal Palace Park, Sydenham Hill, where the match was to kick-off at 3.30 p.m. The huge amphitheatre was bathed in sunshine and the weather at least was calm as the ground filled with more than 62,000 spectators, 3,000 fewer than had watched Aston Villa and Everton the year before but better than the other previous finals since the first at Crystal Palace in 1895; numbered seats in the pavilion were 10s 6d and in the covered stands 5s. The takings were £2,312. It seemed many of the southerners rather than being neutral were lending their support to Derby, perhaps because of the appeal of their superstar Steve Bloomer or else Forest were unpopular after the manner of Southampton's defeat in the semi-final.

Another indignity for the Nottingham side came when team photographs were taken before the match, as was the custom, to make life easier for the official photographer. Both teams were pictured for convenience with and then without the trophy. On this occasion, the photographer was even more particular and required the Reds to wear Derby's white shirts to provide a clearer contrast to their blue shorts. No wonder the players look a touch miffed. Unsurprisingly, the apparently wrong strip has caused no little confusion ever since.

Forest had Danny Allsopp in goal; Archie Ritchie and Adam Scott at full-back; the halves were Frank Forman, John McPherson and Willie Wragg; Tom McInnes and Alf Spouncer were on the wings; Charlie Richards and Arthur Capes the inside-forwards, and Len Benbow led the attack. The Derby line-up was: Jack Fryer; Jimmy Methven, Joe Leiper; John Cox, Archie Goodall, James Turner; John Goodall, Steve Bloomer, John Boag, Jimmy Stevenson and Hugh McQueen.

McPherson won the toss and elected to defend the Palace end. Boag kicked off for Derby and a great cheer went up when Bloomer got on the ball but he could not get the better of Wragg. The early exchanges were fast and furious before the unfancied Forest began to take control. The Reds forced two successive corners as Fryer palmed over a header from the menacing Benbow, who was then heavily brought down by Archie Goodall and required attention from trainer G. Bee.

Forest were in fine flow and there were excellent efforts in quick succession from Capes and Forman followed by a foray by Ritchie. McPherson was a commanding figure in defence keeping quiet the much vaunted pair John Goodall and Bloomer. Still limping, Benbow, despite this handicap, was soon back on the warpath for the Reds and his determined challenge on Leiper won him possession. He sent Spouncer away but the winger was brought down by Methven. Wragg placed the freekick judiciously into the stride of Arthur Capes, who fired a fierce shot along the ground to beat Fryer and give Forest a nineteenth minute lead.

Derby's counter-attacks were few and far between with Bloomer remaining uncharacteristically ineffective. Then, in the thirty-first minute, he punished the Forest defenders for leaving him unmarked as a perfectly-flighted freekick came in from Leiper and he headed past Allsopp, the ball going in off the crossbar.

Undeterred, the Reds pressed forward with purpose and a clever interchange with Richards freed McInnes down the right flank. The winger returned the ball to Richards whose hard hit drive was parried by the alert Fryer. Again, the irrepressible Capes was the man on the spot to guide the rebound firmly along the ground inside the posts. The goal came in the forty-second minute and made the half-time score 2-1. Derby had been lucky. Forest had found the net on two other occasions only for their efforts to be disallowed by referee J. Lewis and a 4-1 scoreline would not have flattered them. Richards thought he had scored in the eighth minute but offside was given – a decision that was deemed decidedly dodgy by the Forest following. Then McInnes was tripped by Archie Goodall and a powerful freekick by Ritchie beat Fryer but did not count as Mr Lewis had seen an infringement.

When the second half began, it was plain to see that, although Benbow had recovered, Wragg was struggling with an injury he had carried for most of the first period. When the wing-half wrenched his knee again, the Reds were forced to reorganize. Wragg was switched to the left wing and was a hobbling passenger for the remainder of the game. Spouncer moved inside and double goalscorer Capes dropped back.

Now, against virtually ten men, Derby sensed their chance and, prompted by Bloomer, took up the offensive. John Goodall tested Allsopp's mettle with a strong header, but the goalkeeper was equal to it. Bloomer was more influential now, but the Derby attack came up against a rock in Forest skipper Jock McPherson and the Reds' rearguard looked impregnable. It was not all Derby. Forman was a giant commanding midfield and he found Benbow dashing forward but a push from behind prevented what was looking like a certain score. The freekick was cleared with difficulty and Fryer had to fist out a crisp shot from Spouncer.

Tension heightened as Derby mounted a frantic late onslaught but Allsopp and his defenders were equal to the task. Then, with five minutes to go, Spouncer forced a corner on the left. Boag got his head to the cross but the ball came to McPherson who held off two challenges and from ten yards out rattled in a shot that gave Fryer no chance of saving. Forest led 3-1 and Derby were broken and beaten.

Forest supporters engulfed the pavilion to see Lord Rosebery present the FA Cup to a great captain, McPherson, and winners' medals to the triumphant Reds. Back in Nottingham the offices of local newspapers were under siege from excited enthusiastic crowds gathered to learn the outcome from the special wires despatched from Sydenham Hill.

Sam Weller Widdowson – who was celebrating his fiftieth birthday– said Forest winning the Cup was the best present he could ever have wished for and Harry Radford, jointly in charge of the team with Harry Hallam, declared it was the proudest day of his life.

∞

Players and committee members stayed in London over the weekend and returned to Nottingham by train on Monday evening. On arrival at the Midland Station they were greeted by such scenes of wild excitement as had never been seen before in Nottingham. Thousands had made their way in droves towards the station so that Carrington and Station Streets were jammed. Foot and mounted police tried to keep the approaches clear but P. S. Clay, the chief constable, had to order entrances to the station to be closed to keep the crowd out. The colour red was everywhere on flags, ribbons, hatbands, ties, sashes and even handkerchiefs.

A sax-tuba band played 'See the conquering hero comes' while the crowd cheered loudly as the players, wearing red caps, crossed the footbridge into Station Street to board a charabanc with McPherson waving the Cup aloft and Secretary Hallam holding high the match ball. Committee members travelled in other brakes and the cavalcade, including a donkey shay representing the lowliness of beaten Derby County's position, began the journey to the Market Square. Spectators perched on lamp-posts, window sills, the branches of trees and 'every coign of vantage' all along the route. Postillions riding gaily caparisoned horses forced a passage through crowded streets.

At St Peter's Gate the church bells rang out thanks to the enthusiasm of committed supporter and campanologist Bob Cobbin. Forest was the ruling passion of this bluff, forthright and autocratic man who became a committee member in 1912 and was the longest-serving club chairman from 1920 to 1948. He donated the Cobbin Cup to the Nottinghamshire Schools' Football Association in 1921. Elected to the FA Council 1923, he served on the FA War Emergency Committee and became an FA Vice President and international selector.

In Market Street 'a new electric automatic device' displayed the message 'Bravo Forest, welcome home.' The players were lifted shoulder-high after descending from their charabanc and carried from Long Row to the club's headquarters at the Maypole Hotel, where chairman and former player Tom Hancock, another lace manufacturer, presided over a celebratory dinner. Notts County chairman H. Heath filled the Cup to toast the club just as Forest's chairman George Seldon had done when County had won the trophy four years' earlier.

Monday's newspaper carried an editorial tribute, it declared,

Victory undoubtedly went to the better team, at all points the Reds were the masters of their opponents and their marked superiority must have come as a surprise to those who were both unable and unwilling to foresee the possibility of any other result than a comfortable walk-over for Derby. It was also the more pronounced by virtue of the fact that for almost three parts of the game they were labouring under the disadvantage of Wragg's limping, while during the whole of the second half they were to all intents and purposes playing with ten men. The Reds were by far the better team, beating their opponents all over the field both in passing skill and general method,

the writer concluded,

There is little to be said for Derby for they did nothing worthy of their reputation or of their much vaunted powers.

Two days later the players were guests of Nottingham Theatre Royal at a performance of the play, *The Sporting Life*, and the FA Cup was exhibited on the stage during one of the scenes. A newspaper leading article suggested that the trophy should be kept in the Castle Museum and not 'hawked about indiscriminately which several previous holders have done.' The paper no doubt had in mind the case of Aston Villa. They beat West Bromwich Albion 1-0 in the first final to be held at Crystal Palace in1895, also refereed by Lewis. Later that summer, Villa allowed the famous trophy to be displayed in a Birmingham sports shop window, from where it was stolen. A £10 reward was offered for its return; a sizeable amount considering the average wage of a player at the time was £3 a week (£2 in summer) and for a worker £1. But the 'little tin idol' was never seen again. Villa were fined £25, the cost of the replacement.

∞

The FA Cup was not the only trophy Forest won that April. Arthur Capes scored the solitary goal when Leicester Fosse were beaten in the Burford Cup Final at the end of the month. They finished eighth in Division One. More importantly during the season plans were being made to move across Trent Bridge and build a new ground on the riverside. The City Ground, which would replace the Town Ground, was to be located between Trent Bridge and Lady Bay Bridge, built in 1878 to carry the Midland Railway line over the river. The line was abandoned in 1968 and in the early 1980s it was converted for road traffic to relieve pressure on Trent Bridge. The bridge was used as a Cold War checkpoint for the 1982 TV drama series 'Smiley's People' based on the spy novel by John Le Carré and starring Sir Alec Guinness.

The City Ground, the club's seventh home in thirty-three years, is on land that is part of The Bridge Estate granted to the Mayor and Burgesses of Nottingham by Edward VI through a Royal Charter of 21 February 1551. The Corporation was expected to raise revenue through rent to maintain and repair Trent Bridge, a crossing believed to have been first erected in AD 920 by Edward the Elder, son of Alfred the Great. Nottingham was awarded city status by Queen Victoria in 1897, her Diamond Jubilee year. The new City Council terminated Forest's tenancy of the Town Ground, which they required for building and redevelopment, and granted the club a twenty-one-year lease of land on the south side of the river for the appropriately named City Ground.

The new ground scheme was adopted at Forest's annual meeting in December 1897. To finance the move the club required to raise £3,000 by subscription from members, supporters and local business men. They were asked to buy bearer bonds in the sum of £5 each. More than £2,000 was obtained in this way and much of it amounted to a gift as many of the bond certificates were never redeemed. There is one in (almost) mint condition preserved in the City Archives. It was given by the executors of the will of bond-holder Mr R. Fleeman of Broad Marsh, Nottingham. The certificate, numbered 405 and dated 15 December 1898, is signed by club secretary Harry Hallam. By comparison, Tottenham Hotspur's White Hart Lane ground, opened on 4 September, 1899, with a friendly against Notts County won 4-1 by the Londoners, set them back £1,200.

If the picturesque setting of the City Ground, with boat clubhouses as neighbours, was remarkable, even more so was the superb playing surface that was soon recognised as one of the best – even the finest – in the country. Forest was fortunate to have as a committee member a nurseryman and landscape gardener named William Bardill. He dug a foundation extending the whole length and breadth of pitch and laid down clinkers to a depth of 2 feet to ensure perfect drainage. The surface was then made up of top quality turf brought up river by barge from Radcliffe-on-Trent. Bardills Garden Centre still thrives on the edge of the city at Toton Lane, just off Brian Clough Way (the A52 between Nottingham and Derby).

8

A Prince From Wales

It was a great day for Blackburn Rovers ... but a touch deflating for Forest. The Reds headed off to Lancashire on 18 November 1998, for a First Division game that also saw the opening of the 'new' Ewood Park after a major rebuilding scheme. To mark the occasion, Rovers presented their visitors with an engraved glass vase on a wooden base. Forest gifted their hosts seven unanswered goals in what proved to be the heaviest defeat of a season that saw them finish ninth just three points behind seventh-placed Blackburn.

A flag proclaiming Forest 'FA Cup winners 1898' was flown proudly over the main stand when the ground was opened with a First Division match on 3 September 1898. On a fine day, the steamboat *Empress* left the landing stage on the embankment opposite bound for the Colwick amusement park down river and a crowd of 15,000 came to watch the game. The visitors were Blackburn Rovers. Of course, Forest lost 1-0. And they had to wait until the middle of October before winning at home against Stoke by 2-1 in front of 8,000 fans.

Form continued to fluctuate but spirits were lifted when Forest invested heavily beating off intense competition to secure the services of twenty-one-year-old Welsh international forward Arthur Grenville Morris from Swindon Town for a fee of £200. Born in Builth Wells, he played for his home town club and also for Aberystwyth, where he worked as an apprentice engineer. Morris, who was awarded his first Welsh cap against Ireland when just eighteen, became a clerk in the drawing office of the Great Western Railway at Swindon before turning professional. He scored 44 goals in fifty appearances for Swindon, including 23 in thirty-one Southern League games, and attracted scouts from all the top clubs but as the Cup-holders and with a new ground Forest had magnetic appeal.

His first game for the Reds ended in a 2-0 defeat at Bury on 3 December 1898, but 15,000 fans came to see his home debut against Derby County a fortnight later when he scored his first goal for the club in a 3-3 draw. Whatever the doubts about the 'huge' transfer fee, Morris had shown he was worth it. He had five international caps when he came to the City Ground and gained his first as a Forester on 18 March 1899, against Scotland at Wrexham. Fifteen more were earned by the Welshman before he retired at the end of April 1913, having scored almost one in every two international games. It was a pattern he repeated in club football, scoring 217 times in 457 appearances for Forest, 199 of them coming in 420 League games. Morris was the Reds' top scorer in nine of the fifteen seasons he spent with the club and for five of them he was captain. He also netted five League hat-tricks and remains Forest's all-time highest scorer.

The famed Billy Meredith was Morris's international partner and said of him, 'He was a great player, a brilliant schemer, a tricky dribbler and a fine shot.' Others dubbed him 'the Prince of inside lefts.' Although he mostly wore the No. 10 shirt, Forest fans saw him as the natural successor of Tinsley Lindley and to them he was 'the Immortal Gren.' A man of outstanding person charm, it was said he never committed a foul tackle and was never known to retaliate.

Of athletic build, according to the Football Post annual of 1907, he stood 5 feet 9 inches tall and weighed 11 stone 5 pounds. And, remarked the writer, but 'for the misfortune of being a Welshman, he would have played for England.' A fine tennis player, he was prevented from playing at Wimbledon because of his career as a football professional but he became a coach for Nottinghamshire Lawn Tennis Association. He was also a coal merchant and so important to Forest that the club allowed him to carry on his business while still a player and to train as it suited him.

League form may not have amounted to much but the first round of the FA Cup on 28 January 1899, brought great excitement to Trentside. Cup-holders Forest began their defence of the trophy against Aston Villa, winners of the Cup and League 'double' in 1897. Arthur Capes and Fred Forman scored the goals that gave the Reds a glorious 2-1 victory in front of 32,070 fans at the City Ground. Both the attendance and the receipts, £1,382, were a record for Nottingham. Second round opponents were Everton at Goodison Park and another Fred Forman goal saw Forest through 1-0. What made it a particularly good performance before a 23,000 crowd was that several members of the team were suffering from food poisoning.

The City Ground attendance record was broken again when Sheffield United and their famous goalkeeper William 'Fatty' Foulke came for the third round on 25 February and 33,500 spectators came, too. But the receipts were £14 shy of the Villa tie takings. After an injury to Almond, United played all the second half with ten men and, according to a contemporary report, were kept in the game thanks to Foulke's brilliant display, topped off by one stupendous save from Capes. Forest were kept at bay and Priest hit the winning goal for the visitors in the 86th minute.

Forest fancied Foulke when he was a slim twenty-year-old and had watched him playing for Blackwell Colliery in a Derbyshire Charity Cup final at Ilkeston on 28 April 1894. On the following Monday, Foulke reported to the City Ground to have a look round and discuss terms. Only then did he reveal that he had already agreed to sign for the Sheffield club. Derby were also interested and equally disappointed when their representative arrived on the scene just as a United director was pocketing the completed transfer papers. Foulke gained one England cap, against Wales in 1897, and spent ten years at Bramall Lane before moving to Chelsea, the upwardly mobile new kids on the metropolitan block. By then, he weighed in at 24 stone and as a 6 feet 4 inches, a giant – sometimes called the Colossus – he was an overweight celebrity who captivated Victorian and Edwardian crowds.

United were back in Nottingham for a Division One match a week later and this time Forest were the victors 2-1 with outside-right Fred Spencer getting both home goals. Only 6,000 were present. And they returned again in March for the FA Cup semi-final against Liverpool. Watched by 21,000, the match was drawn. The tie went to a third replay before the Blades went through to meet Derby County in the final. The newspapers reported on a Bloomer versus Foulke duel and the *Derby Daily Telegraph* commented, 'Bloomer cannot appear to beat Foulke even when he gets to close quarters.' At half-time they were 1-0 down; United rallied and won the Cup by 4-1.

Fred Forman scored a hat-trick as the Reds completed their First Division programme with a 3-0 victory over West Bromwich Albion at the City Ground to finish eleventh. Forest at the turn of the century were among the strongest teams in the country and the committee rewarded the players with a bonus scheme: five shillings a point won at home and ten shillings for every point earned away. Admission charges were set at 6d, 1/6d and 2/6d reserved. Another decision was to revert to wearing white shorts with their red shirts instead of the blue shorts worn in the 1898 Cup Final.

The 1899–1900 season began with a 3-1 victory over Preston North End seen by 10,000 at the City Ground. The game was notable for the debut of twenty-four-year-old stocky inside-right Jack Calvey signed from Millwall with whom he had gained four Southern League championship medals. He scored on his debut and ended the season as the club's top scorer. He led the goal chart for the next two seasons and won an England cap against Ireland in Belfast in March 1902. Fast, plucky and with an excellent shot, he scored 57 goals in 150 appearances for Forest before returning to Millwall in 1904.

Forest had a good season to finish eighth in the First Division table but it was again in the FA Cup that they had most success. Home victories over Grimsby Town and then Sunderland at 3-0 were followed by the

1-0 defeat of Preston North End in a Third Round replay. Arthur Capes scored in the semi-final against Bury at Stoke but the game ended in a 1-1 draw. In the replay at Bramall Lane, Sheffield, Capes and Calvey had put Forest two up and the Reds were cruising with only ten minutes left. But Bury pulled one back and in the last minute won a corner after Forest centre-forward Bob Beveridge had booted the ball 40 yards back over his own goal-line. It was a disastrous mistake. Bury captain Pray waved up the whole team, including the goalkeeper, then took the corner from which centre-forward McLuckie equalized. Bury snatched victory in extra time and went on to win the trophy, beating Southampton 4-0.

Grenville Morris described the semi-final defeat as the saddest disappointment of his career. Curiously, he had been on Bury's books for a short time as a teenager and his first and last League games for Forest were against the Gigg Lane side. There was little consolation to be found in the fact that a Nottingham Forest side, captained by goalkeeper Danny Allsopp, won the National Baseball League championship. The summer league had been set up in 1890 by football clubs led by Derby industrialist Francis Ley (later knighted), who had built the Baseball Ground adjacent to his engineering works. Derby, boosted by a number of experienced American players, had won the first championship. They also held the league title in the two seasons before Forest's success.

The Reds achieved their best Division One finish to date in the 1900/01 season with fourth place only six points behind champions Liverpool. Their own championship hopes were dashed by a disastrous April, when they lost five First Division games including the last of the season to Liverpool. Morris top-scored with fourteen league goals while Harry Linacre, who had been recommended to the club by his uncle Frank Forman, made the goalkeeping position his own. Towards the end of the season, powerfully-built Jim Iremonger made his debut for England at right-back against Scotland. Comfortable using both feet, his second cap came as left-back in Belfast a year later. In all, he played more than 300 games for Forest and was a cricket all-rounder who had seventeen seasons with Nottinghamshire and toured Australia with the MCC in 1911/12 before becoming a coach at Trent Bridge. His brother, Albert, was a Forest trialist but became a local legend as Notts County's goalkeeper, having a road behind Meadow Lane named for him. Another brother, Harold, made eleven appearances in goal for Forest.

Unbeaten in the league at the City Ground until mid-January, Forest dropped a place to fifth in Division One in 1901/02 but another good Cup run saw them again in the semi-final. They knocked out Glossop, Manchester City and Stoke before going down 3-1 to Southampton at White Hart Lane. The attendance was 30,000 kept low because there was a smallpox epidemic in Nottingham and fewer than 200 took the train to London. Southampton became the last club from outside the Football League to reach the final but they were beaten by Sheffield United after a replay.

Grenville Morris scored in eight successive games, three times getting a second goal, but despite his efforts Forest finished in mid-table in 1902/03. Fred Forman went out in a gale, retiring after a storm-battered FA Cup-tie against Stoke in February when, despite the weather, 20,000 fans turned up at the City Ground. The following season Frank Forman announced that he would no longer being playing on a regular basis. In its Football Guide, the *Notts Weekly Guardian* commented,

> His has truly been a brilliant and honourable career. Both to his country and to his club his services have been invaluable and he unquestionably ranks as one of the finest players who has ever played the great winter pastime.

∞

Drama and spectacle did not stop with the final whistle of the season at the City Ground. The Midlands industrial exhibition, a sort of mini world's fair, had opened in May 1903, on land between the football ground and Trent Bridge leased for five years to the operating company by Nottingham Corporation. Trentside was thronged with visitors, many listening to the band of the Manchester Regiment, when at about half past eight on the evening of 2 July 1904, smoke was seen coming from painted wooden scenery at a fairground ride that had been given an unfortunate name change from 'Fairy River' to 'The River Styx'. The covered 'subterranean river ride' wound a serpentine course through imaginary stalactite caves with patrons travelling in little boats. The exhibition buildings 'flimsy and highly inflammable' according to a report in the *Nottingham Evening Post* on Monday 4 July, were soon ablaze but, luckily, there were no casualties. There was slight panic at first and a rush for the exits when the cry of 'fire' was raised but the fear of danger was speedily allayed. The *Post* commented,

> When it was seen that the flames were spreading and it was decided to clear the grounds and buildings the officials had some difficulty in persuading some of the people to leave – such is the fascination of a blaze when the sense of personal risk is removed.
>
> The flames spread with extraordinary rapidity and were, unfortunately, carried to the main pavilion on the ground of Nottingham Forest Football Club, which was completely destroyed.

The loss to the club amounted to £2,000, partly covered by insurance. Firemen were able to save adjacent residential properties in the avenues running from Radcliffe Road, Rosebery Avenue and Pavilion Road. The reporter wrote,

Wisely enough, several of the householders nearest to the danger took the precautions to obtain hosepipes and assiduously cool the walls of their houses [...] In one case, a piece of burning wood fell on the roof of a house where it blazed away furiously for some time until the occupier took extreme measures and broke through the slates for the purpose of reaching and extinguishing it.

The pavilion stand 'was one of the most commodious structures of the kind in the country. Everything contained in the premises was destroyed.' Secretary Harry Hallam was early on the scene and, the paper recorded, Harry Radford and other committee members joined him. But there was nothing to be done and it was simply the case of watching:

The process of destruction work itself out. [Inside the pavilion] the flames roared with a noise like that produced by a forced draught and when the rows of seats, rising tier over tier above one another to the top of the stand, were ablaze from end to end the intensity of the glare was something to remember ... The corrugated roofing withstood the heat for some time but, gradually, the metal sheets bent and dipped towards the glowing mass below, assuming the form of hammocks until bolts and rivets relinquished their task and an end fell from here and there into the flames.

Firemen prevented the flames from spreading to the stand at the Trent end of the ground and kept them away from the boathouses of Nottingham Rowing Club and Nottingham Boat Club.

Earlier, according to the *Evening Post* of Saturday 7 March, gales had 'blown down and totally wrecked' the stand on the 'sixpenny side.' In years to come, the City Ground would endure German bombs, Trent flood and another destructive main stand fire.

Forest slipped to sixteenth of the eighteen clubs in Division One at the end of the 1904/05 season. Below them Bury and Notts County were spared relegation as four newcomers were admitted to the Football League and, consequently, each division was enlarged by two teams. The highlight of a disappointing season was the staging of Aston Villa's FA Cup semi-final replay with Everton at the City Ground on 29 March. Villa won 2-1 and then beat Newcastle United 2-0 at the Crystal Palace to win the trophy for the fourth time. Receipts of £1,444 4s were a new record for Nottingham.

9

Rio de la Plata

As every Nottingham schoolboy knows, Arsenal adopted their red and white colours because former Nottingham Forest players, Fred Beardsley and Morris Bates were founding fathers of the London club in 1886 and Forest provided kits and a ball to help them get started. Not nearly so well known is that Independiente of Buenos Aires, one of South America's most famous clubs, changed its blue and white strip to red in tribute to the Nottingham side.

Independiente was formed in 1905 and in the summer of that year, at the invitation of the Argentine FA, Forest embarked on the club's first-ever overseas tour. The first match was played in Montevideo and then the touring party crossed the River Plate from Uruguay to Argentina, where seven teams were faced.

The Forest centenary book, published in 1965, records that at one of these matches was a young boy, watching football for the first time, who grew up to become President of Argentina. Juan Peron was then ten years old and attending a military school. It is suggested that he recalled the experience when becoming president of the Football Association of Argentina. What is certain is that Independiente's founding president Aristides Langone saw the Reds in action and was so impressed he decided that red should become his club's colour.

Forest was not the first English club to visit Argentina but it was the first Football League club. Southampton, of the Southern League, got there first a year earlier. A crowd of 12,000 at the City Ground on 24 April saw the Reds beaten 2-0 by Everton in the final First Division match of the 1904/05 season. Then Forest won an away friendly with Leicester Fosse 2-1 before the touring party left Nottingham on 19 May and sailed from Southampton on board the steamer Danube. During the three-week Atlantic crossing, the players kept fit by running circuits and playing deck cricket. Accompanied by club vice-president Harry Radford and secretary Harry Hallam, the tourists were England international goalkeeper Harry Linacre, full-backs Charles Craig and Walter Dudley, half-backs Sam Timmins, George Henderson, Bob Norris and Tom Clifford with forwards Tom Davies, Bill Shearman, George Lessons, Tom Niblo, Alf Spouncer and Albert Holmes.

Penerol of Uruguay were the first opponents on 11 June. A crowd of 5,000 at the Gran Parque Central Stadium in Montevideo saw Spouncer hit a hat-trick as Forest won 6-1. Niblo and Shearman also scored and there was an own goal. Five days later, on the Argentinian side of the River Plate, Spencer was again on target as the Reds won 5-0 against Rosario of Santa Fe in front of 1,500 spectators at the Plaza Jewell ground. Davies, Shearman, Lessons and Niblo were the other scorers.

The Sociedad Sportive Stadium in Buenos Aires was the venue for the next six games. First Belgrano were beaten 7-0, Shearman hitting four goals before an admiring 9,700 crowd on 18 June. Lessons (2) and Davies were also on the scoresheet. The biggest victory was against the Britanicos, formed by British 'ex pat' residents. Lessons and Shearman scored four each and other goals came from Spouncer (2), Davies, Niblo and a penalty by Clifford. It finished 13-1 and was watched by 4,000 on 22 June. Rosario tried again two days afterwards but this time lost 6-0. There was a hat-trick by Lessons and other goals from Holmes, Shearman and Niblo. The gate was 2,500.

The joint highest attendance was 10,000 for a game against Alumni on 25 June. That was when Senor Langone of Independiente found red shirts inspirational and irresistible – it is surely possible that the young Peron was there, too. In any event, the Alumni were beaten 6-1. Lessons (2), Niblo, Shearman and Timmins scored. There was also an own goal. Another 10,000 spectators were present for the match on 2 July against Liga Argentina, a representative side selected from the country's leading clubs. It made no difference as Lessons struck another four goals in a 9-1 victory. Niblo (2), Henderson, Timmins and Shearman got the others. Finally, on 5 July Forest played an exhibition game with all thirteen players taking part and, presumably, a few locals making up the sides. The 'A' team beat the 'B' team 2-1, but the venue and other details are unrecorded. Inside-right Bill Shearman, who had top-scored in the First Division season with 13 goals from twenty-nine matches, got 13 goals in eight on tour, but the leading scorer was centre-forward George Lessons with 17. Both forwards twice hit four goals in tour games.

Clifford, who played six games at right-half, is listed as C. Clifford in Ken Smales' records, which provide no further information about him. In fact, he was a twenty-nine-year-old former Celtic player who had been signed by Forest from Motherwell just before the tour began. According to the *Nottingham Evening Post* on Thursday 3 August 1905, Hallam said the trip had introduced Clifford to his new comrades and from what had been seen of him, he gave promise of strengthening the half-back line. The player had sustained a slight knee injury but should have recovered for the start of the season. But Clifford never played for Forest again so perhaps the injury proved more serious than first thought. The forgotten footballer almost became the unknown soldier. Royal Scots Fusilier Tom Clifford was killed at the Battle of the Somme on 19 January 1917. With no identified grave, he is listed in the Memorial to the Missing monument, designed by Sir Edward Lutyens, erected in the French village of Thiepval.

Secretary Hallam regarded Argentinian playing standards as better than Midland League but not quite up to the English Second Division. He said, however, that attendances compared well particularly as admission charges were three times higher than in England. It had been a triumphant tour. Despite leaving at home Welsh wizard Arthur Grenville Morris, who had been the league season's second highest scorer after Shearman, Forest had scored 57 goals in eight matches (excluding the exhibition game) and, without iconic defender Frank Forman, conceded just four.

Forest's tour is described as 'an unmitigated success' by Uruguayan writer Andreas Campomar in a chapter headed 'Battles of the River Plate' at the beginning of his history of Latin American football *¡Golazo!* (2014). A publisher/writer, Campomar, confirms that by the end of the tour: 'Such was the esteem in which Nottingham Forest were held that Independiente copied the club's red strip.' Equally impressed, says Campmar, were the Argentine Football Association who sought to make the summer tour by British clubs an annual event.

∞

After another three weeks at sea, Forest had less than a month to prepare for the 1905/06 season. Perhaps, the players had tired of travelling for, although winning five and being unbeaten in the first seven Division One games at the City Ground, the team failed to win in the league away from Nottingham until Sheffield United were beaten 4-1 at Bramall Lane on 3 March. Forest were in a relegation scrap but a 4-0 victory over Bolton Wanderers watched by 7,000 at the City Ground on 24 March gave hope of survival. One of the scorers was centre-forward Joe Hardstaff, who had made his debut in January. The twenty-three-year-old played nine times in 1905/06 but that was his only goal and did not make up for letting the side down by missing the train for the visit to Stoke a week earlier. Hardstaff made his name on the cricket field, spending twenty-two years at Trent Bridge, appearing in 340 first-class matches for Nottinghamshire and playing for England in five Test matches. His son, Joe junior, was also a famous batsman for Notts and England.

The whipping boys of the division were Wolverhampton Wanderers, who finished eight points adrift at the foot of the table after conceding ninety-nine goals. Forest were caught up in a battle with Bury and Middlesbrough to avoid the second relegation spot. On the last day of the season, the Reds crashed 4-1 to Everton at Goodison Park. This result doomed them to their first-ever relegation. They had thirty-one points, the same as Middlesbrough, who had won three games fewer, but went down by the five-hundredth part of a goal.

Two important signings had been made during the season. Wing-half Jack Armstrong first played at the City Ground representing Notts Junior League against the Irish Junior League on 15 April 1905. He signed as a professional for Forest in August of the same year and made his debut as a twenty-one-year-old in a 4-3 defeat of Everton at the City Ground two days before Christmas. Slight, quick and neat on the ball, he soon made the left-half position his own and went on to make 461 League and Cup appearances in a seventeen-year career with the club, retiring aged thirty-eight. He also played seventy-five times in wartime football. Armstrong also became a great club captain, deservedly in the company of Jack Burkitt, John McGovern and Stuart Pearce.

A more immediate impact was made by the other newcomer Enoch 'Knocker' West, who, like Sam Weller Widdowson before him, was born in Hucknall Torkard. He played for Hucknall Constitutional and after a brief, unhappy spell with Sheffield United joined Forest as a nineteen-year-old centre or inside forward in exchange for a £5 note. His debut came in a 3-2 home win against Bury on 16 September and a fortnight later 10,000 were at the City Ground to see him score his first goal for the Reds, the winner against Preston North End. Young Enoch finished the season as Forest's second highest scorer with fourteen First Division goals from thirty-five games. 'Knocker' also scored three in four FA Cup ties.

'He will not be twenty until March next but it is doubtful if as many hundreds would buy his services now,' Gibson and Pickford commented in *Association Football and the Men Who Made It*. 'He has scored in nearly every match in which he has played'. With Gren Morris hitting 20 league goals in thirty-two games, the wonder is that Forest failed to avoid relegation with two such prolific marksmen in the side. Former BBC radio football correspondent Bryon Butler, in his official centenary history of the football league (1987), described 'Knocker' as 'a bull at large, a force of nature.'

Unrest among members after the relegation shock led to a call for Forest to fall in line with the other Football League clubs and become a limited liability company. It was decided at the annual meeting to issue 1,000 £1 shares and appoint five directors. That nothing was done and the scheme fell through probably owes much to elation at the team bouncing back to the top division at first time of asking and with an impressive record.

The Reds took time to find their feet with two away defeats and a home draw in their first three Second Division matches but then got into their stride with a 3-0 win over Leeds at the City Ground on 22 September. Glamorous newcomers Chelsea attracted a crowd of 22,000 when they came to Nottingham at the beginning of October. They left mussed up by a 3-1 defeat. Forest completed a league 'double' over the

Londoners with a 2-0 win at Stamford Bridge in February, when, it was reported, a crowd of 25,000 saw the game with another 15,000 fans locked out. Both clubs were promoted. After beating Chelsea, Forest won twelve and drew two of their last fourteen matches to take their points total to sixty, three more than the runners-up and twelve ahead of third-placed Leicester Fosse. Morris hit twenty-one league goals and West again fourteen. But 'Knocker' had played the last twelve matches on the left wing to accommodate new signing in January Arthur Green, a Welsh international centre-forward who had been Notts County's leading scorer for the past three seasons. Right-half Eddie Hughes, who won nine caps for Wales as a Forest player, made 36 appearances during the promotion campaign. He was an early exponent of the long throw-in.

Forest ended ninth in Division One in 1907/08 and the first season back was distinguished by 'Knocker' West becoming the League's leading scorer with twenty-eight goals, including all four when Sunderland were beaten 4-1 at the City Ground in November. He had also scored at Birmingham in February but this did not count when the game was abandoned at 1-1 after thirty-eight minutes because the roof of a stand had been damaged by a gale.

The home 'derby' with Notts County on 27 March 1909 was notable for the appearance of the Iremonger brothers, Jim and Magpies' stalwart Albert, in opposite goals. Jim, normally a full-back, was deputizing for Harry Linacre. West beat Albert from the penalty spot to give Forest a 1-0 victory. Linacre was a huge favourite with the City Ground faithful and a crowd of 10,000 turned up for his benefit match against Bristol City on 10 April. He retired two days' later after playing at home against Bury.

So Jim Iremonger found himself back in goal when Forest met Leicester Fosse at the City Ground in the season's penultimate First Division match with the threat of relegation still hanging over them. In the event, the goalkeeper was virtually unemployed on that Wednesday afternoon at the end of April. The Reds thrashed their local rivals by a record score, 12-0. Questions were asked, particularly in Lancashire where Liverpool, Manchester City and Bury were all involved in the relegation dogfight. Leicester, who had been promoted the previous season and playing for the first time in the top flight, were already destined for the drop. Notts County as well as Forest were in the mix. The Reds' win saw both in the clear by two points. Manchester City went down with Fosse. The Forest side was: Jim Iremonger, Walter Dudley, George Maltby, Edwin Hughes, George Needham, Jack Armstrong, Bill Hooper, Tom Marrison, Enoch West, Grenville Morris, and Alf Spouncer. Hooper, Spouncer and West each hit hat-tricks, Morris got two goals and Hughes the other.

∞

Rumour was rife and the outcry in the north west persuaded the Football League to hold an inquiry at Leicester on 12 May. President of the

League J. J. Bentley was chairman of the commission, which met at the Grand Hotel, and the other members were John Lewis, W. McGregor, H. Keys and C. E. Sutcliffe. None of the Forest officials and players were summoned to attend. Witnesses called to give evidence included A.G. Hines (Notts F. A.), referee Jack Howcroft of Bolton, Leicester Fosse secretary G. Johnson and goalkeeper H. P. Bailey, the captain. After the hearing, the commission was unanimous is declaring that 'there was neither corruption, collusion, nor anything to suggest that the game had not been properly fought out.' Its conclusion was that 'the bulk of the Fosse players attended the wedding of R. F. Turner two days before the match and that the celebrations were kept up on the night before the contest.' In the opinion of the commission 'this was inopportune and accounted for the indifferent form of a number of the Fosse players.' The witnesses had agreed that the Forest team was 'in remarkably good form'.

Jim Iremonger played his 301st and last match for the Reds early in the 1909/10 season but continued with his county cricket career at Trent Bridge and was unlucky to miss becoming a 'double' international when he toured Australia with the MCC in 1911/12. Forest again finished fourteenth in the League but had a 6-2 victory in one of the last matches played at Bank Street before Manchester United opened Old Trafford in February, 1910. Morris and West both scored hat-tricks.

'Knocker' was transferred to Manchester United during the summer. In his final season with Forest he scored seventeen First Division goals and four in the FA Cup. Morris had nineteen in the league and one in the Cup. In five seasons, West had scored 104 goals in 183 appearances, 96 of them in 168 league games. He hit four league hat-tricks and another in the Cup. Just as prolific for United, he top-scored with nineteen goals when the Manchester side won the league championship in his first season at Old Trafford. His career came to a sad end when, along with others from both sides, he was accused of deliberately fixing the match against Liverpool at Old Trafford on Good Friday 2 April 1915, when United needed to win to ensure their First Division survival. They did so 2-0 after heavy bets had been placed at odds of 7-1 on that very outcome. After an inquiry West and seven others – three from United and four of Liverpool – were banned for life by the Football Association. In 1919 the FA lifted the bans on seven players in recognition of war service and admissions of guilt but 'Knocker' continued vociferously to deny his involvement and his sentence was not lifted until 1945. In the case of Sandy Turnbull, one of the United men, it was a posthumous reinstatement as he had been killed in action. West's thirty-year ban was the longest suffered by an English professional and by the time of his reprieve he was nearly sixty. He had bankrupted himself suing the FA and went to his grave in 1965, the year of Forest's centenary, still protesting his innocence.

Forest began the 1910/11 season in style with away wins against Preston North End and Liverpool, the defeat of Manchester United at the

City Ground, and a 1-1 draw with Notts County on 3 September, when 27,000 came to the opening of the Meadow Lane ground. On Christmas Eve, a twenty-year-old attacking centre-half from Ellesmere Port named Joe Mercer played his first match for the Reds against Tottenham Hotspur at White Hart Lane. Five years' later, he made his 158th and final appearance in the Garibaldi Red in North London against Arsenal, famously to be captained to an FA Cup triumph over Liverpool at Wembley in 1950 by his England international son, Joe junior.

Morris and Armstrong scored at the City Ground in January, when the double was completed over Liverpool and Forest seemed to be settling for a mid-table finish. But the next seven matches were all lost before they picked up a point with a goal-less draw at home to Manchester City. The disastrous decline continued with the season ending with five more defeats. In their last thirteen matches, Forest had taken just one point from a possible twenty-six. Even so, they were only four points from safety and victory at Bury at the start of that dismal run or at Bristol City on the last day might have meant survival. As it was, Bury ended up third from bottom two points above City, who were relegated with two points more than the Foresters, who had a better goal average than either of them.

Sad Forest even struggled during their second spell in Division Two. They were fifteenth in 1911/12 and fared even worse in 1912/13, when the last eight matches were all lost and they dropped to seventeenth. The great Gren Morris retired at the end of the season to concentrate on his coal business and tennis coaching. He died in West Bridgford, aged 82, in November, 1959. What, one wonders, were his feeling when in May that year he saw his club win the FA Cup for the second time and the players go up to the Royal Box at Wembley each to be presented with the winner's medal that he had so desired.

Centre-forward Jackie Derrick hit a hat-trick as the Reds beat Notts County 5-0 to win the County Cup in January, 1914. The Magpies, though, were promoted as champions in 1913/14 after only one season in Division Two and bottom club Forest had to seek re-election to the Football League along with the two sides above them, Lincoln City and Leicester Fosse. The Foresters topped the poll to secure their place but with war clouds gathering there was great uncertainty.

PART TWO

1915–65

Amongst all the unimportant things in the world, football is by far the
most important.
Pope John Paul II, once a goalkeeper in his native Poland

Football is the last sacred ritual of our time.
Pier Paolo Pasoloni, Italian film director and poet

10

The Victory Shield

Cometh the hour, cometh the man. A club in crisis needs careful stewardship by a strong leader. Bob Marsters had assisted secretary Hallam during his last years of office and also Hallam's successor, former player and committee man Teddy Earp. It was as if he had been groomed to take charge and guide the club through desperate times. The only members' club in a league of limited companies, financially fettered Forest struggled to survive. Long established headquarters at Maypole Yard were given up and the new secretary conducted the club's business from a bedroom at his home before moving the office to the City Ground.

On 28 July 1914, Austria declared war on Serbia in response to the assassination, a month earlier, of Archduke Franz Ferdinand in Sarajevo by a Bosnian Serb. This precipitated the First World War with Germany declaring war on Russia on 1 August and the next day invading Luxembourg. On 3 August the Germans declared war on France and invaded Belgium. One day later Great Britain was at war with Germany. Amid catastrophic chaos, confusion and conflict on the Continent, the twenty-seventh season of the Football League began on 2 September 1914, with Forest at home against Birmingham and a crowd of 5,000 at the City Ground. It was a 1-1 draw notable for a debut goal by John G. 'Tim' Coleman, an England international inside-right who had played for Arsenal, Everton and Sunderland before joining the Reds from Fulham when he was nearly thirty-three. He finished Forest's top scorer with 14 league goals from thirty-eight games. His last game was in a 7-0 Second Division defeat against Arsenal at Highbury on 24 April 1915. While at Everton he was one of the few to defy the Football Association's ban on the Players' Union and keep his membership. After a stand-off, it was the FA who backed down.

Remember the BBC TV comedy series *Blackadder*, written by Richard Curtis and Ben Elton and starring Rowan Atkinson, Stephen Fry, Hugh Laurie and Tony Robinson? A great show, it had a closing episode set on the Western Front in the First World War that touched the emotions more dramatically than many a more serious offering. Atkinson was Captain Blackadder and Robinson his incompetent cook Baldrick. They recall the Christmas truce of 1914 when Fritz and Tommy laid down their guns, emerged from their trenches, shared gifts, sang carols together and played football in no man's land.

'Remember the football match?' Baldrick asks. 'Remember it?' replies Blackadder, 'How could I forget it? I was never offside. I could not believe it.' Then the order comes and they go over the top and charge towards the German lines. The screen fades to a field of Flanders poppies. Surprisingly, perhaps, the Commonwealth War Graves Commission lists six soldiers with the name Blackadder who were killed in action on the Western Front.

Several football matches were reported to have taken place all along the frontline at Christmas 1914 and they are the stuff of legend. But they were no myth. This outbreak of peace was joyous for the combatants of both sides but the brasshats behind the lines were alarmed and hurriedly brought it to an end. During the 2014/2015 winter months, the Royal Shakespeare Company commemorated those events of 100 years ago by commissioning and staging *The Christmas Truce*, a play by Phil Porter drawing on true stories of soldiers in the Warwickshire Regiment who took part in one of the unforgettable matches.

One of those was the cartoonist Bruce Bairnsfather, who worked at the RSC's Stratford forerunner, the Shakespeare Memorial Theatre, as an electrical engineer, and as a First World War officer created the popular comic character 'Old Bill'. The match was witnessed by a Newark soldier and Forest fan serving with the regiment, William Setchfield, who wrote about it to his brother before the authorities censored further information. He also asked his brother to write back with results and details of Forest matches. Setchfield's letters were published in a Newark newspaper in 1915. A German soldier recorded the event in his diaries.

> The English brought a football from the trenches and pretty soon a lively game ensued. This Christmas, the celebration of love, managed to bring mortal enemies together as friends for a time.

On Christmas Day and Boxing Day 1914 Forest played Derby County first at home and then away in the Second Division. Symbolically, the ball burst after thirty-five minutes at the City Ground but a crowd of 15,000 saw a 2-2 draw. Left-back Tommy Gibson, from the penalty spot, and inside-left John Lockton were the home scorers. There was a 14,000 gate at the Baseball Ground the next day, when the Reds were beaten 1-0. Derby ended as champions, Arsenal were fifth and Forest eighteenth, third from bottom and five points better than Leicester. Bottom club Glossop went out of the league.

Forest's goalkeeper William Fiske and outside-right Robert Firth, both reservists, were called up on the outbreak of war. Early on, Joe Mercer gave the lead in volunteering, followed by Gibson, who was said to have been all along keen to join up, and Coleman. All three became sergeants. Lockton attained the rank of second lieutenant and Harold Iremonger was a private. It was claimed that more men enlisted from Forest than from any other club except Clapham Orient. Fiske was killed in action and Mercer died in 1927 after health problems resulting from a wartime gas attack. His more famous footballing son, Joe junior, was then just twelve.

Mercer had joined the 17th infantry battalion of the Middlesex Regiment along with so many professional footballers that it was nicknamed 'The Footballers' Battalion'. England international Frank Buckley, later to manage Wolves and then Notts County, was the first player to enlist after its formation in December 1914. He rose to the rank of major and commanded the battalion. It suffered heavy losses during the Battle of the Somme and Buckley himself was wounded. Northampton Town's Walter Tull became a second lieutenant and the first black infantry officer in the British Army. A memorial to the Footballers' Battalion was unveiled in 2010 in Longueval, France. It had been paid for by donations from fans and the ceremony was attended by members of the Football Supporters' Federation.

Forest's golden jubilee year of 1915 began in deep crisis. Players who had not already left to serve with the Footballers' Battalion accepted a 25 per cent pay cut, the League made a grant of £50 followed by £10 a week to the end of the season, £90 was raised from a public appeal and the City Council waived a quarter's ground rent of £36 16s 6d. Then the League drew up special regulations for war-time football, creating regional tournaments and permitting players not on active service to play for any club provided they did so for sport and were not paid. Secretary-manager Bob Marsters immediately grasped the possibilities. Money was no longer a problem in acquiring star performers. His persuasive powers were enough.

Within three weeks he had assembled a Forest team of 'guest' players that included goalkeeping great England international Sam Hardy, who helped win the Championship for Liverpool and gained two FA Cup medals with Aston Villa. His greatest save was to rescue Nottingham Forest from extinction for his signing was Marsters' master-stroke. Hardy's genius lay in an uncanny sense of anticipation that meant he rarely needed to be spectacular. He played in 35 of Forest's thirty-six competitive games in 1915/16 and the one he missed was a 4-1 defeat at Derby.

Fourteen clubs entered the Midlands competition that season and the Reds romped to the championship five points clear of runners-up Sheffield United. The 'double' was completed with success in the subsidiary tournament, winning at Leicester on the final day to leave Notts County runners-up. Hardy had kept a clean sheet in nine successive matches between 6 November and 8 January. Manchester City were champions in the north and Chelsea in the south. Leeds were the midlands' leaders in the next two seasons, when significantly Forest were without 'Super Sam', who had been 'called to the Colours'. He returned to the Reds for the triumphant 1918/19 campaign.

Star quality was added at Christmas when Marsters brought Danny Shea, one of the greatest of all ball players, to the City Ground. Despite his Irish name, Shea was an England international inside-forward born at Wapping and the greatest playmaker of his day. On a foggy day in East London in January, 1911, his goals for West Ham United had knocked Forest out of the FA Cup 2-1. He admitted afterwards to taking full advantage of the conditions to do a 'double Maradona.' 'I punched both goals into the net in full view of several opponents,' he said. Forest supporters will have forgiven him when on his Christmas Day debut in the Garibaldi 12,000 at the City Ground saw his goals beat Notts County 2-0. Blackburn Rovers paid a record £2,000 to take him from the Hammers midway through the 1912/13 season and he returned to Lancashire after scoring fourteen goals in fourteen competitive games during his five months as a guest Forester. Strangely, although he scored twice, the last Midlands regional match was lost at Barnsley to a goal that, according to Forest's statistical record, was 'fisted in.'

Shea helped win the major prize – the Victory Shield – when the war ended. Forest were again regional champions in 1918/19 with Birmingham and Notts County joint runners-up. Everton, the northern winners, were the opposition in a two-legged final played on a home and away basis. A crowd of 15,000 saw a goal-less draw in the first match at the City Ground on 10 May 1919, when Forest's Noah Burton had a goal disallowed for offside and Everton's Gault missed a penalty trying to beat Hardy but shooting wide. Everton were always favourites and now the trophy seemed destined for Merseyside. Goodison Park was packed with 40,000 fans but this time Burton was not to be denied and got the only goal in the forty-second minute.

Jack Armstrong captained the trophy winners whose team for the City Ground encounter was: Sam Hardy; well established full-back partners Harold Bulling and Harry Jones, who would play for England in a 4-1 victory over France in 1923; former Liverpool captain Harry Lowe, Harold Wightman, who would become Forest's first team manager, and Armstrong; Bill Birch, Danny Shea, Walter Tinsley, Noah Burton and left-winger Harry Martin, who had played for England against Ireland in 1914. There was just one change for Goodison Park; Tinsley stood down for the redoubtable Tommy Gibson, who had just returned from war service.

Marsters, who was on £3 a week at Forest, was offered the post of Everton secretary but preferred to stay on Trentside. He was rewarded later with a benefit match. Match-winner Burton, an amateur on Derby's books in 1915, went back to the Baseball Ground and became the Rams' leading scorer in the first post-war season. Basford-born Burton returned to the Reds in the summer of 1921 and played 319 games, scoring sixty goals, before retiring a decade later.

Another returnee in 1921 was Sam Hardy, for whom Forest paid Aston Villa his highest transfer fee – £1,000. It proved money well spent. The great goalkeeper, although thirty-eight, clearly had much to do with winning the Second Division championship in season 1921/22 for only 30 goals were conceded in forty-two games – a divisional record. He went on to make 110 league and cup appearances, playing his last game on 6 September 1924. Hardy was one of the first students of sophisticated angles and the geometry of goalkeeping and, as film footage shows, a keeper who would have been in the front rank of any era. Legend has it that his anticipation was so sharp he rarely had to dive for the ball and he saved more penalties than any of his contemporaries.

He had been an amateur centre-forward before becoming a professional with his local club Chesterfield in 1903. His wages were 18s a week when, two years' later, he was transferred to Liverpool, for whom he made over 200 appearances. He joined Aston Villa in 1912 and, with his career at Villa Park interrupted by the war, played in 160 games for the Villans before his permanent move to the City Ground. With the exception of England's tour of Austria and Hungary in 1908 and an occasional home international, he was England's regular goalkeeper from 1907 to 1920, gaining twenty-four caps as well as playing in three war-time internationals. After his retirement from football, Hardy became a hotel owner in his native Derbyshire. He died in England's World Cup-winning year, 1966.

Skipper Jack Armstrong, who had won a Second Division championship medal in his first full season, 1906/07, gained another in 1921/22, his last full season at the club. This loyal stalwart's final competitive game ended in the heaviest defeat of the 1922/23 First Division season by 8-2 at Burnley on 4 November. The return match on Trentside a week later was won 1-0 by Forest. Jack played his very last game for the Reds in a friendly against the Corinthians at the City Ground on 24 February 1923. He then had a season with Sutton Town and picked up a winner's medal in the 1923/24 Notts Senior Cup final. A cricket all-rounder with his local club, Keyworth, he played for them until the mid-1930s, when he took up umpiring. He ran a market garden business in Keyworth, kept pigs and poultry and became one of the leading experts on chickens in England.

Forest began the first post-war season in Division Two and, with wartime guests having returned to their clubs, struggled to rebuild the side and finished in eighteenth place. One notable recruit was inside-right Jack Spaven from Scunthorpe who scored on his debut in February, 1920, and became the club's leading scorer for the next three seasons. He had won the Military Medal serving with the Royal Artillery in France. But 1920/21 was another undistinguished season and the Reds were again eighteenth at the end of it. Some indication of the frailty of Forest's finances came on 8 January 1921, when, with a home draw against Newcastle United in the third round of the FA Cup, they accepted an offer of £500 to play the tie at St James Park. They were also guaranteed a minimum £1,500 share of the gate. A crowd of 47,652 turned up and the match was drawn 1-1. The replay, four days later and again at Newcastle, attracted 30,728. This time United won 2-1 so the deal proved a satisfactory one for both clubs.

A 4-1 defeat at Crystal Palace was an uninspiring start to the 1921/22 campaign but, with Hardy back in goal and Spaven knocking the ball in at the other end, the Reds soon found their form. 'Shoot Spav' Forest fans urged one of the hardest strikers of a ball with either foot ever known whenever he was in range of the target. And invariably he did, accumulating fifty goals in 170 games during his six seasons with the club.

Two days after their opening day defeat, the Reds began a record, still unequalled, run of seven consecutive league victories beating Hull City 3-2 at the City Ground with goals from Spaven, Walter Tinsley and Bob Parker. Inside-forward Tinsley had been signed after impressing as a guest and Parker joined from Everton, for whom he had scored no fewer than seven hat-tricks. It was Tinsley who helped Forest gain revenge over Palace, scoring both goals in a 2-1 win watched by a home crowd of 16,000. Then Spaven got the only goal as the 'double' was completed over Hull City. The Reds were not hammering the opposition but Noah Burton's solitary goal was enough at Coventry. In this era many fixtures were played back-to-back and the next week Coventry came to the City Ground, where Parker fired the only goal. The sixth and seventh successive victories came in the same week against Derby County.

A crowd of 22,803 was at the Baseball Ground on 24 September and Spaven scored twice in a 2-1 win. A week later there were 28,000 to see Forest hit three goals without reply to rout the Rams. The scorers were the same trio whose efforts had started the remarkable run on 29 August: Tinsley, Spaven and Parker. Two draws in a week against Leicester saw it end. In the first of these, Leicester led at home 2-0 with eight minutes to go but Spaven and Burton saved a point to disappoint a crowd of 25,000. Five special trains ran from Leicester for the return game but there were no goals for the 30,000 spectators to celebrate. Forest's biggest win of the season came in the snow at Sheffield on 4 February when Wednesday were thrashed 4-0. It rained throughout the match on 22 April when promotion was clinched with a 3-1 victory over Stoke at the City Ground. A week later the championship was secured with a Noah Burton goal that defeated Leeds United at the City Ground.

Curiously, in an account of the 2-0 victory at Port Vale on 26 November it was reported that the ball appeared 'to be painted white'. Was a game played with a white ball yet another Forest first?

The Reds reached the fifth round of the FA Cup before going out at Cardiff before a 50,000 crowd. City lost a semi-final replay to Wolves, who were beaten 1-0 by Spurs in the Stamford Bridge final. Fourteen Forest players were each given a gold watch by the grateful committee in recognition of a remarkable season. They were Sam Hardy, Harold Bulling, Harry Jones, Jack Belton from Loughborough who made 347 appearances despite the interruption of war, Glaswegian Fred Parker a strong tackling centre-half signed from Manchester City, Jack Armstrong, winger Sid Harrold signed from Leicester City, Jack Spaven, Bob Parker, Walter Tinsley, Noah Burton, quick and clever winger Syd Gibson from Kettering Town, and Irish international inside-forward Paddy Nelis.

The renaissance of the Reds was short-lived with life in Division One a relentless struggle. The agony was ended on the last day of the 1924/25 season when a sparse crowd of 6,000 at the City Ground saw championship runners-up West Bromwich Albion send Forest down. The home side had done most of the attacking but the more methodical Albion got the game's only goal. Preston North End were twenty-first and also relegated while Arsenal escaped by the skin of their teeth.

After beating Tottenham Hotspur by a Harry Martin goal at the City Ground on 20 December, Forest played fifteen league games without a win. The spell was broken on 4 April with the 4-0 defeat of Leeds United on Trentside. Tall long-striding left-winger Martin again found the net. Born in Selston, Notts, he had won a championship medal with Sunderland before joining Forest at first as a wartime guest. Against Bolton Wanderers on Boxing Day he saved a point for his team in rare cirumstances. He received a nasty leg injury and was taken to the treatment room. Then Forest, a goal down, were awarded a penalty. There were no volunteers to take it and skipper Bob Wallace rushed to the dressing room. Martin was brought back to the pitch. The 20,000 City Ground crowd went wild as their semi-crippled hero beat Bolton's England goalkeeper Dick Pym from the penalty spot at the Bridgford end, salvaged a point and limped off the field again. Martin was transferred to Rochdale at the end of the season. After retiring as a player, he had a couple of years as manager of Mansfield Town. Nelis and Fred Parker also finished and Sam Hardy had retired in October.

The club also bade farewell to Bob Marsters who, after twenty-one years service, became a respected and often visited Nottingham licensee. Notts County followed Forest down the following season and the city was without top flight football for thirty-two years until, in 1957, the Reds returned as runners-up to Leicester City.

II

The Goose Fair Match

Pele, many say, coined the phrase 'the beautiful game' to describe football. But it was an English amateur defender who put it best. Football was a game 'hurtling with conflict yet passionate and beautiful in its art,' wrote Jolly Jack Priestley as long ago as 1929.

Bradford-born headmaster's son John Boynton (better known as J. B.) Priestley was one of the twentieth century's leading men of letters. A pipe-smoking novelist and playwright, his broadcast talks during the Second World War made him second only to Winston Churchill in popularity with radio listeners. A full-back on the field but a left-winger off it, he influenced the politics of the time, upset Churchill, and supported the new Labour Government in 1945. He was also a founding member of the Campaign for Nuclear Disarmament in 1958.

'Conflict, passion, beauty and art': the quote comes from the opening chapter of his prize-winning and best-loved novel *The Good Companions*, published in 1929. Unusually in English fiction, this first chapter is almost entirely devoted to football with a middle-aged Yorkshireman, Jess Oakroyd, going to watch Bruddersfield United. The core of the story has Oakroyd touring with a concert party. Then, in the closing chapter, he returns to Bruddersfield – an amalgam of the author's home town Bradford and Huddersfield – and goes again to a match. There is an epilogue in which Oakroyd has emigrated to Canada to be with his daughter and grandchildren. But still the highlight of his week is the arrival of the Saturday night football edition of the *Bruddersfield Evening Express*.

Nottingham in those days was a great newspaper city. It had two morning papers, the *Journal* and the *Guardian*, and two in the evening, the *News* and the *Post*. The *Evening News* and the *Football News* were published by Nottingham Journal Ltd from its offices, the Express building in Upper Parliament Street. It's now been converted into shops but the corner entrance with the Express name above the door still stands. The *Journal* was published in the city for more than 200 years. Novelist Graham Greene was a sub editor and Peter Pan's creator J. M. Barrie was a leader writer and columnist on the paper. T. Bailey Forman Ltd, publishers of the *Post*, bought out the *Nottingham Journal* company in 1953. For a time, the *Journal* was merged with the *Guardian* to become the *Nottingham Guardian Journal* and the evening papers were brought together as the *Evening Post and News*. A feature of the Monday morning edition was a back page devoted to pictures from Saturday's home match, either Forest's or County's.

The *Football Post* was a tabloid on white paper and the *Football News* was a pink broadsheet. Remarkably, the speed at which they were produced enabled both to carry full match reports, results and up-to-date league tables and be on the streets in the time it took supporters to walk from the City Ground or Meadow Lane to Slab Square. The *Football News* had the best letters' page. It was the equivalent of today's fan forums on the internet though the correspondence was generally more considered and thoughtful. A regular contributor was Forest fan Harry Durose from New Brinsley. He first saw the Reds as a thirteen-year-old on 3 March 1923, when they were beaten 4-0 in a Division One match at the City Ground despite the presence in goal of the great Sam Hardy.

Harry was among the, then record, 44,166 supporters who packed the City Ground on 1 March 1930, when Second Division Forest faced Division One leaders Sheffield Wednesday in the sixth round of the FA Cup. Queues began to form on Trentside at 10.00 a.m. and the gates were closed over half an hour before kick-off. Receipts were £3,822. The visitors took a two-goal lead in the first seventeen minutes. Outside-left Rimmer surprised himself and Nottingham-born goalkeeper Arthur Dexter with the first, a cross from the wing that swerved several feet in flight before entering the net just beneath the bar in the thirteenth minute. The second goal came four minutes later with a 15-yard header from centre-forward Allen. Inside-left Joe Loftus got Forest back in the game just before half-time, beating two defenders before cracking home a rising right-foot shot. Just on the hour, Bill Dickinson, frequently a left-winger but playing at centre-forward, shot in off the post to equalize. Wing-half Billy McKinlay was reported to be the outstanding player on the field and centre-half Tommy Graham was inspirational in defence. Wednesday won the replay at Hillsborough 3-1. Noah Burton, who had missed the first match through injury, scored for the Reds. Nearly 60,000 saw the game and receipts were £4,100. But Forest were fined £50 for arriving late.

Mr Durose was invited to contribute to a 'Memory Lane' column in the Forest programme in 1952 and chose another FA Cup-tie as his most memorable game. This was the fifth round match against Cup-holders Cardiff City at the City Ground on 18 February 1928. Over 30,000 had seen the Reds beat Derby County 2-0 after extra time in a fourth round replay at the City Ground on 1 February. Right-back Bill Thompson with a penalty kick and inside-right Cyril Stocks scored the home goals in a 2-1 victory to knockout City but Forest were beaten 3-0 by Sheffield United at Bramall Lane in the sixth round.

Four years after writing *The Good Companions*, Priestley set out on an 'English Journey' to examine the state of the nation for another book. His travels brought him to Nottingham on Goose Fair Saturday 7 October 1933, and he went with two local friends to the City Ground for the Forest versus Notts County 'derby' match. And, yes, the mist really was rolling in from the Trent. It was also cold and drizzling with rain but we know from records that 23,828 supporters turned out.

Priestley wrote,

Sitting immediately in front of us was a party of two comfortable middle-aged women and a little elderly man who was like a mouse until some incident in the game roused him and then he barked fiercely. The two women ... were the oddest knowledgeable spectators of a football match I have ever seen. They remonstrated with the players by first name. It was as if the two teams had brought their two mothers with them.

Perhaps curiosity about his neighbours distracted him. Fine writer he may have been but a match reporter? Never. 'Near us we had men who looked at one another with eyes shining with happiness when the County scored,' he continued, 'there were other men who bit their lips because the Forest seemed in danger.' Notts, in fact, failed to score. And Forest won the game 2-0. It was the Reds fifth successive win against the Magpies. The goalscorers were powerfully-built centre-forward Johnny Dent and pacey winger Arthur Masters. But the real strength of the side was the half-back line of Billy McKinlay (uncle of the 1959 FA Cup winner Bob McKinlay), England centre-half Tommy Graham (later club trainer under manager Billy Walker) and left-half Bob Pugh. Bob toured Canada with the Welsh FA eleven and would have become a full international but for the selectors discovering that he had been born on the English side of the border.

So Priestley got the score wrong. But on this occasion it was the crowd that interested him and he knew these fans well. It was easy to understand why the crowds paid shillings they could sometimes badly afford to see professionals kick a ball about. 'They are not mere spectators in the sense of being idle and indifferent lookers-on,' he wrote. 'Though only vicariously, yet they run and leap and struggle and sweat, are driven to despair, are raised to triumph; and there is thrust into their lives of monotonous tasks and grey streets an epic hour of colour and strife that is no more a mere matter of some other men's boots and a leather ball than a violin concerto is a mere matter of some other man's catgut and rosin.' With the absurdities of financial interest, the player transfer system, betting and excessive media attention 'nearly everything has been done to spoil this game,' he commented, 'But the fact remains that it is not yet spoilt and it has gone out and conquered the world.'

It was the Goose Fair that drew Priestley to Nottingham for, he wrote, 'the city always had a name for enjoying itself.' As a boy he had heard tell that the football trippers from the North frequently headed for Nottingham.

> Rumour had it that the place was rich with pretty girls. There were goings-on in Nottingham. The truth is, I suppose, that in the old days the enormous numbers of girls employed in the lace trade were more independent and fonder of pleasure than most provincial young women. Certainly, in my tiny experience of it, Nottingham seems gayer, in its own robust Midland fashion, than other provincial towns.

As for the fair itself, it was a 'romantic illusion' glittering in the dank night.

> Golden Goose Fair. I stayed long enough, still warm from my sweaty progress, to smoke a pipe out as I stared and stared at this bright mirage beyond the black trees, and then I joined the crowd that was hurrying down the road to the trams and buses.

In another book *Delight*, published in 1949, Priestley remembered how as a boy he played football all day during the school holidays. 'I would hear the thud, thud, thud of the ball, a sound unlike any other, and delight would rise in my heart,' he recalled. Even hearing the sound now, as a 'heavy ageing man,' he would long to join in. Many of the boys he grew up with lost their lives in the mud of France. He served in the Army during the First World War and was wounded in 1916 by mortar fire. Priestley understood football and its followers because he was genuinely one of them.

∞

Fifth-place finishes in 1926/27 and 1932/33 were the best Forest could achieve in Division Two from their relegation in 1925 up to the Second World War. Their FA Cup form gave supporters something to shout about. They were seventeenth in the Second Division in 1925/26 but reached the sixth round of the Cup, their best run for seventeen seasons and then took eventual winners Bolton Wanderers to two replays. A crowd of 26,300 at the City Ground on 6 March saw Forest twice come from behind to earn a second chance at Burnden Park. It was all the more deserved as they played the last fifteen minutes with ten men after centre-forward Randolph Galloway tore a cartilage. Cyril Stocks and Noah Burton scored for the Reds. The match at Bolton was goalless after extra time and one goal decided it at Old Trafford. A total of 87,004 spectators watched the three quarter-final matches and aggregate receipts were £6,628.

Galloway's playing career began with Sunderland Tramways and included spells with Derby and Tottenham Hotspur before finishing at Grantham Town. But it is his managerial record in Europe and South America that is most impressive. The clubs he managed included Sporting Gijon, Valencia and Racing Santander in the 1930s, the Costa Rican national team in 1946, Penarol of Uruguay in 1948, Young Fellows of Zurich, Sporting Lisbon, whom he guided to three league titles from 1950 to 1953, and Vitoria SC of Portugal 1954/55. Randolph Septimus Galloway died aged sixty-seven on 10 April 1964, in Mapperley, Notts. Winger Bob Firth, who played 145 games for Forest between 1911 and 1921, was another who found success as a coach in Spain. He took Santander to a runners-up spot in La Liga in 1930/31 and Real Madrid to the championship in 1932/33.

The Forest side against Bolton included two internationals; centre-half Gerry Morgan, who had been capped by Northern Ireland for the first time a month before he was signed from Linfield and gained six more while a Red, and Welshman Charlie Jones, a talented left-winger who gained four caps after moving to the City Ground from Oldham in September, 1925. Herbert Chapman paid Forest £4,850 to take Jones to Highbury in May, 1928, and he won three league championship medals with Arsenal and four more international caps. He became a tenacious ballwinner in the Gunners' midfield after losing his wing place to Cliff Bastin. Jones came back to Nottingham as manager of Notts County in May 1934 but quit in December 1935 after falling out with the directors.

Goalkeeper Len Langford, born at Alfreton, Derbyshire, had joined up as a strapping fifteen-year-old when the First World War began and even then was big enough to be recruited by the Coldstream Guards. In 1921 he won the Household Brigade's middle-weight boxing title and three years later joined Forest, getting only a ten-minute warning that he was to make his debut against Sheffield United at the City Ground. He made 144 appearances for the Reds before handing over the gloves to a much slighter Arthur Dexter, who had been his understudy for five years, and joining Manchester City.

Dexter was a sixteen-year-old apprentice printer who had annoyed his employers, Forman's Printers, by joining the Forest groundstaff in 1921 and he was told in no uncertain terms that he had to serve out his time. He made his debut as an eighteen year old on 1 September 1923, deputizing for injured veteran Sam Hardy and keeping a clean sheet in a 1-0 win over Everton at the City Ground. Arthur stood in again for the lumbago-stricken Hardy at home to Tottenham Hotspur in November and then it was back to the reserves and the print works. He signed for Forest full-time when he was twenty-one and left Forman's on good terms with the promise of a job should he want to return. Weighing just 11 stones 'wet through' in contrast to his beefy contemporaries between the sticks, Arthur was as safe a keeper as he was consistent and retired after fourteen years and 274 games with the Reds. A local newspaper cartoonist portrayed him as 'Dexterous Dexter.'

Forest's leading scorer between the wars was Johnny Dent from County Durham who had been left out of Huddersfield Town's 1928 FA Cup Final team despite hitting 22 goals in forty-eight League games for the Terriers. He moved to the City Ground in October 1929, for a fee of £1,500 and scored in six successive Second Division matches before Christmas, ending the season as the club's top scorer with 15 League and three FA Cup goals, a third round hat-trick at Rotherham. A gutsy, well-built and brave centre-forward, Dent found the perfect strike partner in the cerebral Tom Peacock, a school teacher who had played as an amateur with Bath City and signed professional for Forest in August, 1933. Peacock scored on his debut and struck four goals in a 6-1 home win over Port Vale on 23 December, when Dent also scored and Forest registered a 2,000th Football League goal. Dent was again the season's leading scorer with twenty-seven League goals. Remarkably, despite finishing seventeenth, the Reds totalled more goals than promoted Preston North End. Peacock was top scorer in 1934/35 with twenty-one goals in Division Two and again the following season hitting twenty. He wrote his name in Forest records when he scored four goals in a match three times in the space of nine games before Christmas 1935. The bludgeon and rapier partnership of thrustful Dent and thoughtful Peacock was worth more than 100 goals to the Reds in the 1930s before Dent departed.

Another good Cup run came in 1934/35 with both the fourth and fifth rounds going to replays. Despite the match being played in the teeth of what was described as 'a regular blizzard,' there were 32,862 spectators for the home tie against Manchester United, which ended goalless. Forest won the replay 3-0 in front of 33,851 at Old Trafford. Receipts for the two games topped £5,000. The City Ground gate for the fifth round match against Burnley was 34,180 and receipts were £2,796. This was again goalless but the Reds played the second-half without centre-half Harry Smith, who was concussed. Smith returned to the side at Burnley but the game was lost 3-0. A fourth round tie at Derby the following season drew a record 37,830 attendance at the Baseball Ground and record receipts of £3,356.

Forest crossed the North Sea in March 1931 to meet a Netherlands XI at the ground of Sparta Rotterdam, where a 15,000 crowd saw their visitors win 3-1 and pick up a guaranteed £230. In May 1932 talks about a merger took place between the chairmen of Forest and Notts,

Bob Cobbin and Lord Belper. Several more meetings took place but there was no great enthusiasm for the plan and it was quietly dropped. Most supporters of both clubs will be relieved that it was but Forest fans regret that in 1935 an opportunity to buy the City Ground was lost. Landlords Nottingham Corporation agreed to sell the ground, including tennis courts and car park, for £7,000. The deal was not proceeded with, probably for financial reasons, and Forest remain council tenants.

Dent, then thirty-three, scored twice against Blackburn Rovers and again at Bury in December, 1936, but played his last game for Forest a week later before moving to end his career with Kidderminster Harriers. He had scored 122 goals in 207 appearances in the Garibaldi. Forest already had his replacement in situ. Mercurial Irish international centre-forward David Martin had been signed from Wolverhampton Wanderers for £7,000, then a club record fee. Always known as 'Boy' Martin because of his young days as a drummer with the Royal Ulster Rifles, he scored 29 goals in thirty-seven League appearances in his first season and added two more in the FA Cup. Billy McKinlay and Arthur Dexter both retired at the end of the season though the Scot became a scout and, of course, introduced his nephew Bob to the club.

Martin's most valuable goals for Forest came in the last match of the 1937/38 season at Barnsley. The result would decide which of the clubs would go down with the already doomed Stockport County to the Third Division. They were level on points but Forest's goal average was fractionally better – by two-thousandths of a goal. Smart play by inside-right Meynell Burgin, another former Wolves player, created the chance and Martin finished with style. But a 30-yard strike by Asquith bounced over the diving body of Percy Ashton and Barnsley were level. The normally consistent goalkeeper made another mistake when, having done well to hold a fierce shot, he turned back towards goal and bounced the ball over the line. If that was a demoralizing blow for the visitors, worse was to follow when wing-half Bob Davies was injured and became a limping passenger on the wing before having to leave the field altogether.

Forest's ten men battled on but their cause appeared lost until in the closing minutes. Clifford Binns, the home keeper, held a cross but Martin 'no bustler of goalkeepers in the ordinary way,' according to reporter Arthur Turner 'let loose a full-blooded charge that had Binns rocking and turning … turning into goal with the ball in his hands.' The Forest players danced for joy, Barnsley's frantically appealed. The referee went over to his linesman but adhered to his original decision. 'A goal it was,' wrote Turner. 'A goal that saved Forest from relegation. The goalkeeper walked yards down the pitch, crying bitterly, with his face in his hands.' Even then it wasn't over as Barnsley rattled the Forest bar with Ashton beaten. The rebound was cleared to safety. Forest's goal average was 0.783 and relegated Barnsley's 0.781.

The 1938/39 season's opener was a match at the City Ground against Notts County in aid of the Football League's Jubilee Trust Fund. A crowd of 9,505 saw the Reds win 4-1 but hopes of better things in the Second Division were soon dashed. Forest went eight games without a win and then, after beating Bradford Park Avenue, let slip a three-goal lead to allow visiting Sheffield Wednesday to take home a point. That was followed by a 7-1 beating at Chesterfield. After a 1-1 home draw with Fulham before 9,341 fans on 11 March, the decision was taken to part company with team manager Harold Wightman. He was the first to have that role. Wightman, a Nottinghamshire man who had guested for the Reds during the First World War, had successfully managed Luton Town before succeeding secretary Noel Watson and taking the new job title in 1935. Jack Baynes, who had followed Marsters as secretary-manager in 1925, had limited success with little money and left after four years to take over at Wrexham. Stan Hardy, related to goalkeeper Sam, lasted only until January, 1932, after the team had just ended a disastrous run of nine League games without a win. Former first-class referee Watson was persuaded to take over with Dave Willis, father-in-law of the great Arsenal forward Alex James, as his trainer. Watson remained as secretary, and later also as honorary treasurer, serving the club for thirty years and becoming a life member.

12

Billy Walker's War

Ten days after Wightman's dismissal, Forest appointed Billy Walker as the first club manager. He could not have had a tougher start, away to Blackburn Rovers who would be crowned champions. Unsurprisingly, the Reds were beaten but it was only by the odd goal in five. Jack Surtees, who had been an FA Cup winner with Walker's Wednesday, celebrated their reunion with one of the Forest goals. He was also on target in each of the three wins gained in the next four games and took over the captaincy from the injured Tommy Graham when, once again, Forest faced a relegation battle away from home on the last day of the season. But this time they knew that, with a superior goal average, they could survive a defeat at Norwich so long as it was by fewer than four goals.

'Boy' Martin had left to join Notts County in November and at centre-forward was twenty-three year old Bob McCall, who would later establish himself as wing-half and then full-back before returning to his home town club, Worksop Town, as player-manager in 1952. The home side were restricted to a single goal, scored in the 49th minute. Forest's fine defence had kept them up with the Canaries joining Tranmere in relegation.

A goalscoring inside-forward for Aston Villa and England, Billy Walker got an FA Cup winner's medal with Aston Villa in 1920. As a manager, he won two. The first was at the end of April, 1935, in his second season with Sheffield Wednesday, who beat the favourites West Bromwich Albion 4-2. He was then still in his thirties. The other, of course, was Forest's ten-man Wembley triumph over Luton Town in 1959, when he had been the Reds' manager for twenty years.

In his autobiography *Soccer in the Blood*, Walker wrote of a 'bitter sweet' time at Sheffield. He had spent nineteen years as a Villa player and was thirty-five when he took his first managerial post with Wednesday. He had taken on a daunting task. After five seasons of never finishing outside the top three, the Owls were languishing near the foot of the First Division. They had won only two of their last eleven games and had leaked goals alarmingly, six at Wolverhampton and four at Sunderland. Could the tyro manager restore their confidence? The answer came swiftly. Four victories in a row inspired an unbeaten run of sixteen matches, including four FA Cup-ties, and Wednesday finished the 1932/33 season in mid-table seven points clear of relegation. 'Wednesday were in a pretty bad way when I got there,' Walker wrote. 'They were second from bottom of the league table and morale was about as low as their position.' His secret, he said, was an insistence on the team playing good, passing football – a policy from which he would never waver during a long management career. He paid tribute to the players' part in Wednesday's revival and added, 'As an inside-forward myself, I naturally enough had a shrewd eye for another of the breed and here I was lucky in having on the playing staff that strange genius Ronnie Starling.' Walker built the Wednesday attack around Starling and said it was thanks to the player's 'subtle brilliance' that the FA Cup was won. Sports journalist Henry Rose, who was killed in the Munich air disaster, supported that verdict. Starling, as befits a captain, was Wednesday's inspiration, he wrote.

Things began to go wrong for Walker after four years at Sheffield. He described being 'made a scapegoat' with interference in his handling of the players and team selection. The inevitable relegation and his resignation followed. It seems to have been a bitter parting. Walker said,

> My authority seeped away and a very unhappy period of my life came to a close with this statement issued by the chairman, Mr W. G. Turner, who had spoken so fulsomely when I arrived at the club: 'Mr W. H. Walker handed in his resignation as secretary-manager. This has been accepted and his engagement with the club has been terminated on terms mutually agreed upon. There is nothing further to be said.' There it was then.

After a brief interval in non-league football as the manager of Chelmsford City, Billy Walker was appointed boss at the City Ground. Starling, who had won two England caps, joined him in 1940 and played eleven games for the Reds in wartime regional football, scoring four goals. Walker managed the club for twenty-one years and, on his retirement, joined the committee. His blackest day with Forest was 7 May 1949. Bury were beaten in front of a 26,754 City Ground crowd with a goal by winger George Lee but Second Division survival depended on Leicester losing at Cardiff in a game that started a quarter of an hour later. When the final whistle went on Trentside the Foxes were losing 1-0 but a late equalizer gave them the point that sent Forest down in twenty-first position.

The committee's response was in sharp contrast to the reaction at Sheffield to a similar event just over ten years' earlier. Chairman Jack Brentnall, a musical instrument dealer, knocked on the locked door of Walker's office. The manager opened it reluctantly. But Brentnall had a smile on his face. 'Cheer up Billy,' he said, 'you told me we'd get back in two years if we went down. Well, we're down and I believe you. Remember I'll back you and I'll be out with you if we don't do it.' Patience proves to be a virtue in football as in life. Show it as supporters, players, manager and, especially, as club directors and there's a better chance of eventual success.

Just as Wednesday had been, Forest were in freefall when Walker took over and narrowly avoided relegation. Fans were given some hope of improvement with the signing of wingers Colin Perry and Jack Maund from Aston Villa. The Reds were in eighth place in Division Two when the outbreak of war in September 1939 rang down the curtain on the Football League season. Perry and Maund each scored in one of the three games they played but, as records were expunged on the League's suspension, neither appear on the official list of Forest's Football League players. Maund played a few times during the war but Perry only once. He was killed at Tobruk in November 1942 while serving in North Africa as a driver with the RASC.

Forest went to war heavily in debt to the bank with the committee finding money from their own pockets to keep the club going. Mr H. R. Cobbin, a committee member since 1912 and its chairman until 1948, handed over 'a very large cheque' without a word to his colleagues. 'A crisis meeting was called,' Walker wrote in *The Club in Wartime Football*, his 1947 booklet,

And, although things looked very black, the committee decided they owed it to the boys who were going to war, and as a means of keeping up morale, to carry on.

Players' contracts were cancelled as they went into the Forces, civil defence work, armament factories or back into the pits. Walker wrote,

I decided I had a wonderful opportunity of finding young talent on our own doorstep. In September 1939, I started our Colts team and I am proud to claim that I was the first manager in wartime to embark on such a venture. During the war years I tried out more than 1,000 young local players. Many are still in the game, with Forest or other clubs, many, I regret to say, were killed in the war. Of those 1,000 'discoveries' only about fifty made good.

Billy Walker's lament for lost talent had a poignant sequel in August, 2011, when an email was sent to the club by Laura Tough, who explained:

Shortly before he died last year my grandfather wrote his memoirs, including his experiences serving in the West Yorkshire Regiment in the Second World War. He described an incident in May/June 1940 in which his company was fired upon by German Stuka planes, injuring the colleague next to him who later died from his wounds. According to grandpa's account, this man was a professional footballer for Nottingham Forest and one of the injuries he sustained was his foot being sliced off by a piece of shrapnel. My grandpa wrote that he wished he could remember the brave man's name but that, with the passage of time, he could not.

Ms Tough said that it would mean a great deal to her mum and granny if the club could identify her grandfather's comrade. He was Samuel Grenville Roberts who was fatally wounded during the evacuation of Dunkirk on 3 June 1940. Gren would have been twenty-one on 16 August 1940 had he survived. He was an inside-right, born at Blackwell, who played for Huthwaite Swifts and Huthwaite Colliery Welfare before joining Forest in March, 1937. He made his debut in a 1-0 home win against Luton Town on 15 April 1938, and made five more appearances partnering winger Arthur Betts.

Another Forester killed in action was centre-forward Harry Race, who fell at the battle of El Alamein during the North African campaign on 24 October 1942. Harry was born at Evenwood, County Durham, on 7 January 1906, and played for both Liverpool and Manchester City before coming to the City Ground. He made his Forest debut in a 1-1 draw with Brentford on Trentside in the opening match of the 1933/34 season and went on to score 30 goals in 124 appearances. Three others to perish were young reserves Alf Moult, Joe Crofts and Frank Johnson.

The war ended the League career of goalkeeper Percy Ashton, who had made his debut as a twenty-year-old in a home match with Stoke in September 1930 a month after joining the club. Signed from West Melton Excelsior as cover for 'Dexterous' Dexter after the transfer of Len Langford to Manchester City, he had to wait until halfway through the 1933/34 season for a regular place. He remained number one right up to the war, making 185 League and Cup appearances not counting the three games of the abandoned 1939/40 Second Division season and wartime league games. His last match was against Sheffield Wednesday at Hillsborough on 6 April 1940. The war also effectively ended the footballing career of Tom Peacock though he did score 7 times in seventeen regional games before finally bowing out against Derby at the Baseball Ground in October 1945. He had scored 62 goals in 120 games for the Reds. A flight sergeant in the RAF during the war, back in civvy street he returned to teaching and later became headmaster at St Edmund's primary school, Mansfield Woodhouse.

Throughout the war years, Forest competed in regional football and made use of the 'guest player' system although Walker was not an enthusiast for it. The 'guests' included the Derby County wingers Sammy Crooks and Dally Duncan, Ron Burgess of Tottenham and Andy Beattie of Preston, who was to succeed Walker at Forest on his retirement. The manager himself played for the team in the first two full wartime seasons. In 1940/41 he kept goal in a City Ground friendly against the RAF, which was won 4-1, and a Midlands Cup-tie at Lincoln, where Forest were beaten 2-1. He was then at outside-left when the Reds lost 4-0 in a regional league match at Stoke. In 1941/42 he was again an emergency goalkeeper for a League Cup qualifier at Chesterfield and conceded only the decisive goal.

∞

Straight-backed, six-footer Billy Walker strode through Burton's Arcade and into Slab Square wearing a duffle coat with the bearing of a Grenadier in a guardsman's greatcoat. A little younger and he would have made an ideal recruit for Captain Athelstan Popkess, the city's controversial police chief who insisted on a minimum height of six feet for members of his Force. Walker and Popkess became legendary leaders locally. In conflict they might have been titans clashing. And cross swords they did ... in 1940. It was all over a young police cadet who wanted to play football for Forest on Saturdays. It began with a Post Office telegram handed in at 12.36 p.m. at Nottingham on 15 February 1940. Addressed to 'Richardson, 1 Vernon Ave Wilford' it read: 'Ring 8236 before five after 89048 – Walker Notts (sic) Forest.'

As a result of the phone call, Police Cadet Geoffrey Richardson wrote to his boss, Superintendent Tacey:

> Sir, I respectfully apply through you to the Chief Constable for permission to play for Nottingham Forest FC against Rochdale on Saturday, 17th instant. I am, Sir, your obedient servant, G. Richardson, Junior Clerk, Guildhall station.

The young man applied again this time for permission to act as reserve on 8 June against Grimsby Town. This second application was approved so it's probable that the first one was too. Unfortunately, there is no record of these games though they must have been played as young Richardson clearly impressed. For, on 22 August 1940, Billy Walker wrote directly to Captain Popkess at the Guildhall.

The letter read:

> Dear Sir, During the past ten months I have been personally coaching one of your boys by the name of Geoffrey Richardson, and I would like his services during the coming season. Therefore, I would be delighted if you could help my club by giving him permission to play for us. He has, I may add, the promise of being a future star and is in every way a credit to the Nottingham Police Force. We do not have far to travel this season, Birmingham being the longest journey. With regard to injuries, I

think there is less chance of this when play takes place on a good ground and against restrained professionals, who now have to think of their work first, than in the hurly burly local amateur games. Trusting that you can help us in the matter, Yours faithfully, W. H. Walker, Manager.

On 5 September, Captain Popkess replied through his secretary,

I am directed by the Chief Constable to acknowledge receipt of your letter of the 22nd ultimo requesting permission to enlist the services of Geoffrey Richardson during the coming season, and to say that, with the present national situation, the Chief Constable regrets he cannot agree to this clerk playing football for Notts County (sic) as suggested.

Seventeen-year-old Richardson played for Nottingham Amateurs against Rochdale and Lancashire Amateurs at the City Ground on Saturday, 23 March 1940. The Nottingham side was captained by Frank Knight, who played for Forest for nine years before retiring in September, 1949, and becoming a trainer. Richardson is recorded in former club secretary Ken Smales' official statistical history 'Forest – the first 125 years', as having played in a Christmas Day friendly at the City Ground in 1941 against Mansfield Town. His son, Neil, a Forest season ticket holder, has a programme for a Football League championship against Birmingham City at St. Andrew's Ground on Saturday 7 September 1940. The single sheet official programme, priced one penny, shows Geoff Richardson coming into the side at left-back replacing J. Fillingham. Forest lost the game 2-1 but Smales' record names the substitute left-back as F. Robinson. So did Richardson play under an assumed name to fool his police superiors? For sure, F. Robinson subsequently vanishes from all records.

According to Neil, his father was so upset by Captain Popkess's decision that he quit the police and joined the army. He became a captain in the Royal Artillery and served in France, Italy and Germany. The young man was not forgotten by Forest. On being demobbed and seeking civilian employment, he was given a glowing reference by manager Walker, who wrote:

I have the greatest pleasure in recommending Geoffrey Richardson for a post of sports coach. I have known him for many years both as a player with my team during the early years of the war and since he joined the armed forces. He was a member of the finest young team I ever had. He is also fully qualified to become a cricket coach as he has had experience with the Nottinghamshire County Cricket Club.

He has always proved himself to be a great sportsman and is a gentleman both on and off the field. Should he be successful in obtaining the post for which he is applying, I can assure you that you will be appointing someone both worthy and capable. During his service career, he attained the rank of captain and as sports officer was responsible in coaching many men in the units in which he served.

Geoffrey Richardson collapsed and died playing in an Amateur Football Association cup-tie for Sherwood Amateurs Reserves against Brentham (Middlesex) Reserves on Saturday 30 October 1965. He was 44 and left a widow, Joyce, and children Neil and Lynne. Billy Walker built a redoubtable Forest Colts side in the Notts Amateur League, the only junior competition able to carry on during the war. Captain Athelstan Popkess was the youngest chief constable ever at thirty-seven in 1930 when he took over the Nottingham City force. He was a visionary policeman, founding the country's first forensic science laboratory, introducing walkie-talkies for officers, training police dogs, and coming up with the idea of traffic wardens. He led the city force until 1960 and died in Torquay in 1968, aged seventy-five.

∞

A wartime international match was played at the City Ground on 26 April 1941, when England beat Wales 4-1. Centre-forward Don Welsh of Charlton Athletic scored all four English goals and the half-backs Cliff Britton (Everton), Stan Cullis (Wolves) and Vic Buckingham (Spurs) all went on to become distinguished managers. No Forest players were picked for either side but Ron Burgess, who guested for the Reds, was in the Welsh line-up and Bob Davies played the first ten minutes for Wales until late arrival Dai Astley was ready to take his place at inside-right. The attendance was 13,016. England had played Wales at the City Ground once before, on 15 March 1909, when Sam Hardy was awarded his sixth cap and kept a clean sheet in a 2-0 victory.

Future first team regulars such as Frank Knight, Geoff Thomas, Jack Hutchinson, Bill Morley and 'Tot' Leverton were among Walker's wartime discoveries but other local clubs benefited from his youth programme at the end of hostilities. Ilkeston Town, for instance, formed in 1945 won four successive Central Alliance championships with a side that included captain Les 'Snowy' Smith, Dave Baker, Phil Bibby, Ken Ledger, Jack Ward and Horace Hackland, all of whom had begun their careers in Forest junior sides. A skilful attack-minded half-back, Hackland had been spotted as a teenager with Basford United and Grove Celtic. He was signed by Walker towards the end of the war and, in 1950, by Ilkeston in the office at Oscroft's car showroom on Castle Boulevard, where he worked. Terms of £4 a week were agreed for the part-timer, who was sought after by a number of non-league clubs, but the clincher in the deal was Ilkeston's willingness to provide the player with a pair of contact lenses, making him one of the very few footballers wearing them in those days. Hackland won four championship medals and later became a coach and then general secretary of the Town club.

The Midland Cup was the trophy Forest came closest to collecting during the war when the final was settled by a 'golden' goal. The Reds and West Bromwich Albion shared four goals in the first leg at the Hawthorns on 29 April 1944. A week later 14,438 saw Forest take a 3-2 lead late in extra time and some supporters, thinking it was all over, invaded the pitch to carry the players shoulder-high for the presentation by the Lord Mayor of Nottingham. But there were still two minutes left, police restored order, and Albion grabbed an equalizer on resumption. The sides were deadlocked at the end of extra time and the match continued until a deciding goal was scored. That 'sudden death' goal was put past Forest's 'guest' goalkeeper Ray Middleton to give Albion an overall 6-5 victory.

During the 1945/46 season Forest flew to war-battered Germany to play the Rhine Army team in Cologne. The soldiers were 4-1 winners and their left-wing pair impressed. At inside-left was Billy Steel, who became a Scottish international and a Derby County star before emigrating to Canada. He was unaffordable but his partner George Lee, fast with a powerful shot, was brought to the City Ground a week before the 1946/47 season started. Walker paid York City £7,500 for him and commented: 'I fully believe him to be the best left-winger in the country today.' He also signed the army side's right-back Jim Clarke, who hailed from the manager's home town, Wednesbury in Staffordshire, and went to the same school there. So despite the defeat and an alarming return flight, a hurricane buffeting the plane which had to make an unscheduled landing near the South Coast, the trip was well worthwhile.

Thirty-four years later the Reds would re-visit Cologne's Mungersdorfer stadium on 25 April 1979, and record a famous victory; Ian Bowyer scoring the vital goal that carried them through to the European Cup Final by a 4-3 aggregate after drawing the first leg against FC Cologne 3-3 in the semi-final first leg at the City Ground.

13

Something About a Sailor

One of the shrewdest strokes of business pulled off by Forest's astute manager Billy Walker at the end of the Second World War was the signing of England wartime international inside-forward Robert Albert John Brown from First Division Charlton Athletic.

R. A. J. Brown, who liked to be called Bert but was forever known in football as 'Sailor', had starred for the Londoners in the 1946 FA Cup Final won 4-1 by Derby County after extra time. Deep into the second-half with the scores level at 1-1, 'Sailor' dribbled past five defenders but just failed to find his skipper Don Welsh with a pass that might have produced the winning goal. His ear, as ever, close to the ground, Walker picked up that afterwards there had been a sharp fall-out between Brown and his manager, Jimmy Seed. The player was going to be moved on and, naturally, he wanted to stay in the top flight. His preferred destination was Aston Villa but Seed did not want to see his star go to another Division One club and Forest snapped him up for £6,750.

A year later, 'Sailor' was transferred to Villa for a club record fee of £10,000. Had there been an arrangement? Who knows? But Forest certainly did very well out of it. Brown played forty-five Second Division games for the Reds, scoring seventeen goals. He also featured in four FA Cup-ties and a couple of friendlies, including a 2-2 draw against the Combined Services in Hamburg. Ironically, before Walker's time, the club might have signed him for nothing. On 3 May 1934, Forest played a friendly at Gorleston and won 5-2. Brown was in his home town's side and may have been the reason for Forest's visit because he had been recommended to the club by scout Billy Latham. He was invited to the City Ground for a trial but nothing came of it. Centre-half Tom Graham, who had played against him, suggested he should try again with Forest but by then the youngster was already booked for Charlton.

'Sailor' scored on his debut for Forest at Barnsley on 31 August 1946, but George Robledo got a hat-trick for the home side who won 3-2. His last game on 27 September 1947, was also a defeat in Yorkshire. Despite George Lee putting Forest ahead in the first minute at Hillsborough, Sheffield Wednesday were the victors 2-1. Walker thought highly of him, he wrote in his handbook.

> Bert Brown is the captain and schemer of the side with original ideas on tactics. A vital link in any line in which he plays, Brown can stay the course to the end. Another of Forest's humourists, his forte is dialect stories and verse. Is keen to become a football manager, otherwise is quite rational.

So how did Bert become known as 'Sailor'. Well it was nothing to do with war service since he had been a sergeant in the RAF. Rather, he had a distinctive rolling gait and, with a muscular stocky build, he reminded team-mates of the cartoon character 'Popeye the sailor man' and so, irresistibly, he was nicknamed 'Sailor'. Brown was twenty-three and already making an impact with Charlton, then one of the leading First Division clubs, when the war began in 1939. He captained the RAF team and made half-a-dozen appearances for England alongside the likes of Stanley Matthews and Tommy Lawton in unofficial wartime internationals, for which caps were not awarded. His RAF side, with Matthews his wing partner, beat the Belgian national team in Brussels at the end of the war. He and the great Stanley were described by a Belgian correspondent as 'the two best footballers I've seen in my life.'

Brown scored for England in a 2-0 victory against Belgium at Wembley in January, 1946, and, despite facing competition from such players as Wilf Mannion, Raich Carter and Jimmy Hagan, was in the national team that beat Switzerland 4-1 at Stamford Bridge four months' later. A clever dribbler and a fine pass-maker, 'Sailor' was a talented ball player who featured in Wembley finals in four successive years – for Charlton in the League Cup South in 1943 and 1944, for Millwall in the same competition as a 'guest' in 1945 as well as in the first post-war FA Cup Final.

An injury playing for Villa ended Brown's Football League career in 1949 but he returned to Gorleston to become an inspirational player-manager. He led his home-town club on an impressive run in the early stages of the 1951/52 FA Cup competition. They ended going out to Leyton Orient in a first round proper second replay at Highbury despite scoring four goals – Orient got five.

'Sailor' died at Forres, Morayshire, on 27 December 2008, aged ninety-three. He will never be forgotten by his home town. David Hardy of Gorleston FC said 'Sailor' was voted the club's greatest-ever player in a poll on their website. Following his death, the club renamed one of its stands The Sailor Brown Stand and in pre-season 2009 introduced the Sailor Brown memorial trophy tournament. It's a day-long event with half-a-dozen East Anglian senior teams competing in a round robin league of twenty-five-minute games. Three points are awarded for a win, two for a score draw and one for a goal-less draw. The top two in the league qualify for the final. A youth tournament runs parallel to the main competition. Brown's daughter, Julie, has annually travelled from her home in Scotland to present the trophies.

Unfortunately for Forest, Brown's transfer to Aston Villa coincided with the sensational arrival of England's current centre-forward Tommy Lawton at Third Division Notts County from Chelsea. Walker saw England's inside-right Raich Carter as a perfect City Ground counter-attraction. Silver-haired Carter and blond Irish star Peter Doherty were the 'silver and gold' inside-forward partners who, after being wartime 'guests' at the Baseball Ground, helped Derby win the FA Cup against Brown's Charlton. They were together for the start of the first post-war Football League campaign in 1946/47 but Doherty made only fifteen appearances, scoring seven goals, before moving to Huddersfield. Carter didn't stay at the Baseball Ground much longer. He left in March, 1948, having scored 34 goals in sixty-three appearances. Both had fallen out with the Derby board.

Carter had played for Forest in wartime League South on 12 September 1945, in a draw with Fulham at the City Ground. At the time he was in the RAF and stationed at a pilot rehabilitation centre at Loughborough. So Walker thought he might have a chance of persuading him to come and Derby to sell. He was thwarted by the player's management ambitions. There was an offer from Hull City and Carter reasonably considered his prospects in that direction much brighter on Humberside than on Trentside. And so it proved. Within a couple of weeks Maj. Frank Buckley quit the Hull job to take over at Leeds and, in his place, Carter was appointed the Tigers' player-manager. He led his charges to the Third Division North championship and, ambitiously, signed England centre-half Neil Franklin and Don Revie. When a second promotion didn't materialize, ever the perfectionist Carter resigned in September, 1951. Subsequently, he led Leeds United to the top flight in 1956 but, after ruffling the feathers at Elland Road, was sacked in 1958. He had one more promotion to achieve, taking Mansfield Town out of the Fourth Division in 1963 before finishing his career with three lean years at Middlesbrough.

Forest went into the war having made a loss of £4,877, which doesn't seem much by today's reckoning but was a considerable concern at the time. Profit and loss accounts stayed in the red until 1943, when a profit of £1,571 was made. Profits rose steadily to £2,919 at the end of the 1946/47 season. A comfortable enough sum but Walker had forked out £4,500 on the recommendation of Bert Brown for winger Freddie Scott from York City, a record fee for the selling club. 'Sailor' had partnered him in wartime football at York and Charlton and knew his worth. A former England Boys outside-right, Scott was then only a month from his thirtieth birthday but he went on to play 323 games for Forest and was only a month from turning forty when he made his last appearance in September 1956. With the height and weight of a jockey, Scott had the pace and skill to take on the strongest defender. A fine positional player, he could play on either wing and was shrewd enough to make the ball do a lot of the work. Walker said he would do even better if he cut in towards goal a little more 'and had a crack.' In fact, Scott's 28 goals for Forest included one in his last game which Rotherham won 3-2.

For season 1946/47, Billy Walker introduced a palm-sized four-page card of players' instructions containing thirteen training rules and regulations. The day would begin at 10.00 a.m., they were told, and training would include running, sprinting, skipping, punching the ball, walking, football dribbling and practice games. Any player absenting himself from training would be held to have broken his agreement and his wages would be stopped pro rata. Friends were not allowed in the club rooms and gambling of any description was strictly prohibited. On the back was an admission ticket and players were to carry the pass and show it to the gateman at all home matches. In effect, it was a Forest identity card and, psychologically, it must have given players a sense of belonging.

∞

When Larry Platts died in a Lincolnshire nursing home on 4 September 2006, aged eighty-four, it was said that 'he was a Forest man right up to the end.' He was one of Walker's 'colts' and made his first team debut in goal for a friendly match at Lincoln City on 19 October 1940, just twelve days before his nineteenth birthday. It was won 3-2. Larry was also on the winning side in his last game when the Reds beat Port Vale 2-0 in the Third Division South at the City Ground on 29 April 1950. Wally Ardron and Gordon Kaile scored in a match watched by a crowd of only 5,908. In all, he made seventy-two first team appearances – all but ten of them in wartime football.

But it is Forest's famous FA Cup fourth-round victory over Manchester United on 25 January 1947, that gives him an honoured place in the club's history. Because of war damage to Old Trafford, the game was played at Manchester City's Maine Road ground where there was a 34,059 attendance. Forest were in the lower half of the Second Division with United lying third in Division One. Goals by Eddie Barks and Colin Lyman made Forest giant-killers but it is remembered as 'Larry Platts' match.' Nottingham journalist Arthur Turner reported, 'Platts kept a fantastic goal – it was the game of his life.' Army call-up made that his last for a couple of years.

The Forest team was: Larry Platts, Harry Brigham, Bob McCall, George Pritty, Ted Blagg, Frank Knight, Freddie Scott, 'Sailor' Brown,

Eddie Barks, Jack Edwards and Colin Lyman. Johnny Carey, later to become a Forest manager, was in the United line-up along with Johnny Aston, Allenby Chilton, Jimmy Delaney, Johnny Morris, Jack Rowley and Stan Pearson. The quality of the home side was shown in their next match when they beat Arsenal 6-2 in the First Division at Highbury. The young goalkeeper had made his Football League debut at the City Ground only a week earlier when Southampton were despatched 6-0 with goals by Lyman (2), Edwards, Barks, Brown and Brigham. There were 24,591 present.

Eddie Barks was Walker's first signing for Forest in April, 1939, from Heanor Town. Ilkeston-born Barks was 'one of the best club players I have ever had,' said Walker.

> He is the real 100 per cent player who never gives up; a real tryer. A real glutton for work, he is ready and willing to play anywhere and his whole-hearted efforts in the unaccustomed position of centre-forward, he is really a wing-half, will not soon be forgotten by Forest supporters.

Barks played seventy times for the Reds between August 1946 and September 1948 scoring six goals, and then joined Mansfield Town, making 225 appearances for the Stags.

With Platts now in uniform, Griff Roberts was in goal for the Fifth Round tie against Middlesbrough of the First Division. A crowd of 32,000, paying £3,842, saw England's Wilf Mannion score an own goal in a 2-2 draw. Freddie Scott got the other Forest goal. The replay at Middlesbrough was watched by 27,000. Barks and Edwards scored for Forest but Mannion hit a hat-trick in a 6-2 home win. Lyman became a 'passenger' for the remainder of the match after twisting his knee in the 30th minute. City Ground supporters had seen Mannion in September playing for an FA XI against a Combined XI in a benefit match organised by Billy Walker for Newark-born England star Willie Hall, who had lost both legs after being struck down by thrombosis. In a memorable international match against Northern Ireland in 1938, Hall, formerly of Notts County but then a Spurs player, had lit up a dull November day with a three-minute hat-trick. He went on to score a record five goals in a row as England won 7-0. The FA XI included such stars as Frank Swift, George Hardwick, England captain, Stan Cullis and Billy Wright from Wolves, Tom Finney and Raich Carter. In Combined XI were Ray Middleton, Leon Leuty, Len Shackleton, Jack Rowley of Manchester United and Forest players Bill Baxter, Bob MCall and Tom Johnston. Mannion got a goal and the game ended properly as a 2-2 draw.

Floods, fog and snowfalls during the winter of 1946/47 caused such disruption that the football season ran into the middle of June. Forest's match against Manchester City in November had to be played at Notts County's Meadow Lane because the City Ground was deep under water.

A 32,000 crowd saw the visitors win by an only goal. Trent floods returned with a vengeance in March, when the water crept up almost to the height of the crossbars and swans from the river glided majestically the full length of the pitch. Floodwater swamped the club's offices and important records were lost. No home matches were played that month and those fixtures were postponed until the end of May. The match at Fulham in December was abandoned because of fog with Forest leading by a Barks goal and only fifteen minutes remaining. The match at Millwall in March was finished in a snowstorm.

Forest were not safe from relegation until their last three matches, all at home and all victories. A Johnston goal was enough to see off Chesterfield on 27 May and four days later Plymouth Argyle were thrashed 5-1. Johnston netted another two and Brown, Edwards and Knight also scored. It was raining heavily and only 8,429 turned up when Forest ended the season with a 4-0 victory over Bradford Park Avenue at the City Ground on 14 June. Versatile Tom Johnston, who had been a part-time pro with Peterborough United and joined the Reds during the war, scored a hat-trick taking his goal tally to twelve and making him the season's second highest scorer after 'Sailor' Brown on sixteen.

A significant newcomer who made his debut in a 1-1 draw at Fulham on 26 May was 'Mr Consistency' himself George Henry 'Harry' Walker, who had helped Portsmouth win the FA Cup against Wolves at Wembley in May 1939. 'As safe as houses', he was tall and confident in judgment and handling. An ever-present in Forest's Third Division South championship-winning side, he played 304 games for the club before injury forced his retirement aged thirty-nine in May, 1955. Walker warded off challengers for his place like Reg Savage, Griff Roberts, Harry Orgill and, of course, Larry Platts.

Walker wanted his team to play a high-speed passing game and, needing a schemer to replace the departing Brown, paid Brentford £7,000 for thirty-year-old George Wilkins, who was described as 'a clever, calculating craftsman.' He scored on his debut in a 4-2 home win over Doncaster Rovers on 27 December 1947, and averaged a goal every four games but, plagued by injuries, his appearances became increasingly spasmodic. The father of Ray Wilkins of Manchester United, Chelsea and England, he managed only twenty-six starts in nearly two years. Another thirty-plus Londoner proved a more enduring signing. Blond centre-half Horace Gager cost a record £8,000 fee to Luton Town but became the pillar of the Forest defence for the next seven years before retiring in 1955 after playing 258 league and nine FA Cup games. He scored the penalty goal that gave Forest a 2-2 draw at Barnsley on 17 April and made them safe from relegation.

It was a temporary respite for, despite a final flourish with six wins and a draw in their last nine games, they were doomed on the closing day of the season to go down in twenty-first place with bottom club Lincoln City.

With one game remaining, the Reds were two points behind Leicester but with a superior goal average. Forest were at home to Bury while City had to travel to fourth-placed Cardiff. A 26,754 crowd at the City Ground saw a second-half goal by George Lee give Forest both points. All now depended on the result at Ninian Park, where the game had kicked of a quarter of an hour later. Cardiff were holding a first-half lead but then, two minutes after the City Ground game had finished, Forest fans were crushed as the Foxes' centre-forward Jack Lee grabbed a saving equalizer.

Walker himself was in despair and described that last Saturday of the season as 'the blackest of my whole career.' In his autobiography he wrote,

> From the beginning I was so nervous of the outcome that I went into my office and stayed there. So much depended on every kick of that game that I could not bear to see a single one of them. All I could do was to sit there and listen to the roars of the crowd from time to time and wonder for whom they were roaring! At times like these the position of the manager of a club that has been having a bad time is almost the same as that of the captain of a ship that's in trouble. As I sat there trying to forget the game and its dire potential, I was fortified by one voice out on the terracing. This voice kept up the morale-boosting shout of 'Come on, Forest' that did my heart good.

The next day he went to the ground in some trepidation for a meeting with the committee, he wrote,

> It was hard to believe from the way they behaved that we had just been sent into the Third Division [...] You might have thought we had won promotion! It did not seem possible that seven men could look as happy as these did in these circumstances but I knew my great friend Jack Brentnall had created this atmosphere especially to help me.

His chairman and the committee showed they believed in him. 'I thanked them and went home at lunchtime a very much happier man.'

A highlight of the season had been an FA Cup third-round tussle with Liverpool, which went to a replay. A crowd of 35,000 at the City Ground saw Forest, 2-0 up at the time, reduced to ten men after seventy minutes when Walker was concussed and inside-left 'Tucker' Johnson had to take over in goal. The game finished 2-2 after extra time. Centre-forward Bill Hullett, who had pulled a muscle, went in goal for the last half-hour to allow Johnson to go forward and Forest's ten men looked to most likely to score. They almost regained the lead when George Lee had a shot cleared off the line. It was a different story in the replay at Anfield. Wilkins missed a penalty for Forest, who were well beaten 4-0. A future inspiring FA Cup winning captain Jack Burkitt, then twenty-two, played in both games having made his first team debut at Coventry two months earlier.

Six-footer John Love joined from Albion Rovers for £7,000, a typical Billy Walker fee, at the end of February. His seven goals from inside-right in thirteen games had much to do with the Reds improvement towards the end of the season but was not enough to keep them in Division Two. He was, however, second highest scorer to Lee, who had ten from thirty-six appearances. The Scot had served with Bomber Command as a flight lieutenant but gained the DFC as a glider pilot wounded but staying at the controls during the crossing of the Rhine in 1944. He scored 20 goals in sixty games for Forest

These were the days of post-war shortages, ration books and clothing coupons. Forest were in the unfortunate position of having to appeal to supporters so that kit could be bought and more than 200 responded. Ill health had been a factor in the retirement of Bob Cobbin after twenty-eight years as chairman. He had played a considerable part in keeping the club afloat through difficult times. Forest was his ruling passion and he was honoured as a life member. Dapper, pipe-smoking Jack Brentnall, with dark, wavy hair brushed straight back, succeeded to the chairmanship and immediately struck up a strong relationship with manager, who was rarely seen without a cigarette.

The new chairman's whole-hearted support, and that of the committee, was just the encouragement Billy Walker needed. Relegation led to him losing two of his best players. George Lee went to West Bromwich Albion for £11,500 and Jack Edwards to Southampton for £10,000 but in goalkeeper Harry Walker and centre-half Horace Gager he had two-thirds of a rebuilt team spine. The final part would be gutsy goal-scoring centre-forward and he was about to be added. A golden decade was dawning.

14

From Pit to Pinnacle

'The bravest centre-forward who ever drew breath.' That was TV chat show host Michael Parkinson's take on Wally Ardron in his 1968 book *Football Daft*. Well, Wally was certainly manager Billy Walker's most significant signing and one of Forest's all-time greats. He made a promising start in the Garibaldi with a goal at the Goldstone Ground to earn a point from the opening match of the 1949/50 Division Three South season, a 2-2 draw with Brighton and Hove Albion. Unfortunately, it was not so happy for inside-left Tommy 'Tucker' Johnson who had to go off after half-an-hour and then hobbled on the left-wing for the whole of the second half. An x-ray subsequently revealed that he had broken his leg.

'Tucker', a Geordie, had been another £7,000 signing and joined from Gateshead in August 1948, on the recommendation of Freddie Scott. A classy inside-forward, he was a clever ball player yet also forceful with a hard shot – just Walker's type. Stocky and sturdy, he was easily picked out by his fair, floppy hair. He scored 30 goals in seventy-three appearances for Forest despite suffering a second broken leg and the removal of a cartilage. His last game for the Reds was a goal-less draw against West Ham United at the City Ground on 3 November 1951, and he retired at the end of the season.

During close seasons, 'Tucker' had taken coaching engagements with Myllykosken Pallo-47 (commonly known as MyPa) in Finland, and these led to Forest having a distinguished supporter in Kensington Palace Gardens, London. No. 14 is the official residence of Finland's ambassador and in 2012 His Excellency Mr Pekka Huhtaniemi, a MyPa follower, said this connection had made him choose Forest as the English team to support. The ambassador sent the club a MyPa magazine, pennant and badges. MyPa's colours are also red and white. Coincidentally, Tom Johnston coached Finnish team Valkeakoski Harka in the summer of 1957 after leaving Notts County and before joining Birmingham City. Johnston had been equally prolific for the Reds with 26 goals in sixty-six games before his transfer to Meadow Lane at the end of the 1947/48 season.

Ardron was then a part-timer and worked as a fireman on the railway but he had scored 230 goals in nine seasons, including wartime, for Rotherham and the thirty-eight in the first season after the war is still a club record. The deal was done at The Crown Hotel, Bawtry, convenient for both clubs, and chairman Brentnall accompanied the manager. But, first, Ardron had a question for them. He wanted to know if they realised how old he was and, according to the player in his autobiography *Goals Galore*, Walker's reply was, 'Yes, you are thirty-two and you will do me for five seasons.' Ardron comments, 'This I, in fact, did and scored nearly 130 goals for him. Rotherham were happy, too – the money they received, £10,000, enabled them to buy their Millmoor ground from British Railways.' Wally's age on signing may have been slightly exaggerated. According to former club secretary Ken Smales's records, he was born on 19 September 1919. Another source makes the year of birth 1918.

Not particularly tall, but stocky and powerfully built, as befits a champion shot-putter and useful pugilist, Ardron could handle himself all right. Bruce Woodcock was the first post-war British heavyweight champion and held both British and Empire titles from 1945 to 1950. Wally was his mate and sparring partner.

Manager Walker insisted that his new centre-forward give up his railway job and the player responded magnificently to becoming a full-time pro. He scored twenty-five goals in his first season and became so influential that Walker acted on his advice to buy left-wing pair Tommy Capel and Colin Collindridge. Ex-Royal Marine Capel, then twenty-six, came from Birmingham City in exchange for a £14,000 cheque, the largest Walker had signed, and made his debut on 5 November 1949, when 18,471 turned up at the City Ground for a 2-0 victory against Crystal Palace, John Love scoring both goals. Capel had a powerful left-foot and made his presence felt with 9 goals in twenty-four league games in his first season.

Tommy Lawton-led Notts County were still, of course, the big boys in town. On 26 November when 15,567 were at the City Ground to see Forest beat Bristol City 1-0 in the first round of the FA Cup, there were 28,584 at Meadow Lane for the Magpies' cup-tie against non-league Tilbury. Forest played the Essex port town's team in a City Ground friendly at the end of the season to raise funds for Hyson Green children.

The first-ever Third Division matches between the Nottingham clubs and the first in the League for nearly fifteen years resulted in home and away defeats for Forest in front of huge crowds. Notts were top of the table with Forest hard on their heels when the two sides met at the City Ground on 3 December before a crowd of 38,903. In the 28th minute the Magpies took the lead with goal headlined in the *Daily Express* as 'Lawton's Leap.' Here is how reporter Crawford White described it,

From a corner Broome placed a high dropping centre rather farther from goal than usual. No greyhound ever left a trap quicker as he darted in to take his chance. He made a spectacular leap, timed the flight of the ball uncannily and nodded his head. The next thing the crowd saw was the ball hurtling past the Forest goalkeeper. Even dyed in the wool Forest fans had to applaud this piece of soccer sorcery.

Former Aston Villa and Derby winger Frank Broome made it 2-0 after the interval and, with only three minutes remaining, Tommy Capel pulled one back for the Reds.

The return match on 22 April attracted an all-ticket crowd of 46,000, breaking the Meadow Lane attendance record. Jackie Sewell headed Notts in front after fifty-eight minutes and two minutes later Lawton got another – with a header, of course. The 2-0 victory gave the home side their first ever double over Forest. It also assured promotion. Lawton was the division's top scorer with thirty-one goals. Wally Ardron was second highest, six behind the Magpies' captain. Forest finished fourth with forty-nine points, nine fewer than the champions Notts.

In May, Forest went on a six-match tour of the Netherlands, West Germany and Belgium. There were 1-0 victories over Gool Hilversum and Sparta Rotterdam, 2-2 draws against Gottingen 05 and Osnabruck with a 6-1 defeat by S.V. Bremen in West Germany, and a 6-0 thrashing by Belgian side Racing Club Malines. Racing Club came to the City Ground a year later for a match to mark the opening of the Festival of Britain, which was intended by the Labour Government of the time to lift the spirits of a people still recovering from war and to show the world that the nation was facing the future with enterprise and optimism. Most of the activities were centred on London's South Bank side of the River Thames. The site was signalled by the Skylon, a vertical cigar-shaped structure appearing to float above the ground with no visible means of support – a bit like the economy, critics said. Now the Festival Hall is all that survives. Though in Nottinghamshire, just a few miles west of the city, lies Trowell, somewhat surprisingly chosen as the Festival Village. Trowell had no pub – until the Festival Inn was built – and views across the industrial spoil tips of Stanton Ironworks.

Forest supporters had lots to celebrate. After two seasons in Division Three South the club had been promoted as champions, six points clear of runners-up Norwich, scoring a League record 110 goals while conceding only forty. Walker had fulfilled his promise. What's more, the reserves had won the Midland League nine points clear of second-placed Rotherham United after scoring 103 goals against forty-five. In the letters column of the Football News on Saturday 5 May 1951, habitual correspondent Harry Durose pointed out that Forest were the highest scorers in all four divisions (including Third Division North) of the Football League and had conceded fewer than any other League club.

In a programme note for the Festival match, chairman Brentnall remarked on a 'truly wonderful season' just passed and looked forward with confidence 'in the knowledge that ours is a happy club with the family and team spirit paramount.' Introducing the visitors, the programme revealed that Racing Club had been formed by the four Dogaer brothers, who had fled from Malines to London during the First World War and the oldest of whom had played in Chelsea's reserves side. On their return home in 1918 the latter became Racing Club's coach and was then its president. Belgian international Van der Auwera was described as an 'old-fashioned attacking centre-half and inside-right de Saedeleer was acknowledged one of the most highly-skilled in Europe. Forest lined up with Harry Walker in goal, Bill Whare and Geoff Thomas at full-back, captain Horace Gager at centre-half flanked by Bill Morley and Jack Burkitt, with the forwards Freddie Scott, 'Tucker' Johnson, Wally Ardron, Tommy Capel and Colin Collindridge. This had been the first-choice eleven all season. A festive crowd of 18,000 saw the game. Substitutes were allowed. John Love went on for Collindridge and scored in the 3-1 victory with the Reds' other goals coming from Capel and Johnson.

Forest signed Collindridge just in time for the start of the promotion season. Earlier they could have had him for no more than a £10 signing-on fee but his transfer from Sheffield United was secured for £12,000. They were not alone in missing his talent. Rotherham had released him shortly after his seventeenth birthday. Wolverhampton Wanderers also let him go and he declined Forest's offer of only part-time terms. After serving in the RAF, he helped Sheffield United win the League North title in the transitional 1945/46 season, scoring sixteen goals in nineteen games. He was also the Blades' top scorer in each of the three postwar seasons. When Walker heard that Collindridge was keen on a move to Preston, he stepped in with an offer knowing that the player had married a Nottingham girl during his RAF service and hoping that he might like to live in the city. The approach was successful and a week after signing he scored on his debut in a season-opener at Newport. Johnson got the other goal in 2-0 win. A cheery character and an excellent club man, the winger was a huge favourite with Forest fans who admired his speed, skill, direct play and powerful left-foot shot.

Collindridge struck up an immediate rapport with his inside partner Capel and the goals began to flow from all along the forward line. Forest hit seven without reply against Aldershot at the City Ground at the end of September. Ardron hit a hat-trick, Scott got two with one each from the left wing pair. In the middle of November a crowd of 20,639 on Trentside saw Capel hit four, a hat-trick from Ardron and Johnson score two in a 9-2 trouncing of Gillingham. A week later, it was Johnson's turn to register a hat-trick as Torquay United were beaten 6-1 in the first round of the FA Cup. When Crystal Palace were beaten 6-1 in south London in January every Forest forward scored. Johnson got another hat-trick in a 5-0 win at Exeter and the Reds finished the season with four successive victories, two at home and two away.

Wally Ardron had revelled in having Scott and Johnson to his right with Capel and Collindridge on his left flank. He scored a still-standing club record thirty-six goals. Capel hit twenty-three, Collindridge sixteen, Johnson fifteen and Scott nine goals. 'Tot' Leverton, who deputized chiefly for the injury-prone Johnson, contributed 6 goals in twenty-two appearances. It wasn't all down to the attack, of course. Forest had an outstanding half-back line with captain Horace Gager at centre-half and two home-grown wing-halves Bill Morley and Jack Burkitt. In front of the reliable goalkeeper Walker were full-backs Bill Whare and Geoff Thomas, who went on to establish a sound, long-lived partnership. Jack Hutchinson at full-back, former Manchester United wing-half John Anderson, and inside-forward John Love made up the promotion-winning squad.

On 1 May 1951, Billy Walker received a letter from the chairman, Jack Brentnall, that he said was 'as much a treasured possession as my own Villa cup medal'. The chairman wrote,

Dear Billy,

I felt that I would like to write to express my gratification and sincere appreciation of your untiring efforts to bring about the Championship that we have just obtained.

I am fully aware of the anxiety and numerous difficulties throughout the season that have caused you to be so uneasy and restless. Along with you I have, as you know, at times been very concerned, but your personality and confidence on these adverse occasions, which you have always been so ready to pass along to me, have been reassuring. We, together, have seen dark days, but at the moment I feel the times are going to be much better, and with your valuable help and experience, which as you know I have always appreciated, gives me confidence to say that the set-back we had two years ago has been overcome and the future, without a doubt, is going to be much brighter. No committee man and chairman could have had a better guide than yourself. We both may have been doubted by some of our colleagues and supporters on many occasions but my confidence was never shaken.

I am so pleased that we have been able to stick together to retrieve our position and I sincerely trust we shall be together many more years to further same. Whatever happens, and in football as you know it is very difficult to foresee the future, I hope we shall be the staunch and true friends that we have been in the past.

Very many thanks, Billy.

(signed) Jack Brentnall, Chairman

Walker wished 'that all club executives could think and talk so sweet'. He recalled that twenty-five years earlier as an Aston Villa player he scored a goal that sent Forest down into the Second Division.

That far-back game was a particularly mixed day for me because, by that time, my old colleague Sam Hardy, the greatest goalkeeper of them all, was playing for Forest, and it was my goal that beat him and Forest.

Now, with the First Division well in our sights, was a time of tremendous exhilaration, and that summer flew past on wings. But, in spite of the fact that I had put Forest back into the Second Division with the help of my committee and my players, the nigglers were still at it. They wondered if we should go straight forward, or if we should go back. They wondered if we had a good enough team, if we'd a good enough ground (although it is, in my opinion, the best ground and the best piece of turf in the country). And so it went on, harassingly, from the kind of people who are never satisfied. Well, it did not take very long for us to show them.'

One wonders, do those remarks by a great former manager give pause for thought to the internet fan forum and Twitter grumblers and rumour-mongers of the present day.

Walker was confident that his promotion-winners would do well in the higher division and added only wing-half Alan Orr from Third Lanark and Dubliner Noel Kelly, an inside-forward from Crystal Palace, to his squad. The Reds did so well that they led the division for six weeks until defeated by West Ham on 22 March 1951. They might have had back-to-back promotions but for bad luck with injuries to key players including skipper Gager and, even more damagingly, Collindridge, who broke a leg in December and did not return to the side until Good Friday to play only the last five games of the season. Winger Alan Moore was signed from Hull City and made his debut in a 3-2 win over Notts County at the City Ground on 19 January. There was a crowd of 40,000, four thousand fewer than there had been at Meadow Lane in September, when the Magpies had scored twice in the last five minutes to force a draw. Forest finished their first season back in Division Two a creditable fourth.

Tommy Lawton came to the City Ground in September 1952, this time leading the Brentford attack but without success as the home side were comfortable 3-0 winners. Jack French, a wing-half signed from Southend United for £10,000 and inside-forward Tommy Martin, a record £15,000 buy from Doncaster Rovers, made their debuts against Rotherham United at Millmoor at the beginning of November in an attempt to end a run of five defeats in seven games. It succeeded but Forest dropped to a seventh place finish.

Now in his middle thirties and becoming more prone to injury, Wally Ardron made just 14 appearances in 1953/54 but still managed to score ten goals. Alan Moore was top scorer with nineteen and Tommy Capel got eighteen. When Forest beat Notts 5-0 at the City Ground on 10 October the visitors fielded five former Reds – Aubrey Southwell, Bill Baxter, Jack Edwards, Tommy Johnston and 'Tot' Leverton. The 4-2 defeat of Derby on 7 November was Reds' ninth successive home win. Forest had regained fourth place when the season ended but Tommy Capel and Colin Collindridge had played their last games for the club, the left-wing pair being transferred to Coventry City during the summer.

∞

It's puzzling how a player can shine with one club yet struggle at another. A prime example was one-time carpet fitter Garry Birtles, who joined Forest from Long Eaton United for £2,000 in March, 1976. A true local hero, he was twice a European Cup winner and gained three England international caps before being sold to Manchester United for £1.25m in October, 1980. And the goals dried up. After scoring thirty-two times in eighty-seven First Division games for Forest, he seemed to take a lifetime to open his Old Trafford account. Birtles made twenty-eight appearances for United in his debut season but did not get his first goal until the 1981/82 campaign. He had scored eleven goals in fifty-eight games before Brian Clough brought him back to Trentside for £250,000. United chairman Martin Edwards 'would have carried me on his back over broken glass across the Pennines back to Nottingham,' Birtles comments in his entertaining autobiography *My Magic Carpet Ride*.

Another spectacular failure was Forest's attempt to replace the irreplaceable Wally Ardron, when the still revered centre-forward was forced to retire through injury, with Reading's highly-rated Ronnie Blackman, who was signed for £8,000 for the start of the 1954/55 season in the expectation that he would become Ardron's successor. He arrived with a big reputation. His manager at Reading the former England international centre-forward Ted Drake had seen the tall dockyard worker's potential playing non-league football with Gosport Borough. And Drake's view was seconded by the renowned cricket and football writer and broadcaster John Arlott, a Reading supporter. In his book *Concerning Soccer*, published in 1952, Arlott wrote a chapter of studies of players. His subjects included Tommy Lawton, Stanley Matthews, Eddie Baily (then of Spurs), Roy Bentley of Chelsea, Arsenal's Jimmy Logie, Jimmy Hill of Fulham, and Ronnie Blackman.

Of the Reading player, Arlott wrote,

> Blackman's rare value is that he is one of the half-dozen centre-forwards today with the natural blend of timing, positioning, single-mindedness and dash to get to the high-crossed ball and then the courage to throw his head in through the ruck of goalkeeper's fists and jumping defenders to strike the goals that count.

Blackman scored 39 times in the 1951/52 season and 158 League goals in all for the Berkshire side, both feats still club records. Unfortunately, his move to Nottingham did not work out. He was never the same player on Trentside and admitted he had not wanted the transfer and been unable to settle. He had played just eleven games and scored three goals when he was offloaded to Ipswich Town, then of the Third Division South, in May, 1955.

Ardron played his last match for the Reds across the river at Meadow Lane on 12 February, 1955, but did not score and Notts were the victors 4-1. He and Tommy Lawton were rival but very different centre-forwards though both were accomplished headers of the ball. Who had the biggest impact? Lawton drew the crowds to the Lane and inspired promotion to Division Two but County slumped after his departure. Ardron's goals and grit drove Forest forward and they were able to build on his achievements. He is remembered reverently still in the stands at the City Ground, where his ashes were spread on the pitch after his death in 1978.

'Billy Walker told me he wanted First Division soccer and the FA Cup,' Ardron wrote in his book. 'Both were achieved but, unfortunately for me, after my enforced retirement through injury.' Although Forest were fifteenth in 1954/55 they reached the Fifth Round of the FA Cup and took eventual winners Newcastle United to a second replay. The match at the City Ground on 18 February ended 1-1 with new outside-left Peter Small, from Leicester City, who had been injured and taken to hospital for an X-ray, returning to the field to put Forest ahead with just five minutes left. Two minutes later Jack Milburn equalized. The attendance was 25,252. Across the river on the same afternoon Notts County's Cup clash with Chelsea attracted nearly 42,000. At St James' Park, the Reds were two down at half-time but came back with goals by Jim Barrett and Fred Scott. A coin was tossed to decide which club would stage the second replay and it fell for Newcastle. Tommy Wilson shot Forest ahead in the twenty-second minute but the home side equalized and got the winner in extra time.

Judging by comments in his 'The Manager's Review' in a Forest programme in March, 1953, Billy Walker stored what he had seen in his memory for future action. Here's what he wrote after an eight-match unbeaten run had been ended at Upton Park:

> In the West Ham side last week I saw for the first time their young inside-forward, Barrett, who is the son of old Jimmy Barrett, the former West Ham centre-half, who had some twenty years service with the club. While old Jimmy stood about 6 foot and weighed something like 15 stone, young Jimmy is 5 foot 8in and only about 11 stone. He is unlike his father in build but, on last Saturday's display, he is a grand player, very constructive, and always having a crack at goal.

Walker signed Jim Barrett from West Ham in December, 1954, for £7,500. He top-scored for Forest for three successive seasons. In the promotion-winning season 1956/57, young Jim hit 30 league and cup goals.

In time Walker came to appreciate that Ardron's natural successor was the local boy Tommy Wilson, signed in 1951 from Cinderhill Colliery, but before claiming the number nine shirt as his own he had to see off lively competition from Peter Higham, brought in from Preston North End. It was immediately obvious, however, that Bobby McKinlay was the player to take over from Horace Gager, who played five times in 1954/55 before retiring. Gager had made 268 appearances in a seven-year career at the City Ground. Outside-left Stewart Imlach was a new recruit in the summer. The Scot, who had built up his fitness and speed running on the beach at Lossiemouth, was unhappy and unsettled at Derby. He found the Wembley-sized pitch at the City Ground much more to his liking than the cramped Baseball Ground. A prelude to promotion, Forest climbed back to seventh place in 1955/56. With Doug Lishman having been signed from Arsenal on transfer deadline day in March and Eddie Baily to join him in the Garibaldi early in the new season the key the First Division door was in Forest's hands.

Barrett scored seven goals in the Reds' first three games of the 1956/57 season as they romped to 4-1 and 5-1 away victories first at Leyton Orient and then Bristol City before beating Fulham 3-1 at home. In February Forest recorded 7-1 victories on successive Saturdays. The first was at Port Vale, where Barrett hit a hat-trick and five goals came in twelve minutes. Next Tommy Wilson scored four goals to delight a City Ground crowd of 25,994 as Barnsley suffered the same fate. In addition to winning promotion, the Reds reached the sixth round where they met the previous year's Wembley finalists Birmingham City and took them to a replay. The first match at St. Andrew's was goalless and the Blues won the replay by the only goal to disappoint a 36,486 crowd at the City Ground. Barrett scored twenty-seven Second Division goals and three in the Cup. Lishman delivered sixteen and Wilson posted just as many including two in the Cup. Imlach in his debut season scored twelve. Forest's ninty-four goals was a club record for the Second Division and Barrett's total of thirty was the best by an inside-right.

Billy Walker asked:

What do records matter at a time like this? Forest were back in the First Division again – back to the heady highlands of the game after thirty-two years in the scrubby foothills.

15

Eldorado

When the reigning champions, the famous Busby Babes of Manchester United, came to the City Ground on Saturday 12 October 1957, they faced a newly-promoted Forest side that had taken the First Division by storm by winning eight of the first eleven games played. The victories had included a 7-0 drubbing at the City Ground of star-studded Burnley, full of internationals including centre-forward Ray Pointer and winger John Connelly of England, goalkeeper Adam Blacklaw (Scotland) and Northern Ireland inside-forward Jimmy McIlroy and led by wing-half Jimmy Adamson. All five Forest forwards scored with two each for Wilson and Imlach.

A then record crowd of 47,804 came to welcome Manchester United to the City Ground, some of them sitting on bench seats in the new East Stand in use for the first time. Others were allowed to sit on the pitch-side of the concrete wall in front of the terraces. No health and safety fears then – and no football hooligans. Don Davies of the *Manchester Guardian*, who wrote under the nom de plume 'The Old International', reported that:

> This was the perfect occasion, a case where the flawless manners of players, officials and spectators alike gave to a routine league match the flavour almost of an idyll.

With United in an all-white strip, Forest in their blood red shirts and the sun shining, there was the tingling sense of a great event. Forest fell behind within four minutes of the kick-off. Winger David Pegg, deep in his own half, was picked out with a throw by goalkeeper Ray Woods and he raced seventy yards down the touchline before delivering an accurate cross for Billy Whelan to volley into the net. But, as Davies admitted, if they had not 'squandered scoring chances as freely as they made them' Forest should have been ahead at half-time.

A minute after the restart Stewart Imlach

crept up behind Blanchflower unawares and gave that Irish international the shock of his life by suddenly thrusting a grinning face over his shoulder while he nodded a long, high centre from Quigley unerringly home.

Imlach's equaliser was answered twelve minutes later when Dennis Viollet restored United's lead. After that, reported Davies, there seemed almost a continuous bombardment of the United goal with only the broad bulk of Duncan Edwards and the safe hands of Ray Wood intervening to save their side from disaster. He concluded:

Forest supporters will take some convincing that Foulkes, Blanchflower, Byrne and Edwards were enjoying the shots that bruised their ribs. But what will be acknowledged without dispute is that this was a great exhibition of football, in which skill was the final, the only, arbiter, and where the splendour of the performance was enriched by the grace of sportsmanlike behaviour.

Stapleford-born Peter Watson made a rare appearance in place of Bobby McKinlay, a victim of influenza, and with great style subdued England centre-forward Tommy Taylor. The Forest XI was: Thomson; Whare, Thomas; Morley, Watson, Burkitt (captain); Gray, Quigley, Wilson, Baily and Imlach. England captain Roger Byrne led the United side of: Wood; Foulkes, Byrne; Colman, Jack Blanchflower, Edwards; Berry, Whelan, Taylor, Viollet and Pegg. The match ball, signed by both teams and their famous managers Billy Walker and Matt Busby, is a prize item displayed still by Forest. It is made all the more significant as four months after that classic encounter came the disaster at Munich airport on 6 February 1958, an air crash that shocked the world and tragically ended the lives of twenty-three people including eight of the Busby Babes.

Fate dictated that Forest would be Manchester United's first league opponents after Munich. United had only two survivors from the pre-disaster squad, goalkeeper Harry Gregg, who had been signed a few weeks before the crash and was hailed a hero for his rescue efforts at Munich, and full-back Bill Foulkes. They had recruited inside-forward Ernie Taylor from Blackpool and half-back Stan Crowther from Aston Villa and had won an FA Cup-tie against Sheffield Wednesday. There were 66,346 people at Old Trafford for the match against Forest on 22 February 1958, the biggest crowd since the war. Before the kick-off and at half-time collection boxes were passed along the terracing and through the stands. In a snowstorm that conjured up memories of television pictures from Munich, the Dean of Manchester conducted a short memorial service for the dead and then a welter of noise and tumult was unleashed as the game began.

The Forest players answered the understandably fanatical fervour they faced with cultured football and commendable restraint. After half-an-hour Tommy Wilson chased a poor United clearance out to the right and cut the ball back to the edge of the penalty area. Imlach instinctively drifted in from the left and from twenty yards drove the ball past Gregg into the net. It was the first goal against the stricken club and was met with silence. In an emotional second-half, United surging forward to a continuous roar of support got the equalizer they deserved when Alex Dawson forced in a corner before the final whistle. The fighting furies of United were: Gregg; Foulkes, Greaves; Goodwin, Cope, Crowther; Webster, Taylor, Dawson, Pearson and Brennan. Forest's eleven were: Thomson; Whare, Thomas; Morley, McKinlay, Burkitt; Gray, Quigley, Wilson, Chris Joyce (Barrett was absent with 'flu) and Imlach.

Billy Walker made just two signings during the close season in preparation for Forest's new start in Division One and they proved bargain buys. Billy Gray came from Burnley initially to fill the right wing position mainly occupied by Higham or Small in the promotion side and Charlie ('Chic') Thomson arrived from Chelsea to replace Harry Nicholson in goal. The total outlay was about £10,000. Gray, on the small side but quick and strong, had won the Northumberland schools boxing title for four years in succession before 'kicking a tin around' and turning to football. He was a first team regular at Chelsea and then joined Burnley, becoming their top scorer in his first four seasons. But he went on to make 223 appearances for Forest, more than for any previous club. Thomson, whose father had been a Scottish League goalkeeper, joined Chelsea from Clyde in 1952 and had four seasons at Stamford Bridge, keeping goal for the last sixteen games of their 1954/55 championship season to qualify for a medal.

Their pace-setting start made Forest early leaders. Barrett scored in seven consecutive games. Then, on 7 December, 1957, the player and the club suffered a severe blow when the main marksman tore ligaments in his right knee just twenty-six minutes into a home game with Sunderland. Wilson scored twice to give the Reds a 2-0 victory but Barrett's season had ended. Again he had been in brilliant form and scored twelve goals in seventeen games. Forest were tenth in the table at the end of the season and went off on tour to West German, Belgium and Holland, during which they played Flamingo in Liege and drew 2-2 with the Brazilians. In March the Reds took an Italian break when they went to Florence where they had the support of a contingent of sailors from Royal Navy ships anchored at Livorno but could only achieve a scoreless draw with Fiorentina. Making his debut at centre-forward was a Northern Ireland international Fay Coyle signed from Coleraine. He made his First Division start in another goal-less draw at Chelsea on 4 April and then played two more league games at Sunderland and Arsenal before going off with the Northern Ireland squad to the World Cup finals and winning his fourth cap against Argentina. He returned homesick to Coleraine that summer without playing a single game at the City Ground and in 1964 captained Derry City, his hometown club, to an Irish Cup final victory over Glentoran and, consequently, into European competition for the first time in their history.

It was a busy summer for Billy Walker, who made three key signings in July. In order of arrival they were full-back Joe McDonald from Sunderland, winger Roy Dwight from Fulham and wing-half Jeff Whitefoot, a former Busby Babe, from Grimsby Town. As every pub quiz contestant knows, Dwight was the uncle of music star Elton John (real name Reg Dwight). He was also the costliest recruit at £14,000. The fee paid for Whitefoot was £10,000 and Sunderland accepted just under their asking price of £5,000 for McDonald, a Scottish international who had played for Great Britain against the rest of Europe in an Irish FA anniversary match at Windsor Park, Belfast, in 1955. Dwight had been Fulham's top scorer in each of the past two seasons. Walker had wanted to sign Whitefoot from Manchester United eight months' earlier and a transfer had been agreed by all parties but the player wanted a guarantee of first team football and went to Grimsby for £8,000. His family could not settle there and so, having liked Nottingham and the house offered them, Whitefoot welcomed Walker's second approach. It proved a happy move.

A former schoolboy international, Whitefoot was one of the original Busby Babes and had learned how to control a ball playing with his father outside their home in a cobbled cul de sac in Cheadle. He became the youngest to play in the League for United when he made his debut against Portsmouth in April, 1950, aged sixteen years 105 days. A member of the championship-winning side of 1955/56, he gained an England Under-twenty-three cap against Italy in Bologna and made nearly 100 League and Cup appearances for his club. With Forest, Whitefoot played 285 League and Cup games before retiring after a stay of ten seasons. McDonald made 124 League and Cup appearances in three seasons and fully repaid Walker's faith in him while Dwight, despite the sickening blow that was to come at Wembley, scored twenty-seven goals in fifty-three games for the Reds.

After an opening day shock 5-1 defeat by Wolves at Molineux despite a debut goal from Dwight, and a 3-0 drubbing by Manchester United in front of a 44,971 crowd at the City Ground, Forest found their shooting boots to beat Portsmouth 5-0 and West Ham 4-0, both at home. Dwight, Wilson and Quigley shared the goals. Then Quigley hit a hat-trick as Manchester City were beaten 4-0, also at the City Ground. After a second-half hat-trick by Dwight on a foggy November afternoon had given the Reds their first win at Leicester for fifty years, they stayed in a challenging position in the league table as the FA Cup campaign loomed large.

It began on 10 January on a deeply rutted pitch that was icy and covered with snow at the small Sandy Lane ground of amateurs Tooting and Mitcham United, who had already knocked out two League sides, Bournemouth and Northampton. This was their first-ever appearance in the Third Round and the ground was packed with a record attendance of 14,300. The home side mastered the conditions early on and were two up by half-time. After the break they were forced on the defensive and wing-half Murphy, who had scored Tooting's second goal in the 35th minute, put through his own goal seventeen minutes later. Tooting's misfortune continued when a defender handled the ball in the penalty area and Billy Gray sent the spot kick high to the right of the goalkeeper's outstretched hand to equalize with fifteen minutes remaining. The kick-off for the replay a week later was at 2.00 p.m. to allow for possible extra time and even more respect for the amateurs was shown by a City Ground attendance of 42,320. This time the result was never in doubt with Dwight, Wilson and Imlach taking Forest through. They were in the Fourth Round and met Grimsby Town of Division Two at the City Ground only four days later. The tie was virtually decided by half-time. Whitefoot scored after three minutes and Gray got two in six minutes, including a penalty a minute before the break. Wilson made it four on the hour before winger Scott got a consolation goal for the visitors in the 76th minute.

Whitefoot, Dwight and Wilson gave Forest a comfortable home win against Bolton Wanderers in the league on 7 February to set them up for a Fifth Round visit a week later to St Andrew's, where 55,000 saw Birmingham City a minute away from victory but a spectacular Wilson header dramatically saved the day. The replay drew a crowd of 39,431 to the City Ground on 18 February. It was goalless at full-time. Then John Gordon put Birmingham ahead in the fifteenth minute of extra. With five minutes to go, Roy Dwight lobbed the keeper to force a second replay. This took place on the afternoon of Monday 23 February, at Leicester's Filbert Street before 34,458.

Here's how Jeff Whitefoot saw it:

We were a good footballing side ourselves but so too were Birmingham. They had some fine players at the time and we knew it would be a tough tie to get through. In all honesty, I think we felt as though we were going out in the first two games but there was a great spirit in the Forest side and we managed to keep going and get vital equalizers to see us through. We expected it being just the same at Filbert Street but it was just one of those days when everything went well for us. I remember Roy Dwight scored an early goal, which helped very much, and after that we kept playing our football. And the goals came. Roy ended up with a hat-trick and Billy Gray scored the other two, including a penalty. A nap-hand. Fantastic.

After three matches and 300 minutes play, Forest had eclipsed the Blues with a dazzling display. The irony was that just over two weeks later the Reds met Birmingham at home in the First Division and lost 7-1. Whitefoot recalls,

> It certainly brought us down to earth. I remember us having a goalkeeper called Willie Fraser, who came in for Chic Thomson for that game and another match against Luton that we lost 5-1 just before we met them at Wembley. I don't think he played another game for us and, after those two experiences, you wouldn't have been surprised to have heard that he had a nervous breakdown. But, as everyone knows, it all turned out well and gave us some very special memories.

Billy Walker later commented,

> This was easily our best performance in the Cup and on that day we would have beaten anybody. It was a team triumph with no one player better than another and everyone pulling together for the team. That's as I like it.

Reigning Cup-holders Bolton Wanderers came to the City Ground for the quarter-final tie. It was an all-ticket game and 44,414 fans saw Tommy Wilson score for the Reds after only three minutes and add another two minutes after half-time. Bolton were limited to a 62nd minute reply through winger Brian Birch. Bill Ridding, their manager, was generous in his post-match comments, anticipating continuing success, 'We could not wish to hand the Cup over to a better bunch of footballers and sportsmen. This was their day and I hope it's the same at Wembley.' Walker agreed that this was 'one of the most sporting games I have seen for many a long day'. Bolton, he added, 'were most chivalrous in defeat and made the match as near a classic as could well be.' He had special praise for full-backs Bill Whare and Joe McDonald for restricting crosses from the wings and for centre-half Bob McKinlay for keeping quiet the man the manager had identified as the main threat, England centre-forward Nat Lofthouse.

Nearly 66,000 paid £16,484 to watch the semi-final with Aston Villa at Hillsborough on 14 March. It was a special day for the Forest manager. In 1920 he had won the Cup with Aston Villa, his only Football League club as a player, and fifteen years later he had won it again as a manager with Wednesday. Now he was one step away from another final and, possibly, another Cup triumph. Walker had noted that this Villa side played a deep, defensive game. Forest would have to be patient. They were. And in the 65th minute were rewarded. Walker described it thus,

> Tommy Wilson crossed over to the left to take Jimmy Dugdale away from the middle, so letting in Johnny Quigley to take up a position

around the centre. While Dugdale waited, Wilson slipped the ball across to Johnny, who quickly brought it down from his chest to his feet and, all in the same movement, hit it wide of Nigel Sim's right hand. It was a perfect goal taken by a lad who showed that he at least did not suffer from Cup nerves – and that after only eighteen months out of junior football.

There was overdue recognition in the Press that 'Billy Walker has built a team of talented ball-players'. Earlier they had been referred to as 'Billy Walker's misfits, a team of reach-me-downs'. Walker admitted,

> I did not want any ready-made stars. You have only to look at the performances with Forest of the players I brought to Nottingham and against the background of what they had achieved in their previous clubs to realise that all they needed was proper organisation in which they could find their true level. This we sought to find for them and in this, as the record shows, we succeeded. We know precisely what we want and even if we have to wait we will get it. We have so far – and I can see no reason for the supply of Forest type material ever to dry up. With this supply of experienced but unappreciated players from other clubs, and with the youngsters whom we are constantly finding and developing around our own doorstep – well, there'll always be a Forest!

First Division form dipped and Forest finished thirteenth, four places above Luton Town, who would be their Cup Final opponents. They had played an unchanged eleven throughout the Cup competition. In the league, however, Walker had been ready to give opportunities to other squad members. Three weeks before the final the Reds crashed 5-1 at Luton and the home side's Scottish international inside-forward Allan Brown scored four of them. He later managed both Luton and Forest. The 'rehearsal' defeat might have been seen as a good omen. Before beating Derby County to win the Cup in 1898, Forest had lost 5-0 in a league game at the Baseball Ground. During Cup Final week Forest set up training headquarters at Hendon. Walker announced a line-up unchanged from the previous rounds: Thomson, Whare, McDonald, Whitefoot, McKinlay, Burkitt, Dwight, Quigley, Wilson, Gray and Imlach. Luton were also able to name a first-choice team: Baynham, McNally, Hawkes, Groves, Owen, Pacey, Bingham, Brown, Morton, Cummins and Gregory. Syd Owen, Burkitt's opposite number as captain, was chosen as Footballer of the Year by the Football Writers' Association.

And so to Wembley.

16

Glamour and Glory

Two girls, who in the 1950s worked together as clerks at the Prudential assurance company offices at the junction of King Street and Queen Street in Nottingham city centre (across the road from where the Brian Clough statue now stands), became friends because they were keen Nottingham Forest fans and their fathers both played for Boots Athletic, a company club. They travelled all over the country supporting the Reds and followed the team on the road to Wembley in 1959. Marian Hickling was eighteen and Margaret Scott nineteen when they were picked out of the Cup Final crowd by a press photographer whose picture of them at the Forest end of the stadium standing on the wall holding a banner in front of cheering supporters has become a favourite, almost iconic, illustration of football fandom.

Margaret and Marian captured the headlines as the 'Nottingham Glamour Girls' and some claimed, falsely, that they were not true fans but models. The fact is that they were strikingly outfitted in clothes they had put together themselves. As well as red and white bobble caps, Margaret wore a red skirt with a white top and Marian a white skirt with a red top. The garments were decorated with red and white rosettes and red and white scarves hung from their shoulders. Each girl wore one red sock and one white one with one white shoe and one red. Their costumes and good looks attracted the attention not only of the photographer but outside Wembley Stadium before the game of BBC TV's commentator Kenneth Wolstenholme. He interviewed them for the pre-match build-up programme and they were seen on television by their families back in Nottingham.

Marian still has her scrapbook of the 1958/59 season. It includes The Forest Cup Story, a souvenir produced by the players, the *Nottinghamshire Guardian* 'Wembley Triumph' souvenir and cuttings from the *Nottingham Evening News*, *Nottingham Guardian Journal* and the *Football Post*. Margaret and Marian had to make special arrangements to get the day off work to go to Forest's fifth round second replay at Leicester and the next Saturday they were at the City Ground to see the victory over Bolton Wanderers. Then our intrepid travellers were at Hillsborough for the semi-final against Aston Villa. To Margaret's delight the winning goal was scored by her favourite player Johnny Quigley. The girls were decked out in the red and white outfits and carried home-made mascots at all the cup-ties.

They were thrilled by Forest's fantastic start to the Cup Final with early goals by Roy Dwight and Tommy Wilson. Then Dwight was carried off with a broken leg. 'That was a heart-stopping moment', Marian said. And they had their hearts in their mouths for the remainder of the match as the ten-man Reds held on to win the FA Cup 2-1. Marian's scrapbook contains her semi-final and final tickets, the first priced 2s 6d and the other 3s6d It also has a copy of the song sheet for community singing handed out by the *Daily Express*. The songs included 'There's a long, long trail', 'The Happy Wanderer' and 'The End of the Road'. There was also, of course, the Cup Final hymn 'Abide with Me'.

∞

In their dressing room before the match, the Forest players were going through their usual rituals – Billy Gray taking a cold shower, Joe McDonald having a smoke in the washroom, Stewart Imlach cracking an egg into a glass of sherry before downing it – when in walked a suited committee man. Unassuming as Frank Chambers was, he was not really welcomed half-an-hour before kick-off even though he had brought a gift for each player – a pair of frilly knickers for their other halves. Frank, who normally kept in the background being shy of personal publicity, was a lingerie manufacturer and the knickers had been specially made at his factory in Forest colours and with lace rosettes on the sides. 'It was madness but it broke the tension,' said Chic Thomson. 'I've never seen players so relaxed before a big game.'

Ten minutes had not passed when Forest, playing flowing, accurate, passing football, took the lead with a five-man move. Left-back Joe McDonald headed a long kick by the Luton goalkeeper infield to wing-half Jeff Whitefoot who played the ball on the bounce for inside-left Billy Gray to glance it on with a flick of his head into the path of left-winger Stewart Imlach. Five defenders tracked back but Imlach cut them all out with a cross pulled back for Roy Dwight, racing in, to strike the ball first time with his left foot and send it crashing into the roof of the net. Five minutes later skipper Jack Burkitt stroked the ball to Imlach who found Gray on the flank. Gray dummied inside, stepped back, and lofted the ball for Tommy Wilson, whose bulging neck muscles showed the power of his header into the net – a header to equal the fabled 'Lawton's Leap.'

It was all Forest until the 32nd minute when the dreaded Wembley injury hoodoo, which to a lesser degree had affected Arsenal full-back Wally Barnes, Bolton wing-half Eric Bell, Leicester defender Len Chalmers, Manchester City's full-back Jimmy Meadows and goalkeepers Bert Trautmann of City and Ray Wood of Manchester United, removed Roy Dwight from the fray and into hospital. Astonished patients gathered in their dressing gowns on chairs in front of a television set had seen him carried off the field on a stretcher. Now they saw him brought into their ward unbooted but otherwise still in his full kit, lifted into a bed with a cage to keep the blankets off his right leg and settling down to watch the second half with them. With Jack Burkitt struggling with a dislocated shoulder but still inspirational, the exhausted, depleted Reds conceded a sixty-second-minute goal but flagging yet still fighting found the energy to hang on for a Wembley triumph never equalled first for grace and elegance and then for determination and endeavour.

It was estimated that 200,000 people saw the Cup come home to Nottingham after sixty-one years. A bedecked open-topped coach took the players and committee from the Midland Station on a route encircling the city centre past Chapel Bar and into Angel Row to the Old Market Square. There the players disembarked and led by Jack Burkitt, carrying the FA Cup, walked slowly down the Processional Way to the steps of the imposing Council House. Roy Dwight was with them in a wheelchair, having gained his release from hospital to join in the celebrations. In appreciation an iced cake in the shape of Wembley Stadium was sent by the club to the nurses who had looked after him.

The Cup-winning team was never to play again. Dwight took nearly a year to recover from his injury and, although he scored on his return to the side in a 1-1 draw with Preston at the City Ground at the end of March, 1960, he played just two more games for the club. Stewart Imlach made his last appearance at the same time in early April and Tommy Wilson bade his farewell to the City Ground against Newcastle United in September, 1960, after manager Walker had moved 'upstairs.' Jim Barrett, put out of Cup reckoning by injury, returned for the end-of-season tour of Portugal and Spain. He scored his last Forest goals at Valencia in front of a crowd of 75,000 and Atletico Madrid, taking him to a total of 69 in 117 appearances during five seasons in the Garibaldi. Valencia would loom large in the Forest story in coming seasons.

∞

Marian Bestwick (née Hickling), accompanied by her son Steve, was a special guest of the club at a Championship match in 2012 but, unfortunately, Margaret Baker (née Scott) and her husband Gerry, who live in York, were unable to be there. Gerrard and Margaret had recently celebrated their golden wedding anniversary. He was on the Forest

playing staff when they first met having been an amateur with Wigan
Athletic and Bolton Wanderers before signing for the club in December
of Cup Final year, when serving in the Army at Chilwell. A full-back he
made no senior appearances for Forest and in July, 1963, was transferred
to York City. There he was an extremely popular player making 214
first team appearances before injury forced his retirement, aged thirty-
one, in September, 1969. City gave him a testimonial a month later. The
Wembley 'glamour girls', Margaret and Marian are still firm friends and
meet regularly. Their attendance at Forest matches ended with Margaret's
departure for York but Marian, who lives in West Bridgford, still looks
out for the Reds' results.

Johnny Quigley, who so impressed Margaret, was determined,
industrious and a typical wee Scottish ba' player. He stood just 5 foot
8 inches tall and weighed 11 stone but with the ball at his feet he could
withstand the challenges of the heftiest of opponents and surprise them in
turn with the ferocity of his tackling. He had the toughness that seemingly
comes from being born in the working class district of Govan, a couple
of miles west of Glasgow city centre on the south bank of the Clyde and
once the centre of the Clydeside shipbuilding industry. Other Govanites
include Sir Alex Ferguson, Kenny Dalglish and, more surprisingly,
Leo Blair, father of former Prime Minister Tony Blair. Govan people
claim to be Govanites first and Glaswegians second. The local answer to
the question 'Are ye from Glasga?' is 'Na, a cum fae Govan.'

Johnny was spotted by Billy Walker who was on a scouting mission
north of the border in mid-August 1957. Quigley had begun his career as
a 'provisional' signing by Glasgow Celtic, who farmed him out to local
Scottish junior club St Anthony's. Celtic didn't retain their interest in
him so he joined non-league Ashfield. Walker watched Ashfield against
Linlithgow and was so impressed he immediately signed the twenty-two-
year-old. The Scot's impact at the City Ground was similar to that of
Irishman Roy Keane, who was signed by Brian Clough in the close season
of 1990 and given his debut against Liverpool at the end of August.
Quigley scored two goals for the Reds' first team against an All Stars XI
in a testimonial match for trainer Tommy Graham at the City Ground
on 23 September and made his First Division debut at White Hart Lane
at the beginning of October, scoring again in a 4-1 victory. A week later
he played in the classic match against Manchester United's Busby Babes.

Quigley went on to make twenty-one Division One appearances
in his first season, with three goals, and playing three FA Cup games,
scoring once. He was a key player in the 1958/59 FA Cup-winning
season, scoring twelve goals in thirty-nine First Division appearances
and appearing in all nine FA Cup games, including the replays. He
scored just once in the Cup but what a crucial goal it was coming in the
semi-final and taking Forest through to Wembley. In the same season he
had become the first Forest player to score a post-war hat-trick with goals

in the 57th, 74th and 81st minutes in the 4-0 defeat of Manchester City. After six years as a first-team regular he lost his place to John Barnwell, newly arrived from Arsenal, and in February, 1965, he was transferred to Huddersfield Town. From there he joined Bristol City in October, 1966, and later became captain of the Ashton Gate club. Johnny also skippered Mansfield Town, whom he joined for £3,000 in 1968. He converted from inside-forward to wing-half though in truth it wasn't much of a change since in modern terms he had always been an attacking midfielder.

Quigley was in the Mansfield team that in 1969 beat a West Ham United side, including several of England's World Cup winners, 3-0 to progress to the quarter-finals of the FA Cup before losing to Leicester City. He made over 470 Football League appearances for his four clubs, including 236 games with fifty-one goals for Forest. After being assistant manager at Mansfield, he had a spell coaching Doncaster Rovers before going to the Middle East to coach in Kuwait and Saudi Arabia for five years. Johnny died in Nottingham on 30 November 2004, aged sixty-nine.

∞

Quigley was a typical Walker player but how did the team view their manager? He was 'a likeable rogue,' the Govan man told Gary Imlach, Stewart's son, in an interview for the award-winning book *My Father and other Working-Class Football Heroes*. Quigley added, 'He wouldna gi' you too much, man.' The quote comes in a chapter about the Forest players' pool, set up before the final to make a little extra cash from their appearance at Wembley, as all teams did. They posed in their kit with the dray horses of the local brewery, Shipstones, opened fetes and held a pre-final dance. Billy Walker had offered to act as the players' agent and seek commercial opportunities. The players turned him down. 'Nobody now can remember how much money the players' pool generated,' wrote Gary Imlach. 'Whatever the sum, Billy Walker had been denied his agent's commission.'

Did the manager want his cut of whatever was going? Possibly, he was careful with money. This is his autobiographical reflection,

> Football is more than a game to me. It is more than a profession. It is a way of life. I played football because I had an inner compulsion to do so. Nothing else mattered. Fame, fortune – I never considered these. It was the game that mattered. Anything I have now has not been derived directly from football. When I was starting out, my grandfather said to me, 'Will, when you get a bit of money put it into bricks and mortar.' I did what he told me.

And that was advice he passed on to his players. Perhaps the pool would have been larger with agent Walker.

A journalist and TV sports presenter, Gary Imlach was rightly praised for a heartfelt and hard-hitting appraisal. But there are two sides to every story. Here's Walker's version,

> I've never been one to see the odd bawbee go by but I have never allowed the business of securing the future of myself and my family to interfere with my obligations both to my team and to myself. Now Nottingham is a comparatively compact city. Everywhere our players moved in the Cup-mad town they were pleaded with, cajoled and pestered. Our form began to suffer. Our old smooth rhythm went and defeat followed defeat.

After being beaten by 'an ordinary Chelsea side' Walker told his players the 'perks' had got to stop. 'I told them this without bluster, for that is not my way, but as man-to-man. Soccer was no longer to be a side interest.'

Gary Imlach felt his father had badly treated when he was transferred to Luton, especially as the *Evening Post* seemed to have been told about the deal before the player. He is understandably critical of Forest's manager but the record shows that his father was at his peak in Nottingham with the freedom to express himself Walker gave him. And he was at his happiest, as Gary Imlach acknowledges. Stewart, a Derby discard, won two promotions, a Cup-winners medal and four international caps during his five years at the City Ground. He scored 43 goals in 147 games for Forest, including 5 in eighteen Cup-ties. His career dipped at Luton, Coventry, Crystal Palace and non-league Dover and Chelmsford but he later coached Notts County, when Billy Gray was manager there, Everton, Blackpool and Bury.

With Billy Walker's health failing, 1959/60 was a season of decline. Heaviest defeat was 8-0 at Burnley yet a week later Leeds United were beaten 4-1 at the City Ground. The Reds reached the fourth round of the Cup but were then beaten 3-0 by Sheffield United at Bramall Lane. Tommy Wilson then scored in six successive games, which brought two wins, two draws and two defeats, but they were still battling against relegation until the penultimate Saturday when Newcastle United were beaten 3-0 at the City Ground. The last match at Leeds on 30 April was Walker's last league match as manager. His team was: Thomson, Patrick, McDonald, Whitefoot, McKinlay, Burkitt, Barton, Quigley, Iley, Younger and Gray. Roy Patrick, signed from Derby in August, was the only change from the Cup Final defence – replacing Bill Whare – with Quigley and Gray still in the forward line. Forest lost the game 1-0 but it was Leeds who were relegated along with Luton Town.

Jim Iley had been signed from Spurs for £16,000 in the summer and was seen as Burkitt's eventual replacement. He took the injured skipper's place for the FA Charity Shield match with champions Wolves, who won 3-1 at Molineux, their own ground. With Burkitt fit again for the

Tinsley Lindley
Corinthian and Forester, 1904.
© EMPICS

Harry Radford
peerless administrator, 1905.
© EMPICS

Frank Forman, Forest and England, 1904. © EMPICS. Inset Grenville Morris, Prince of inside-forwards, 1906. © EMPICS

Jack Armstrong
Forest captain, 1921. © EMPICS

Harry Hallam
Forest secretary, 1906. © EMPICS

ASSOCIATION CUP WINNERS
NOTTS FOREST, 1898

1898 FA Cup Final Card
Heads of the Nottingham Forest team which won the FA Cup in 1898, beating Derby County 3-1: (left to right, top to bottom) Archie Ritchie, Dan Allsop, Adam Scott, Frank Forman, Willie Wragg, Tom McInnes, John McPherson, Arthur Capes, Chas Richards, Len Benbow, Alf Spouncer.
© Player's Cigarettes/EMPICS

Billy Walker
1954, twenty-one years Forest manager.
© EMPICS

Jack Brentnall
1954, Forest chairman. © EMPICS

Bob McKinlay
Centre-half, 1969. © EMPICS

Johnny Quigley
Player, 1957. © EMPICS

Sam Hardy
Forest and England goalkeeper,
1920. © PreEMPICS

Peter Shilton
Forest and England goalkeeper,
1978. © EMPICS

Below: Forest Glamour Girls
Forest fans Marian and Margaret at
Wembley, 1959. © PA Photos

Roy Dwight Celebrates a Goal
Forest's Roy Dwight (left) celebrates as his shot flies past Luton Town goalkeeper Ron Baynham for the opening goal, FA Cup Final, 1959. © PA Photos

Tommy Wilson Heads a Goal
Forest's Tommy Wilson (right) heads his team's second goal at Wembley, 1959. © PA Photos

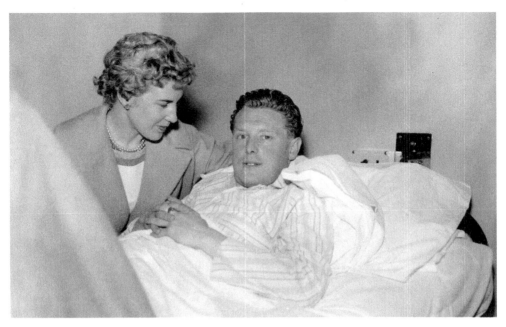

Roy Dwight and his Wife, Connie
While the rest of the team celebrates at the Savoy Hotel, Forest outside-right Roy Dwight
has a quiet chat with his wife, Connie, who was visiting him at Wembley General Hospital.
Dwight broke his leg after he scored the first 1959 Cup Final goal. © PA Photos

Jack with his Wife
Still holding the coveted FA Cup, Forest captain Jack Burkitt gets a congratulatory kiss
from his wife at the team's victory celebration at the Savoy Hotel in London. © PA Photos

Jack Burkitt with Queen Elizabeth
Forest captain Jack Burkitt turns to show the FA Cup to Forest's jubilant fans after Queen
Elizabeth II has presented the trophy. © **PA** Photos

Trevor Francis vs Malmo
Trevor Francis heads the European Cup winning goal past Malmo goalkeeper Jan Moller
in Munich, 1979. © EMPICS

Colin Barrett with the
European Cup
Colin Barrett with the European
Cup. © John Sumpter

The Munich Team with Cup
European Cup winners, 1979.
© John Sumpter

John Robertson Celebrating
John Robertson celebrates his European Cup winning goal against Hamburg in Madrid, 1980. © John Sumpter

Dressing Room Celebrations
Dressing room celebrations in Madrid. © John Sumpter/JMS Photography

Left: Viv Anderson
Player, 1979. © EMPICS

Below: Hillsborough
After Hillsborough. Nigel Clough
and Lee Chapman at the hospital
bedside of a Liverpool supporter.

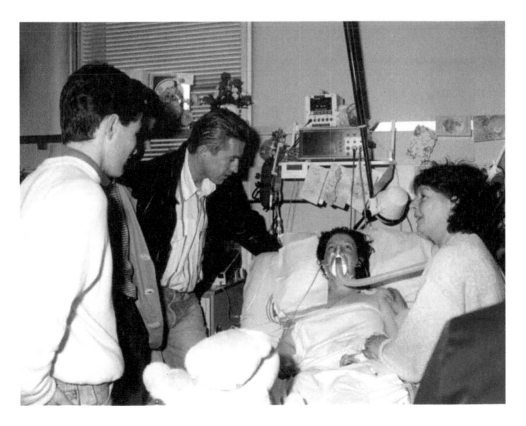

Princess Diana, Brian Clough and Stuart Pearce
Brian Clough and Stuart Pearce meet Princess Diana at the 1991 FA Cup Final.

Facing: Brian Clough Statue
Barbara Clough stands with a statue of her late husband, Nottingham Forest's legendary manager Brian Clough, which she unveiled in the city centre in 2008. © PA Photos

Dave Bassett
Forest manager Dave Bassett from the Council House balcony shows the First Division championship trophy to massed fans in Slab Square.

Nigel Doughty
Chairman Nigel Doughty celebrates promotion from Division One with the players.
© John Sumpter

Fawaz Al Hasawi
Chairman Fawaz Al Hasawi at the City Ground. © John Sumpter

opening First Division match, Iley played at inside-left and scored on his league debut but Forest were beaten 2-1 at Manchester City. He had lost his place at Tottenham when Spurs signed Dave Mackay from Hearts. For Forest he played 105 games, operating in both wing-half positions, at centre-forward, inside-left and on the left wing, before leaving for Newcastle in September 1962. His transfer fee had been the highest Forest had paid until Walker splashed £20,000 on Colin Booth from Wolves after a run of five defeats. This was ended as the former England Under-23 international made his debut in a 3-1 defeat of Chelsea watched by 30,268 at the City Ground on the last day of October. He scored 8 goals in twenty-four games and was the Reds' second highest scorer behind Tommy Wilson on eleven. Booth moved on to Doncaster Rovers at the end of April 1962, after scoring 43 goals in ninety-nine appearances for the Reds.

Relegation having been narrowly avoided, Billy Walker retired after twenty-one years as manager and accepted an invitation to join the committee. It was a summer of change with club secretary Noel Watson giving up after thirty years, later to become president. Ken Smales succeeded him and held the post for the next twenty-seven years. Smales had recently retired after 148 matches for Nottinghamshire County Cricket Club. An off-spin bowler from Yorkshire, he had taken 389 wickets for Notts, including all ten for sixty-six against Gloucestershire in 1956, a county record. Having failed to persuade Harry Catterick to leave Sheffield Wednesday, Forest, on Walker's recommendation, appointed former Scotland and Preston North End full-back Andy Beattie as his successor. Beattie had guested for the Reds during the war and had been manager of Stockport when they knocked Forest out of the FA Cup in the second round match at the City Ground in December 1949.

Beattie took charge for the trip to Birmingham City on 24 September and his first seven game were all defeats. Despite recruiting twenty-year-old inside-forward Colin Addison from York for £12,000 in January, it was mid-April before First Division safety was assured with four matches to spare. The last game was at Stamford Bridge where Jimmy Greaves scored all four Chelsea goals before his transfer to AC Milan. Addison got his 7th goal in fourteen Division One appearances. He proved a splendid acquisition. Top scorer in three out of four full seasons with the Reds, he hit 62 goals in 149 games before going to Arsenal in September 1966 for £45,000. Later, as player-manager he guided Hereford to a famous televised FA Cup victory over Newcastle United in 1972. Jimmy Greaves was proving a real bugbear for Forest and, having returned from Italy, he took the shine off a good start by Forest 1962/63 by hitting four goals for Spurs in a 9-2 thrashing at White Hart Lane at the end of September. The Reds finished a respectable ninth and reached the quarter-finals of the FA Cup but suffered another trouncing at White Hart Lane, where they lost 5-0 in a second replay to Southampton of

Division Two.

There were recriminations in the dressing room and discontent on the terraces over Beattie's defensive tactics. After the ending of the Cup run, eighteen team changes were made in the next three games and, despite a finish in the top half of the table, the committee were losing confidence in him and the manager resigned.

Billy Walker scored 244 goals in 531 appearances for his only League club, Aston Villa. He captained club and country. In his last international, he led England to a famous 4-3 victory over the Austrian 'Wunderteam' at Stamford Bridge in 1932 and was so captivated by their playing style that he would continue to consult European coaches as a manager and keep up-to-date with their techniques. A professorial leader long before Arsene Wenger at Arsenal, he saw it as his responsibility to encourage and develop young players and, along with stability, two promotions and an FA Cup triumph, this was his legacy to Forest and his successors. He was a teacher who let his players express themselves and he was a listener, willing to take on board the advice of senior professionals. All of this made his Reds one of the most attractive teams in the country. The Walker era ended with his death on 28 November 1964, four years after his resignation as a manager and elevation to the committee. Fittingly, it coincided with a victory, Forest winning by 2-0 at Blackpool.

17

Jack and Bobby

Two senior citizens are playing bowls together on one of the greens on Skegness seafront, enjoying each other's company, having a laugh and sharing memories, and to a Forest supporter they look familiar. They don't seem to have changed all that much. You can imagine them in their glory days: Bobby McKinlay winning the ball in the air, nodding it down to Jack Burkitt and the skipper taking control to find the perfect pass to turn defence into attack.

Forest's longest-serving and most successful managers – Billy Walker, twenty-one years from 1939, and Brian Clough, eighteen years from 1975 – had much more than that in common. They shared the same football philosophy. It all boiled down to keeping possession by passing the ball on the ground to feet and picking players willing to take responsibility and knocks. No-one in a shirt of Garibaldi red embodied those qualities more than Brian's son Nigel, his No. 9. Neither Walker nor Clough had time for coaching theories. They would agree that's football's a simple game so why complicate things. They let their players know what was expected of them and insisted they concentrate on their own game whoever the opposition.

Both managers understood that captaincy was more than calling heads or tails before kick-off and they wanted players they could trust. Brian Clough chose John McGovern, who won a League championship medal and was twice a European Cup winner with Forest. Eventually, McGovern was succeeded by Stuart Pearce, who captained England. Billy Walker surprised a few people when he promoted a tough twenty-nine-year-old unrelenting half-back to be his captain when Horace Gager, his stylish, experienced centre-half, retired in 1955. But the manager knew best. Freddie Scott, the next in line, was six months' older than Gager, and Burkitt had six good seasons in the League team behind him. Jack more than justified his manager's confidence leading the Reds back to the top flight and showing true leadership at Wembley when the FA Cup was won with the handicap of being down to ten men for two-thirds of the final after losing Roy Dwight with a broken leg.

Some programme notes from early in 1952 indicate that Burkitt had long been groomed for the captaincy. He had given up an apprenticeship as an engineering draughtsman to become a professional as a nineteen-year-old in 1946. In the 1947/48 season he captained the Forest 'A' team to a league and cup double. After a short spell in the reserves, Jack got his big chance against Coventry City on 20 October 1948, and never looked back.

The programme notes described him as 'a hard, industrious worker, always giving his best for the team'. Against Bolton Wanderers, he gave 'a classic display'. However, it was difficult to pick out any particular match as being outstanding, so well was he playing. 'Well built, Jack is 5 feet 10 inches and weighs 11 stone 5 pounds He is married to a Darlaston girl and is never happier than when he is with his wife and young son in his Nottingham home', it was noted.

It was also announced that 'Forest Freddie' was at the ground to give 5 s prizes to lucky holders of the programme. 'If he taps you on the shoulder, show him your copy. He will do the rest', it stated. Previous winners had been asked, 'what do you think about our playing pitch?' W. Gooch of Grantham had replied, 'Best in the country'. N. G. Jones of Rugby said, 'Beautiful.' Mr. Charlie Harris of Underwood commented, 'Get the stumps out'. Five bob says he was the same Charlie Harris who was Nottinghamshire's opening batsman along with Walter Keeton. Charlie had a reputation as a joker. It was said that after the break for tea at Trent Bridge during a county championship match, he walked to the wicket striking matches to suggest to the umpires that they should draw stumps because of bad light. Keeton, incidentally, played five Second Division games at inside-right for Forest from September to December 1932.

Jack Burkitt, like his manager, was born in Wednesbury, Staffordshire, and both spent their early years in nearby Darlaston, playing in their youth for the Town football club. Town won the Birmingham Combination in 1945/46 with Jack, then nineteen, playing a major role as centre-half. His brother, Bill, told Darlaston Town historian Neil Chambers for the club history in 2011 how Jack came to join Forest.

Bill recalled,

Darlaston were playing Nuneaton away in the FA Cup on 21 September 1946, when a Nottingham Forest scout was watching the Nuneaton centre-forward. Jack had the centre-forward in his pocket and although Darlaston lost 3-1 the scout reported back to Forest manager Billy Walker that he should not pursue the Nuneaton centre-forward but should sign the young Darlaston centre-half.

Walker decided to see for himself and went to Darlaston, whose ground, strangely enough, has been called the City Ground since 1900 when the club's nickname was the Citizens. Bill said,

> Jack was on the verge of signing for Worcester City but Walker came to watch him and decided he wanted to sign him [...] The deal took place in the White Lion pub in Darlaston and the club received £500 and an agreement to a testimonial game for Herbert Hunt, who played for Darlaston for about fourteen years and was a good friend to Jack.

Burkitt joined the Reds in August 1947 and went on to make 503 senior appearances, captaining the side for six seasons. After his playing career ended in 1962, he stayed on as a coach and gained a Full FA coaching badge. It was from Jack that a young Henry Newton learned the basics of solid tackling. In 1966 Burkitt crossed Trent Bridge to manage Notts County for a year and then joined Derby as a trainer under Brian Clough. Jack had already bought a post office in Oakdale Road, Bakersfield, Nottingham, and on leaving the Rams in 1969 worked there until his retirement. He died on 12 September 2003, in Brighouse, Yorkshire.

∞

Jack's defensive partner at Forest and later good friend and bowling companion, Bobby McKinlay is remembered for the manner in which he played the game. A stopper with style, he played nearly 700 games and was never sent off, receiving just two cautions. 'That's one every ten years', he told me, with a smile, when I interviewed him for a football magazine after his retirement. He had become a prison officer at Lowdham Grange near Nottingham, then an institution for young offenders, and lived with his wife, Pauline, at a house in the grounds, where his neighbour and a colleague was former Notts County wing-half Gerry Carver. The Lowdham boys could not have had better role models.

Bob had just turned nineteen when he made his first-team debut in a Second Division game at Coventry on 27 October 1951, replacing veteran captain Horace Gager at centre-half. Billy Walker said,

> There is only one way, in my opinion, to bring on a young player and that is by gradual experience. He will be in for one game and the next time for two or three games. The chief consideration for all young players is the physical side. They must not overtax their strength. Bobby will learn this vital lesson. He must at all times give 100 per cent concentration to his game, must think and act that fraction quicker than an opponent and, above all, keep cool and calm. He must not let himself be rattled by the talkative, experienced adversary that he will meet. He alone can accomplish this. I can only assist him.

It was not an auspicious start for young Bobby. Nottingham-born Peter Taylor, who was to share Forest's European glory as assistant manager to Brian Clough nearly thirty years later, was in goal for Coventry and the home centre-forward Ted Roberts scored a hat-trick in a 3-3 draw. After the match, Walker commented,

> I am quite satisfied with Bobby's display. Roberts, a tough centre-forward, took the three chances that he had but he never once had Bobby rattled. I realised that it would be a big ordeal for this boy but was certain he would rise to it and I am sure you are going to hear about this lad for a number of years.

Those two sets of quotes speak volumes for Walker's management style. In my interview with him, McKinlay had this to say about his old boss,

> Billy Walker was never a tracksuit manager. Team talks were brief and to the point. There was virtually no coaching but we knew to play the passing game. He always said that if we were good enough for him to pick us for the team, we were good enough to know how he wanted us to play and to recognize the strengths and weaknesses of the opposition. There is no doubt, however, that Walker knew how to build a team. He had a fair eye for a player

Talking to Bobby reinforced my impression of the similarities in the football philosophies of Billy Walker and Brian Clough. 'The game is football, play to feet' – Walker. 'If God had wanted us to play football in the clouds, he'd have put grass up there – Clough. Neither had much time for coaching but, of course, the game has moved on.

Uncle Billy introduced the sixteen-year-old Bobby to Forest in 1948. Billy had been a wing-half for the Reds when they had one of the finest half-back lines in the country. The famous trio was made up of an Englishman, a Welshman and a Scotsman: centre-half Tommy Graham, Bob Pugh and Billy McKinlay. Recognised as one of the most creative players in the game, Billy played 357 senior games for Forest in ten years and later became a club scout. The McKinlay family in Lochgelly, Fife, was steeped in football tradition. Bobby's father, Rab, was a semi-professional centre-half with Cowdenheath. Bobby was playing for Fife junior side Bowhill Rovers as a right-winger and it was in that position that he had a week's trial in Nottingham. At the City Ground, coach Bob Davies, a former Forester and Welsh international centre-half, switched him to the middle of the defence.

Bobby returned home to his job with a local garage wondering whether he would get the chance of a football career in England. Seven days later came the good news that he was to be signed as soon as he was seventeen. Rab and Billy McKinlay were at the signing ceremony on 15 October

1949. Bobby was still not convinced that he would make the grade and decided to look upon his move over the border (coming to Nottingham was the first time he had been out of Scotland) as probably 'a year's paid holiday'. In fact, he stayed with Forest twice as long as Uncle Billy had done and played in double the number of matches.

Incredibly, McKinlay never gained a Scottish international cap, though the selectors made headlines for their failure to choose him. His best chance of recognition came towards the end of the 1950s when Glasgow Rangers' George Young finished. Forest's first game in Division One after winning promotion in 1957 was at the City Ground against Preston North End and Bobby found himself facing – at centre-forward – the great and versatile Tom Finney. A 33,000 crowd came to see the encounter. The Reds scored after only three minutes through Jim Barrett. Six minutes' later Preston equalized but Billy Gray got what proved to be the winner in the 28th minute. The headlines dubbed McKinlay 'Tom Finney's Shadow' and 'The Man Who Tied Finney In Notts'. Bob was now firmly in the spotlight. 'It makes me mad to read of Scottish selectors coming south to watch this man and that when the player they should be watching is McKinlay,' said Billy Walker. 'I wouldn't swap Bobby for any centre-half in the country.'

Typically, Bob's own lasting memory of his First Division debut was of unfairly stopping Finney. It was the only time the England man got away and he halted him with a rugby tackle, gripping Finney with both arms round his middle and pulling him to the ground. Bobby told me,

> Finney got up, adjusted his shorts, and never said a word – but he gave me a look that made me feel as small as a worm...
>
> I vowed to myself there and then that I would never do a thing like that again. Billy Walker always said I didn't go in hard enough. Personally, I have never been one for fierce tackling. I prefer the method of intervention, getting to the ball before the need for body contact. I had a healthy respect for my opponent's limbs and I expected him to think likewise. Fortunately, the vast majority did and I missed only about half-a-dozen matches through injury in twenty years.

As the search for Young's successor hotted up, the seven Scottish selectors were each assigned one candidate to watch. In contention were Bobby Evans (Celtic), Willie Toner (Kilmarnock), Doug Cowie (Dundee), Willie McNaught (Raith Rovers), Ken Thomson (Stoke City), and Jim Fotheringham (Arsenal) as well as McKinlay. Scotland's *Sunday Post* had the players checked and drew up 'The George Young League.' Bobby McKinlay earned a 90 per cent rating to head the table, followed by Evans with 85 per cent. The *Post* reporters found that,

> In recent matches McKinlay has succeeded in blotting out England and Preston centre-forward Tom Finney, Manchester City's Bobby

Johnstone and Birmingham City's Eddie Brown.

But the red-headed Celtic player got the selectors' votes. Then Arsenal boss, George Swindin, told the press,

Scotland must be darned well off for centre-halves when they can afford to ignore Bobby McKinlay. He's the best in England.

To get to Wembley in 1959 Forest had first to knock out the Cup-holders Bolton Wanderers in the sixth round. Under the heading 'Nat v Bobby Is The Key To Bolton Tie', Harry Langton of the *Daily Express* wrote:

It is on the old Lion of Vienna, Nat Lofthouse, that Bolton pin their hopes of a second successive trip to a London final in May. But it is a duel that could clinch Bobby McKinlay's place in Scotland's team – a place many think has been long overdue.

After the Reds 2-1 win, the Sunday Express headline reported, 'Bobby McKinlay Blocks Out Nat – And Bolton'. Beneath it, John Macadam wrote,

It was Mr. McKinlay's day. The big centre-half virtually played Lofthouse out of the game and, without his inspiring opportunism, the Bolton forwards were indeed unhappy Wanderers. A Scottish selector who came to watch McKinlay and Forest inside-forward Johnny Quigley saw plenty.

Capel Kirby, in another Sunday morning report, said,

Special praise for Bobby McKinlay, the Forest centre-half, who was not only the master tactician but completely subdued Nat Lofthouse. In doing so he may have won himself the prospect of two visits to Wembley, one for the Cup Final and the other in a Scottish jersey against England. McKinlay's anticipation, interception, tackling and distribution, could not have failed to impress Mr Jimmy Gordon, the Scottish selector.

Chelsea manager Ted Drake, the former England international centre-forward, added his voice to the debate, 'McKinlay is brilliant,' he said. 'He is the best centre-half I've seen this season and if Scotland have a better one, they are dead lucky.' But it was left-winger Stewart Imlach, Bobby's room-mate when staying in hotels on away trips, who became Forest's first-ever Scottish international player.

Bobby McKinlay made 685 appearances for the Reds, and Jack Burkitt 503. Another left-half Ian Bowyer had 564 and another centre-half Steve

Chettle 526. Left-back Stuart Pearce, a future captain, played 522 games for Forest and scored 88 goals. He became the club's most capped player with seventy-eight and captained England ten times. McKinlay became a Forest coach under manager Matt Gillies after retiring in November 1969 but was sacked when Dave Mackay took over three years later. 'Forest treated me well and I have no bitterness', he told me. 'But it is sad that in this game a man with twenty-two years' loyal service to one club can be thrown out by a newcomer, who himself stays for no more than a year before accepting an offer from a rival club and moving on.' Mackay left Forest in October 1973 to join Derby County as Brian Clough's replacement.

Jack Burkitt was given a testimonial in 1961 against Swedish side Malmo who, eighteen years later, were to meet Forest in the European Cup Final in Munich. On a cold, foggy November weeknight 7,800 hardy City Ground diehards turned up to support Jack but the game was abandoned after seventy-nine minutes with the Reds leading 5-1 through Colin Addison, Johnny Quigley, Geoff Vowden, 'Flip' Le Flem and Colin Booth. There were more than 18,000 at the testimonial match for Bobby McKinlay against Glasgow Celtic in April 1965, a victory for Forest with Addison and Alan Hinton the scorers.

18

The Channel Islanders

Guernsey-born Matt Le Tissier, who spent his entire 16-year career with Southampton and won eight England caps, is the best-known player to arrive in English football from the Channel Islands. But thanks to the talent-spotting of former physiotherapist Ted Malpass, who had played with Billy Walker at Aston Villa and lived in Guernsey, Forest had a string of Channel Islanders recommended to the club from the late 1940s to the early 1960s.

They included right-back Bill Whare, who could break opposing wingers' hearts by, when they thought he was left behind, winning the ball with recovering sliding tackles that left them flat on their faces. Their feelings were hurt but never their limbs. Whare always played fairly. He was born in Guernsey in 1925 and made his debut for Forest a few weeks before his 24th birthday in a 2-2 draw in front of a 27,000 crowd for a Division Two match at the City Ground on 23 April 1949. It was his only first team appearance in a relegation season. And he was at left-half. Whare got back into the side at the end of October in his preferred full-back position. There was competition from veteran Jack Hutchinson but he chalked up 298 first team appearances before ending his League career against Burnley at Turf Moor on November 21, 1959. It was not the send-off he would have wanted. Forest lost 8-0 with Jimmy Robson scoring five goals for the home side.

During Bill's decade in the Garibaldi red shirt, Forest rose from Division Three South to the First Division but the highlight was playing his part in the Wembley triumph of 1959. Whare's Cup Final partner at full-back was Joe McDonald but the best-remembered pairing was with Geoff Thomas, who had been signed from a Derby youth club. They played together through three divisions of the Football League and for a total of 204 games.

The Guernsey-born Farmer brothers were recruited from Jersey side St Aubins. Goalkeeper Bill Farmer made his debut in a 2-0 win against

Hull City in a Second Division match at the City Ground on 16 September 1953, when left-winger Colin Collindridge scored both goals. He made 44 Division Two appearances in his three seasons on Trentside and played six games in the FA Cup in 1954/55 including the fifth round tie against Newcastle United, which went to two replays. Bill had left for Loughborough Brush Sports before his brother, wing-half Ron Farmer, made his Forest debut against Gillingham at the City Ground in the FA Cup third round on 4 January 1958, a game won 2-0. Ron played only nine games for Forest before being transferred to Coventry City at the end of the season. With the Sky Blues, he played 285 matches, scoring forty-eight goals, before returning to Nottingham to spend two seasons with Notts County in the Fourth Division.

Although born in Barnsley, Geoff Vowden was brought up in Jersey and came to Forest as a teenager. He scored two goals in his first team debut in a friendly against Scottish Cup winners St Mirren at the City Ground on 23 September 1959. Three days later, as an eighteen-year-old he made his First Division debut at inside-right in a 2-0 home win against Bolton Wanderers. Geoff scored thirty-eight top flight goals in ninety games for Forest and also got eight goals in seventeen FA Cup and Football League cup-ties. He scored in his last game for the Reds on 19 September 1964, a 3-2 defeat at the City Ground by Fulham, for whom full-back Jim Langley struck a 50-yard free-kick past goalkeeper Peter Grummitt. Vowden was at centre-forward and scored in a 3-1 victory at Cardiff when Forest's fifth Channel Islander eighteen-year-old Richard 'Flip' Le Flem made his debut.

Le Flem delighted supporters and frustrated opponents in the manner of his predecessors on the Forest left-wing Colin Collindridge and Stewart Imlach, establishing a tradition of individual brilliance in that position that was to be carried on by Ian Storey-Moore, Duncan McKenzie and John Robertson. And he scored one of the greatest goals ever seen at the City Ground. In their pre-match pub debates, many Reds' fans would put the 7-0 defeat of Burnley on 18 September 1957, as a newly-promoted Division One side as the best of all home performances. Manager Walker described that display as 'one of the most sparkling exhibitions of team football I have had the pleasure of witnessing for a long time – all played their parts to perfection.'

The match against Burnley four seasons' later when Le Flem scored his wonder goal was much tighter but a stirring struggle seen by 34,000 fans at the City Ground on 1 December 1962. Burnley were unable to take advantage when Forest went down to ten men for twenty minutes during the first half after right-winger Trevor Hockey damaged his arm and shoulder in a heavy fall. A big factor in this was the way Jeff Whitefoot, normally known for his creativity at wing-half, shackled the great Irish inside-forward Jimmy McIlroy. Then, with the team back to full strength, just before the interval young, blond centre-forward David Wilson met a cross and headed the ball down for inside-left Johnny Quigley to drive Forest ahead. From a 52nd minute corner, conceded after a period of heavy pressure, the visitors equalized through another blond centre-forward England international Ray Pointer.

From then on it was a tremendous battle, settled by Le Flem's brilliant individual goal. He received Wilson's pass on the left flank just inside the Burnley half and set off on an amazing dribble, leaving five defenders in his wake including England internationals John Angus and Brian Miller as well as the visitors' captain Jimmy Adamson. It was finished off by a superbly struck right foot shot past Adam Blacklaw, Scotland's goalkeeper. The crowd rose as one to acclaim 'Flip' and the applause went on for minutes afterwards. The goal shattered the visitors and jolted their championship hopes. Burnley finished third and Forest ninth in Division One.

Richard 'Flip' Le Flem was born in Bradford on Avon, Wiltshire, in July, 1942, his parents having left the islands during the German wartime occupation. A successful schoolboy athlete and footballer, he arrived from Jersey with Vowden to sign apprentice forms just a month after the 1959 Cup Final. Word soon got round Nottingham about this tricky young ball player Forest had signed and numbers of supporters went down to the Victoria Embankment pitches specially to see Le Flem play for Forest Colts in the Notts Thursday League. It was a competition that pitched the young pros against physically stronger amateurs determined to make the most of their afternoons off from work. His exceptional talent was soon apparent but not always appreciated by some team-mates who, like their opponents, could not anticipate what 'Flip' would do next and who berated him for hogging the ball.

Le Flem made the left-wing spot his own after his First Division debut in a 3-1 victory at Cardiff on 10 September, 1960. During his three-and-a-half seasons in Nottingham, 'Flip' made 151 appearances and scored twenty goals. He also played in an England Under-23 victory over Holland in Rotterdam with Bobby Moore as captain. In January, 1964, Le Flem was swapped by manager Johnny Carey for Wolves' winger Alan Hinton. 'Flip' struggled to settle in Wolverhampton. He felt himself that he had not reproduced the form he had shown on Trentside. He said,

> I had difficulty with the Molineux pitch. The surface at the City Ground was fantastic – like a billiard table – but Stan Cullis [Wolves' manager] liked the ground heavier and had it watered a lot. He didn't want it rolled so it was liable to become bumpy, which wasn't good for a touchline runner like myself.

On the day before being due to report for pre-season training at Molineux in 1964 Le Flem contracted jaundice. 'I was fishing with my brother off the harbour at St Peter Port, Guernsey, and we both contracted the illness,' he said. 'The incubation period is thirty days and I couldn't play until late October – it was that debilitating. Jimmy Greaves had it as well and struggled to get over it.' It was a misfortune Le Flem could ill afford. He moved on to Middlesbrough and then Leyton Orient before returning to Guernsey, where he became an export specialist for an electronics company and then a mains and services executive with Guernsey Water.

∞

With Walker still on the committee, Johnny Carey was the next to take on the manager's role he had filled for so long and with such distinction. Carey had played 344 games for Manchester United and had captained the great post-war side that won the FA Cup in 1948 and the League Championship in 1952. An outstanding left-back, he was credited with caps for both Northern Ireland (seven) and the Republic (twenty-nine), captaining not only club and country but also the Rest of Europe against Great Britain in 1948. He was Footballer of the Year in 1949. As a manager he piloted Blackburn Rovers back to the First Division in 1958 but was later sacked by Everton after guiding the Goodison Park club to fifth in 1960/61, the Toffeemen's highest finish since the war. In 1962, he took Leyton Orient to the top flight for the first time in their history They were immediately relegated but Forest were sufficiently impressed by his record to invite him to follow Andy Beattie at the City Ground.

Forest's opened the 1963/64 season at home to Aston Villa with a new centre-forward, Frank Wignall, as well as a new manager but it was his opposite number, a former Meadow Lane favourite, Tony Hateley who got the only goal. Wignall, an Everton reserve, had been signed at the end of Beattie's reign for a Forest record outlay in the region of £20,000. He repaid his fee with more than fifty goals in nearly 180 games for the Reds before moving to Wolverhampton Wanderers for a handsome £50,000 in March 1968. He later had spells with Derby and Mansfield before going into management with Burton Albion. In 1980 Wignall was appointed national coach by Qatar. Finally, he managed Shepshed Charterhouse from 1981 to 83.

Wignall scored his first goal for the Reds in a 2-1 victory against Liverpool in front of a crowd of nearly 49,000 at Anfield on 24 August. A 4-1 defeat at Tottenham, including another Greaves hat-trick, and a goalless draw in the return match with Liverpool was followed with five successive wins that took Carey's Forest to the top of the First Division in late September. Wignall formed an effective partnership in attack with Addison. He scored 36 goals and his partner 33 in the two-and-a-half seasons they played together.

Versatile Calvin Palmer, signed by Walker as an eighteen-year-old from Skegness Town in 1958, had made more than 100 first-team appearances for the Reds, mainly at wing-half, when he was transferred to Stoke City for £35,000 in September. His replacement was another Walker apprentice Nottingham-born Henry Newton, a city schools' player, though it was as Whitefoot's deputy that he made his debut in a 2-0 win against Leicester at the City Ground on 8 October, when Wignall and Addision got a goal each. Newton, Burkitt trained, was a strong tackler but also supremely confident on the ball and he gained four England Under-23 caps and was on the verge of selection for the 1970 World Cup squad. He had played 315 times for Forest when he was transferred to champions Everton for £150,000 plus Northern Ireland international Tommy Jackson. Forest had blocked a move to local rivals Derby County but Newton got there by a circuitous route three years later when he became Brian Clough's last big signing for the Rams.

Jackson gained nineteen caps as a Forest player between 1970 and 1975, as many as Peter Shilton was awarded by England during his five years at the City Ground. Yet he was never a first-team regular, featuring in nearly 100 games, mostly at wing-half but also on the wing, at inside-forward and twice as a full-back. He was given a free transfer by Brian Clough in the summer of 1975 but was taken on by Manchester United boss Tommy Docherty who wanted him to captain his reserve side. Surprisingly, he broke into the United first team for a season before retiring in 1977 aged thirty-one. Jackson became a successful manager in Ireland and won no fewer than sixteen trophies in six years with Glentoran.

Another debutant was Walker's discovery Sammy Chapman from junior football in Walsall who, at seventeen years and five months, became Forest's youngest-ever player when he came into the side at inside-left against Stoke at the City Ground in mid-January. He went on to make 422 appearances, mainly as a defender, before moving across Trent Bridge to Notts County in 1977. He also played in the United States for Tulsa Roughnecks.

Carey biggest transfer deal in his first season was to pay a then record out-going fee of £30,000 for twenty-five-year-old wing-half or inside-forward John Barnwell from Arsenal. An England Youth and Under-23 international, he had scored 24 goals in more than 160 games for the Gunners but was to play his best football for Forest in a deeply-lying role linking defence with attack as a genuine midfielder. He made over 200 appearances for the Reds and served them splendidly for six seasons. After retiring as a player, Barnwell became an efficient manager and administrator, guiding Wolves to a League Cup final victory over Forest in 1980 and later being appointed chief executive of the Football League Managers' Association.

Forest ended Carey's first season thirteenth in the First Division. Wignall was top scorer with a modest sixteen goals, including his first senior hat-trick in a 3-2 victory at Bolton, and Addison scored ten. The manager's first silverware was the County Cup when Notts were beaten 5-1 at Meadow Lane, where Wignall hit another three. Hinton, with a pile-driver, and Addison got the other two. Wignall and Hinton both gained England caps and appeared together on 18 November in a 2-1 win over Wales at Wembley. Wignall scored both goals in this match, the first time Forest had supplied two players to the England team since the Forman brothers in 1898. Hinton was also in the England team that drew 2-2 with Belgium at Wembley and scored one of the goals. Wignall got his second cap in a 1-1 draw with Holland in Amsterdam.

Right-winger Chris Crowe was signed a few days' before the start of the 1964/65 season for another £30,000 fee from Wolves. Newcastle-born, he played for Scotland as a schoolboy, while living in Edinburgh, and then for England at youth, under-23 and as a full international with a cap against France in 1962. Forest showed they meant business by scoring three times in the last seventeen minutes to snatch a 4-3 victory at home to Birmingham on the opening day of the season. At the end of September they ended Leeds United's run of thirty-three unbeaten home games with goals by Wignall and Hinton in a 2-1 win. At the end of the season, Leeds were deprived of the championship title by Manchester United only on goal average. Forest finished fifth, with a club record forty-seven points (two for a win).

Forest were guests at the May Day celebrations in Austria and beat Rapid Vienna 2-0, Addison and Crowe scoring. The Reds retained the County Cup, beating Mansfield Town, 5-0 on 8 May but just a minute after half-time the game lost its gloss when Frank Wignall sustained a broken leg.

Goalkeeper Peter Grummitt, discovered at Bourne Town, Lincolnshire, had made his debut as an eighteen-year-old replacement for Chic Thomson and what a shock he got when in the first minute of his first game Jim Iley scored an own goal against him. This was in front of nearly 19,000 fans at the City Ground on 12 November 1960. But Colin Booth spared the blushes of both team-mates with two goals to earn a draw with Bolton Wanderers. Peter never did have time for introspection. He was one of the most acrobatic goalkeepers of his time, relying on agility and amazing reflexes. Many an opposing forward has held his head in his hands as Grummitt saved a seeming certainty at point-blank range. He missed only one First Division match in 1964/65, a 3-0 victory at Arsenal. Henry Newton played every League and Cup match and Bob McKinlay completed a fifth consecutive 'ever-present' season.

PART THREE

1965-2015

Soccer is one of the most unifying activities amongst us.
Nelson Mandela

This simple and elegant game, unhampered by complex rules and
equipment, made its way through the world, entirely on its merits.
Eric Hobsbawm, Cambridge Marxist historian

19

High Noon in St Louis

Forest's centenary year North American tour was the lengthiest and most successful ever undertaken by the club. It was marked by overwhelming hospitality, successes on the field, memorable sight-seeing and an itinerary covering thousands of miles with matches in New York, St Louis, Chicago, San Francisco, Los Angeles, Vancouver and Toronto.

Club captain Bobby McKinlay led a squad that included goalkeepers Peter Grummitt and Jimmy Cargill, defenders Peter Hindley, Dennis Mochan, Brian Grant and Bill Taylor, midfielders Jeff Whitefoot, Henry Newton, John Barnwell and John Winfield, wingers Ian Storey-Moore, Alan Hinton, Chris Crowe and Mike Kear, with strikers Colin Addison and David Wilson. Manager Johnny Carey and former skipper Jack Burkitt, then trainer, were in charge of the tourists and were accompanied by chairman Fred Sissons, vice-chairman Jack Levy and committee men Harold Alcock and Tony Wood.

Forest began with an 8-2 victory over Hartford SC in Connecticut on Friday 14 May, Storey-Moore scoring four, Crowe hitting a hat-trick and Addison getting the other goal. The Ukranian Nationals in Philadelphia on Sunday 16 provided stronger opposition but Crowe, Barnwell and Kear scored in a 3-2 win. Three days later the Reds beat Boston Metros in Chelsea, Massachusetts, 4-2 with two goals each from Storey-Moore and Hinton. The run of victories ended in New York where the West German side Hannover 96 beat Forest 3-1 at the Randall's Island stadium on Sunday, 23 May. Hinton was the Reds' scorer.

And so to St Louis, Missouri, popularized by the 1940s Hollywood musical *Meet Me in St Louis*, starring Judy Garland and directed by Vicente Minnelli. St Louis has a long history as one of the major hotbeds of soccer in the United States and, in 1904 – when the film was set – it held the St Louis World's Fair and also hosted the Olympic Games. The city's first professional soccer team, the St Louis Stars, played in the now defunct North American Soccer League. The Stars were unusual in recruiting mainly local players but still won the Southern Division in 1972 and were beaten only 2-1 by the famous New York Cosmos in the championship final. Six St Louisans were in the United States squad that went to the 1950 World Cup finals in Brazil and five (PeeWee Wallace, Charlie Colombo, Gino Pariani, Harry Keough and goalkeeper Frank Borghi) played at Belo Horizonte where the USA sensationally defeated 1-0 an England side that included Stanley Matthews, Tom Finney, Alf Ramsey and Billy Wright.

On Thursday 27 May, Forest attracted a crowd of 5,400 in St Louis when they beat the All Stars 6-1. Hinton and Crowe got two each with Addison and Wilson also scoring. Dave Lange's recent book, *Soccer Made in St Louis,* traces the history of the game in the city back to 1875. Along with Dave Wangerin's *Soccer in a Football World* it's a must-read for anyone who thinks the beautiful game has no roots in the United States. McKinlay later recalled that the most unusual game he ever played in a long career was in downtown St Louis on this trip. It took place not on a football field but on Eighth Street, which was closed to traffic at mid-day (high noon, he said) while the Reds played St Louis Catholic Youth Council All Stars at head tennis.

Forest then moved on to Chicago, where they got revenge against Hannover 96. A crowd of 9,000 at Soldier Field on Sunday 30 May saw the West Germans beaten 2-0, Wilson scoring both goals. Two more games against Hannover 96 were played in California and both were won. In San Francisco on Wednesday 2 June, the West Germans were beaten 6-2 in front of 15,000 fans. Hinton scored a hat-trick, including two penalties, with other goals coming from Addison, Barnwell and Crowe. There was another big crowd in Los Angeles on three days later when 10,000 saw Hinton and Addison ensure a 2-1 victory.

The touring party travelled north to Canada and on Wednesday 9 June, British Columbia All Stars were beaten 2-0 in Vancouver. The attendance was 7,500 and Forest's goals came from Hinton and Barnwell. Three days' later, the Reds lost 2-1 to Hibernian. Addison got the goal against the Edinburgh side. The tour ended in Toronto on Monday 14 June, when a no doubt tiring side scraped a 1-0 victory over Ontario All Stars thanks to a Barnwell penalty.

∞

A twenty-six-year-old Brazilian international centre-forward (impressively) named Waldo Machado da Silva inspired probably the best display by a foreign side at the City Ground. There were 36,158 fans on Trentside to see the first round second leg tie against Valencia in the Coupe Internationale des Villes de Foires (the Inter-Cities Fairs Cup) on Wednesday, 4 October 1961. Forest had some work to do, having been beaten 2-0 three weeks earlier in the magnificent Gran Mestalla stadium, then one of the biggest and most luxurious in Spain. Waldo, a new signing, had scored both goals in the first half.

Valencia is the capital of the province of the same name and is a large city of over 500,000 people on the River Turia and the Mediterranean coast. The football club was formed in the early 1900s by a group of Englishmen aided by local students. Forest had met Valencia for the first time when, after winning the FA Cup, the team went on tour to Portugal and Spain. The tour began on 20 May in Lisbon, where a Billy Gray penalty earned a 1-0 victory. Crossing the border, the Reds were beaten four days' later by the same score at Oviedo. It might have been two but for a penalty save by Chic Thomson. Then, on 27 May, Forest arrived in Valencia. The home goalkeeper, Ignatio Eizaguirre, was playing his final game for the Spanish side but his farewell was spoiled when Jim Barrett struck the winning goal. Barrett scored another the next day against Atletico Madrid but Forest were heavily beaten 6-1. The tour ended in Cadiz with a 3-0 defeat by Athletic Bilbao.

Back to the Fairs Cup (Forest were eligible for the competition because of the annual Goose Fair). In Spain the team had lined up: Peter Grummitt, Calvin Palmer, Billy Gray, Jeff Whitefoot, Bobby McKinlay, Jim Iley, Geoff Vowden, Colin Booth, Johnny Quigley and 'Flip' Le Flem. For the home leg, Doug Baird came in for Palmer at right back and Billy Cobb, just turned twenty-one and from Newark, replaced Vowden. Le Flem gave Forest encouragement early on with a thunderbolt across goal that had goalkeeper Jose Ginesta scrambling. But home hopes were shattered by two quick goals. By Waldo, who else? He gave Valencia the lead in the 11th minute, driving in a centre from right winger Hector Nunez. His second in the 13th minute was a stunner. With the Brazilian some distance out there seemed little danger but he crashed in a tremendous 30-yard drive, surprising goalkeeper Grummitt who managed to touch the ball on to an upright but it spun into the net. Then Waldo set up Nunez for the only other goal of the first half. Just before the break, Le Flem saw two of his crosses dropped by Ginesta with Quigley close to forcing the ball home each time. But three minutes after the restart Nunez got his second goal and Valencia's fourth.

Billy Cobb scored Forest's first goal in a major European competition in the 57th minute with a curling free-kick from the right wing after he had been fouled. It deceived Ginesta and the ball dipped inside the far post. Nunez had the last world for Valencia, completing his hat-trick in the 71st minute. Cobb scored 7 goals in thirty-seven appearances for Forest. He was what then called a utility player. In 1962/63, his best season, he played in six different positions in sixteen First Division appearances before going on to play for Plymouth Argyle, Brentford, Lincoln City and Boston United.

Relations between the two clubs remained friendly and Valencia helped Forest mark the centenary year with a special match at the City

Ground on Tuesday 28 September 1965. A crowd of 18,922 saw the Reds line up: Peter Grummitt, Bill Brindley, Dennis Mochan, Henry Newton, Bobby McKinlay, Jeff Whitefoot, Ian Storey-Moore, Chris Crowe, Frank Wignall, Colin Addison and Alan Hinton. Waldo had suffered a thigh injury in Valencia's 3-0 victory against Real Madrid on the Sunday before the game but he had an injection to enable him to start so as not to disappoint his many admirers in Nottingham. He played the whole of the first half before being replaced.

It was a memorable game fit for the occasion. After only five minutes Forest went in front from a penalty by Chris Crowe after a linesman had spotted a handball offence. Vicente Guillot, a masterly inside-left, equalized in the 19th minute. He darted through the middle, shrugged off two tackles and beat the advancing Grummitt. The ball struck a post, bounced back in the air and Guillot scored with a diving header. Valencia tired in the second half but despite Forest pressure there were no more goals and the game ended all square, causing a Valencian director to comment afterwards, 'A most diplomatic result.'

Before the match, Denis Hill-Wood, chairman of Arsenal, presented Forest with a set of red shirts, recalling the help the club gave to the fledgling Gunners some eighty years earlier. Arsenal also gave Forest a ceramic gun, which occupied an honoured place in the City Ground boardroom but was lost in the main stand fire of 1968. It was replaced by Arsenal in another pleasing gesture.

∞

Forest's first home Division One match of the centenary year resulted in a fine 4-2 victory against Manchester United watch by 33,744 fans, Addison scoring twice with Wignall and Hinton also getting goals. David Wilson became the first Forest substitute to score when West Ham United were beaten 5-0 at the City Ground on 9 October. The Reds failed to maintain the momentum, however, and ended the season eighteenth in the table. Manager Carey made two significant signings who were to make a big impact once they had settled in on Trentside. Welsh international wing-half Terry Hennessey arrived from Birmingham for £45,000 in November. A strong tackler and telling distributor of the ball, he won fifteen caps as a Forest player and captained both club and country. When he left the Reds, after three good seasons, it was to become Brian Clough's first six-figure signing for Derby.

Carey paid a club-record fee of £65,000 for Arsenal's England international centre-forward Joe Baker in March. With a dashing, head-on, style, he quickly became a fan favourite and was nicknamed 'The King' by the City Ground faithful. Baker scored a goal every three games for the Reds and there was outrage when Carey's successor, Matt Gillies, sold him to Sunderland in the summer of 1969. Liverpool-born but with a strong Scottish accent, he received a tremendous welcome when he returned to the City Ground as a guest after suffering a heart attack in 1994.

Carey and his silver-haired trainer-coach Tommy Cavanagh, a drill sergeant of a Liverpudlian, shaped a side capable of challenging for the League and Cup double in 1966/67. Defeats at home to Stoke City and next at Chelsea did not make for an auspicious start but once they got into their stride, the Reds became a formidable force. In January they registered their sixth successive win and in February the thirteenth consecutive First Division match without defeat. Also during this run Dukla Prague were beaten 3-1 in a City Ground friendly. Hennessey with his acute positional sense was the anchor, the creative Barnwell the key figure in midfield, Wignall the ideal target man and, playing off him, 'Zigger Zagger' Baker capable of upsetting any defence with his sudden bursts of acceleration. And there was young forward Ian Storey-Moore described by *The Sunday Telegraph* as 'probably the most talented ball player in the country when Georgie Best is not on song'.

In front of the excellent Grummitt were full-backs Peter Hindley, who played in fifty-two League and Cup games that season, and John Winfield, with fifty appearances. Both were former Walker juniors. Hindley's father, Frank, had been a Forest centre-forward who scored 3 goals in eight games in 1938/39 before joining Brighton and having his career disrupted by the war. Peter began as a centre-forward before being switched to the defence by Andy Beattie. He made 416 appearances, scoring 11 goals, and partnered Winfield, 410 games and 5 goals, at full-back well over 200 times. Bob McKinlay, of course, was an ever-present, and Henry Newton played 39 league games and 9 in the cup. Chris Crowe, who made only 7 league appearances, scored all of his three goals in one match – and that was against Manchester United. A 41,854 crowd at the City Ground at the beginning of October saw his first go in after just fifteen seconds and another was from the penalty spot. Forest won 4-1, with Wignall the other scorer.

The Reds' First Division form was carried into the FA Cup. Plymouth Argyle were beaten 2-1 and Newcastle United 3-0, both home ties, but progress was delayed by Swindon Town who held Forest to a goal-less draw in front of a 45,878 crowd at the City Ground in round five. It was 1-1 in the replay at Swindon, where Hindley scored, but winger Barry Lyons, Baker and Barnwell got the goals to put Forest through 3-0 in front of a 52,596 crowd for the second replay at Villa Park. Then came the sixth round clash with Everton that Carey called 'Just fantastic.'

Martin Tyler, now Sky Sports' top football commentator, and Richard Widdows chose it as one of *The Sixty Memorable Matches* (1973).

Never the wealthiest of clubs, Forest had to buy men below their best and coax something extra out of them or develop whatever talent they could find on their own doorstep. Cavanagh took much of the credit for this. The players worked for him willingly and with success came new assurance; their skills were blended so successfully that their shortcomings did not matter,

wrote the authors. The Everton side that had won the Cup the previous year had one most important addition – that of 1966 World Cup star Alan Ball, signed from Blackpool for a British record of £110,000.

20

Mist Rolling In

Saturday 8 April, was a misty day on Trentside and the City Ground was filled with 47,510 fans determined to lift the gloom. And when Joe Baker raced typically at the heart of the visitors' defence almost from the kick-off the crowd roared its support but he was stopped and the Trent End silenced by a sliding tackle from Brian Labone that left 'The King' rolling over in acute pain. After that he could hardly bend his left leg and every kick, every tackle, was agony. He said later it was the most painful injury he had ever had. Yet he carried on for another half-hour before being replaced by Alan Hinton.

With Forest still trying to reorganize, Alan Ball split the defence for Jimmy Husband to beat Grummitt with a flick inside his left-hand post. Storey-Moore had been moved inside to partner Wignall and it was their combination that proved crucial. Just past the hour, Wignall unleashed a low shot that goalkeeper Andy Rankin could only parry and Storey-Moore gleefully pounced to slot the ball into an empty net. Two minutes later the crowd went wild again. Barnwell put Hinton in possession and the winger's cross was nodded down by Wignall to the feet of the onrushing Storey-Moore who hit a screaming shot wide of Rankin's left hand to give his side the lead.

Now the tension was unbearable. The pace quickened. With Newton tackling like a demon, Barnwell delicately placing passes for Hinton and Moore to run on to, Hennessey and the full-backs pumping long balls for the ever-willing Wignall to chase, the momentum was with Forest. It changed in a moment. Ball sent Sandy Brown away on the right and his cross was turned in by Husband in the 78th minute for his second goal of the game and Everton's equalizer. The Blues were now scenting the kill like pack of hounds. Johnny Morrissey struck a marvellous shot that Grummitt tipped over the bar. The Reds regained their rhythm. McKinlay headed the ball beyond Rankin but Colin Harvey was there to head off the line. Despite the best efforts of both sides time was running out and nervous supporters were anticipating a replay.

'Still the most agonizing moment of an unforgettable soccer experience was to come,' wrote Tony Pritchett in his *Nottingham Evening Post* report. With less than a minute left Winfield sent a long, high centre into the Everton penalty area and found the head of Wignall who deflected the ball down to Storey-Moore. 'His first shot hit Wilson, his second hit the goalkeeper, then his header hit the bar and, finally, at fourth attempt, he headed in', Pritchett reported. What a climax, what a match. It was the first hat-trick of Storey-Moore's career. The headline written over the account by Tyler and Widdows read: 'Some Game, Some Goal, Some Finish'. 'It was probably our finest hour as a team if not my finest game,' the player told David McVay, an ex-professional turned author and journalist.

I remember the atmosphere was electric and they allowed the kids to come over the terracing and stands to sit beside the pitch. The last goal was fortuitous to say the least but Frank Wignall was the 'man of the match' for me. He caused them so many problems and had a head in all three of my goals.

The thought that this would be the team's 'finest hour' did not occur to the thousands who queued all night on Trentside for Forest's allocation of semi-final tickets. Not only the Cup but the double was within range. It had to be the impish Jimmy Greaves, who had long figured in their nightmares, who dashed those dreams at Hillsborough on 29 April. Greavsie's goal was a body blow and Spurs triumphed 2-1 to go to Wembley and there win the trophy. Hennessey scored a fine opportunist goal for the Reds but only after Frank Saul had got Tottenham's second. Greaves just loved playing against Forest. He scored twenty-nine goals in total against them, including hitting four on three occasions. His semi-final goal came from a long clearance by centre-half Mike England that was headed down by Alan Gilzean. As the ball bounced towards him, Greaves turned away from Hennessey and struck it left-footed on the half-volley from about 25 yards out. His shot went in off Grummitt's right-hand post.

Forest lifted themselves with a fine First Division win against Aston Villa at Villa Park, where the 41,468 attendance on 2 May was a record for a match between the two sides. Storey-Moore scored twice and Barry Lyons got the other goal in a 3-0 victory. But four days' later the Reds' title hopes were dashed by a 2-1 defeat at The Dell to relegation strugglers Southampton. Sammy Chapman scored twice in a 3-2 victory at Craven Cottage against lowly Fulham on the last day of the league season to enable the Reds to ward off Tottenham Hotspur and Leeds United and hang on to the runners-up spot. Level on points with Spurs, Forest had by 0.082 the better goal average. Manchester United won the championship by four points, scoring eighty-four goals, twenty more than Forest. In 1967/68 United went on to become the first Football League club to win the European Cup, beating Benfica 4-1 in the final with a team that included three European Footballers of the Year – Bobby Charlton, George Best and Denis Law. Forest were not quite left empty-handed. Lyons scored both goals against Notts County at the City Ground to win the County Cup before a 22,581 crowd, a record for the competition, on 9 May. They then went to Spain and beat Barcelona 2-1 but were beaten 1-0 by Valencia.

Forest got off the a great start in 1967/68, beating Sheffield United away, Arsenal at the City Ground and Coventry City home and away. They were again in the Fairs Cup and, in the first round on 20 September beat Eintracht Frankfurt thanks to a Joe Baker goal in a game played in torrential rain in Germany. Frank Wignall was sent off. The Nottingham leg on 17 October was a romp. The Reds won 4-0, had three goals disallowed and hit the woodwork three times. Baker scored twice with the other goals coming from Chapman and Lyons. This set up a second round clash with FC Zurich. A goal by Henry Newton and a penalty converted by Storey-Moore ensured a 2-1 home win in front of 32,896 fans on 31 October. Zurich led 1-0 at the final whistle in Switzerland on 14 November. The Nottingham players remained on the pitch expecting extra time. It never came. Forest officials had misread the rules of the competition. Zurich were through on 'away goals' thanks to scoring at the City Ground.

Between the two European rounds, there was a magnificent 3-1 win over the champions, Manchester United, in front of a City Ground record crowd of 49,946 on 28 October, when Baker got a brace and Wignall was the other home scorer. Then form declined and Forest failed to score in four successive defeats. There was a brief recovery with a Christmas double over Stoke City, 37,577 watching a 3-0 Boxing Day victory at the City Ground, which was followed by a 3-1 win in the Potteries.

Wignall had to go in goal when Grummitt was injured against Manchester City early in January and Brian Williamson was signed from Leeds as cover. It was a fortuitous move as a month later Grummitt's arm was broken in an FA Cup fourth round defeat at Leeds. He did not return until the start of the 1968/69 season and in the 82nd minute of the second First Division match at Chelsea on 14 August he broke a thumb. One of the greatest of all Forest goalkeepers, he made only 18 appearances that season and just two in the next before being transferred to Sheffield Wednesday. Alan Hill was recruited from Rotherham United with Grummitt sidelined and made himself Forest's number one until, in his forty-sixth game, the goalkeeping hoodoo struck again and he suffered a serious arm injury that ended his career. Ex-Magpie Tony Hateley scored a hat-trick as Liverpool trounced the Reds 6-1 at Anfield to end 1967/68 First Division campaign leaving them an unremarkable mid-table side.

∞

Don Revie's Leeds United were leaders of Division One when they came to Trentside on Saturday 24 August 1968. They had Gary Sprake in goal, Paul Reaney and Terry Cooper at full-back, Jack Charlton at centre-half with Billy Bremner and Norman Hunter either side of him, Mike O'Grady, Rod Belfitt, Mick Jones, Eddie Gray and Terry Hibbitt. Terry Yorath was the substitute. Forest had youth international Colin Hall leading the attack in place of the injured Joe Baker. Brian Williamson was in goal with Peter Hindley and John Winfield at full-back, Bobby McKinlay was centre-half with skipper Terry Hennessey and Henry Newton either side of him, Barry Lyons, John Barnwell, Ian Storey-Moore and Dave Hilley. Sammy Chapman was the substitute. Malcolm Sinclair of Guildford was the referee and the game kicked off in front of 31,126 fans.

The 'David and Goliath' duel between the energetic Hall, at 5 feet 8 inches, and towering England international Charlton was an early highlight as Forest piled on the pressure. Both sides attacked adventurously with the visitors gradually getting the upper hand. In the thirty-fifth minute Bremner held off Hennessey and McKinlay to cross for Belfitt to beat Williamson with a glancing header. The Reds showed fight and urgency to equaliser within three minutes, Hilley heading home superbly from Storey-Moore's perfect centre. Now Forest tore at Leeds like furies. Bremner had to clear off the goal-line from Hall and Hilley. Newton collected the clearance and fired just over the bar from fifteen yards. Then Storey-Moore beat Sprake with a close-range header but the ball rebounded off the crossbar. It was a tremendous finish to the first-half and it was Leeds who were relieved to hear the referee blow for half-time.

Forest seemed to be setting themselves up for a first win after three draws and a defeat. Then fire swept through the main stand to cause a sensational abandonment. The first signs of danger came as the players trooped off for the interval. Wisps, then clouds, of smoke were seen rising from beneath seats near the centre of the stand. Players found the dressing rooms ablaze. Season ticket-holders began moving quickly from their seats under police direction. Flames were now visible through the cracks between the timbers and then they licked the woodwork at the back of the stand but there was no panic. Fans vaulted the surrounding waist-high wall to congregate on the pitch as the fire took hold. Reporters yanked phones out of their connections, grabbed their portable typewriters and left the press box at the back of the stand to join the orderly queues being ushered to safety. An ATV camera crew, perched beneath the roof of the stand, filming their *Star Soccer* programme, scampered for their lives, leaving behind thousands of pounds' worth of equipment. One cameraman had to shin down scaffolding to escape the flames.

Two young professionals watching the game from their usual vantage point in the players' pen went down the tunnel to the dressing rooms a few minutes before half-time to make sure everything was set out – tea, water, new studs if needed – for the home team. They were Alan Buckley and

Duncan McKenzie, who in his autobiography *The Last Fancy Dan*, recalled,

> As we made our way to the bootroom, suddenly the pair of us were in the midst of smoke, which engulfed the corridors. I put my white synthetic training coat over my head. Bucks grabbed the back of my coat and followed me along the wall towards the fire door that opened out on to the car park. Above us, the corrugated roof at the back of the stand was ablaze. Flames were everywhere and sparks were flying down. A copper yelled for us to get back inside but we shouted back, 'No way!' He had no idea what was behind the door as we put our coats over our heads and legged it away from the ground. Neither of us has ever run so fast in our lives.

Mr K. Beale, an engineer in charge of the City Ground floodlights, told the *Nottingham Guardian* Journal that at about 4.00 p.m. he went under the stand to remove electrical fuses to prevent shorting when the water jets were turned on. 'There were flames shooting out then,' he said. 'The trouble was the terrific draught under the stand that made it go up like a tinderbox.' Forest secretary Ken Smales explained that although steelwork and concrete decking had been erected in an extension in 1965, a large part of the structure of timber and brick was original from when the City Ground opened in 1898. It was sad to see the stand reduced to rubble in such a short time but he thought that since there were no injured it was perhaps a blessing in disguise. The rebuilt stand met the Ground Safety Regulations soon to be introduced.

Unfortunately, though, the fire had moved so quickly that all the club records, trophies and momentos were destroyed. 'There was not a pencil left,' Ken said. A few artefacts were later rescued from the strong-room. Personal items lost included Jack Charlton's World Cup watch and the Leeds players returned home in taxis still wearing their white strip. Birthday presents for one of the Forest office girls were also lost.

A headline in new soccer weekly *Goal* published the day before the match ran, 'Leeds ready to set fire to Forest.' It was only the magazine's second edition and a prediction it never equalled. In the same month Russian tanks invaded Czechoslovakia and Tom Jones topped the charts with 'Delilah' – later to be adopted as the Stoke City fans' anthem. So why? Why? Why, Delilah? Opposition supporters often ask that question of the Stokies. According to Stephen Foster, who wrote a book on being a City fan, it came about simply from a policeman quietening down loud supporters in a pub and telling them that if they must sing choose cleaner lyrics. The 'Delilah' track was next up on the juke box and it struck a chord. It's an anthem of defiance in the face of betrayal and reflected how Stoke supporters felt about their club's board and authority in general at the time. *Goal* ran for 296 issues before the final edition in June 1974.

∞

Notts County made Meadow Lane available to their stricken neighbours while rebuilding work took place across the river. Six 'home' games were played there and Forest didn't win a single one. The Reds won only one of the first sixteen First Division matches played after the fire, beating West Bromwich at the Hawthorns 5-2, and this despite Storey-Moore finding the net in six successive games. During this period they were forced because of injuries to field four different goalkeepers in four matches. They were Brian Williamson, Peter Grummitt, Brian Sherratt, who played one game on loan from Oxford United, and Gordon Marshall, for whom they paid Newcastle United £17,500. An England Under-23 international, Marshall was born in Surrey but began his career in Edinburgh with Hearts. He never settled in Nottingham and was transferred to Hibernian for £2,500 after playing only seven matches. Later he had one game with Glasgow Celtic and that was in the European Cup.

Form slumped alarmingly and, with the team second from bottom having gone half a season without a home win, manager Johnny Carey was dismissed in December, 1968. He'd been unlucky. The disruption caused by the main stand fire was a factor but, perhaps, even more so had been the signing a year before of Jim Baxter, a legendary Scottish ball player and drinker, from Sunderland for £100,000 – a deal said to have been brokered by Forest chairman Tony Wood rather than the manager. The late Tony Pritchett, who covered the Reds for the *Nottingham Evening Post*, recalled a conversation with Wood on the flight back from Zurich after the Fairs Cup debacle. 'Mr Wood had grandiose plans for Forest', Pritchett told a Scottish newspaper. 'On the flight from Zurich he turned to me and said, 'You know, Tony, I'm going to make major signings for Forest. And one of them will be Jim Baxter.' Carey, Pritchett said, 'didn't have it in his nature to stand up to Tony Wood.' The manager was quoted as saying, 'That's the best Christmas present I've ever given anybody.' He was understood to have been referring to the cheque to Sunderland rather than the faded star for Forest fans.

Baxter was born in Fife on 29 September 1939. He was twenty-one when Glasgow Rangers signed him from Raith Rovers for a fee of £17,500, then a Scottish record. He was one-footed and used his right only for standing on but with his left he was a magician. 'Treat the ball like a woman. Give it a cuddle, caress it a wee bit, take your time and you'll get the right response', he promised. After England had won the World Cup in 1966, Scotland beat England 3-2 at Wembley and Baxter gave a mesmeric performance. 'It was so good it could have been set to music', Sir Alex Ferguson said. In his five years with Rangers they won three league championships, three Scottish FA Cup victories and four Scottish League Cup tournaments.

Manager Carey disapproved of Baxter with his reputation for drinking and gambling and didn't want him disrupting the team. But Wood thought the Scottish star would double gates and inspire the Reds. A crowd of 30,500 saw Baxter's debut at the City Ground on 16 December, when a goal by Dave Hilley was enough to beat Sheffield United. The attendance was 6,000 more than for the previous home game against Leicester City but that may have been more to do with the weather than the Scot's arrival. Ice had caused that match to be abandoned after an hour. Although he was only twenty-eight, Baxter admitted that his best days were behind him. He was no longer the 'Slim Jim' idolized in Glasgow. 'Training was becoming harder and harder. I let the club and the supporters down', he acknowledged in later years. He was rumoured to be gambling and drinking until the early hours and this was reflected in his performances, no longer managing the full ninety minutes. Less than two years after signing for Forest, having made just fifty appearances, Baxter returned to Scotland to rejoin Rangers on a free transfer for one last hurrah. He retired to become a licensee and died at the age of sixty-one. At his funeral service in Glasgow Cathedral in April, 2001, he was remembered by friends and fans with a grievous sense of loss.

21

The Trickiest Tricky

Having written off £100,000, the biggest deficit on any transfer by an English club at the time, the Forest committee turned to the manager of one of the only two clubs below them in the First Division table, Matt Gillies from Leicester, as Carey's replacement. A mild-mannered Scotsman who had played centre-half for Bolton Wanderers during and just after the war, he had been transferred to Leicester and joined City's coaching staff after retiring. Becoming manager, he led the Foxes to League Cup glory in 1964, beating Stoke over two legs, and to FA Cup Finals in the 1961 and 1963, losing to Spurs and Manchester United, respectively. He resigned in protest at the sacking of his coach Bert Johnson and two months' later joined Forest, bringing Bert with him.

The club was selling its best players to balance the books. The likes of Hennessey, Newton and Grummitt were all allowed to go and others became discontented so it was hardly surprising that the threat of relegation was a constant worry during his four seasons in charge. Storey-Moore remained until all hope of First Division survival had gone. His parting gift to the Forest fans was a goal that he ranked as the best of his career. There were 42,750 in the City Ground for the visit of Arsenal on 27 December 1971. They saw Storey-Moore receive the ball from a throw by goalkeeper Jim Barron and begin a run that took him more than seventy yards into the Arsenal 18-yard box chased most of the way by Alan Ball, recently signed by the Gunners for a British record £220,000 from Everton. What stuck in Storey-Moore's mind was not Ball's ginger hair nor his yellow away shirt but a pair of white boots thudding on the turf behind him and trying to catch up. There were still half-a-dozen defenders confronting him but he twisted and turned to find an opening and then beat goalkeeper Bob Wilson with a shot inside his near post.

Although he was to score twice more for Forest, in defeats by Leicester City at home and Southampton away, that goal was the golden memory he left behind. His last game in Garibaldi red was at the Baseball Ground on 19 February 1972, when Derby put Forest to the sword 4-0. Storey-Moore had come to the club as an apprentice eleven years earlier. He made his First Division debut as an eighteen-year-old in a 2-1 victory against Ipswich, the team from the town where he had been born. Top scorer in the four seasons leading up to his controversial transfer, he scored 118 goals in 271 Forest appearances. Capped only once at senior level by England – against Holland in 1970 – he played in two under-23 internationals and twice represented the Football League.

Forest had begun 1972 with a respectable 2-2 draw against Manchester City at Maine Road but then came a run of eight successive defeats including one in an FA Cup-tie at Millwall. The dismal sequence started with a 1-0 loss to Crystal Palace in front of only 19,000 supporters at the City Ground on Saturday, 8 January. That was the point at which relegation became a real probability – and Storey-Moore's departure a certainty. How Forest's situation was viewed nationally was illustrated by the cynical coverage of the game by the South London Press. Tony Rickson's match report was headlined, 'Palace Had Much More'. The scoreline read, 'Ian Storey-Moore 0, Crystal Palace 1'. And Rickson emphasised that teamwork and effort were the keys to Palace's success while Forest relied entirely on 'the occasional brilliance of Ian Storey-Moore.'

Gillies accepted a bid for him of £200,000 from Manchester United manager Frank O'Farrell and so began a 'Tug-o-Moore', perhaps one of the most unedifying of all transfer sagas. Brian Clough pounced when it seemed the player could not agree personal terms. He matched the United bid and got Storey-Moore's signature. The Forest player was paraded at the Baseball Ground as a new signing and watched the Rams beat Wolves. But no transfer forms had been signed by Forest officials and they refused to confirm the transaction. Storey-Moore went home to Bingham and there he was visited by O'Farrell and Matt Busby, then a United director. A deal was done.

Jonathan Wilson in his Clough biography *Nobody Ever Says Thank You*, writes that, 'furious' at the turn of events, the great BC sent off a four-page telegram to the Football League in protest but he was not supported by his chairman, Sam Longson, who apologised on Derby's behalf. It did not prevent his club being fined £5,000 and Clough receiving a warning about his conduct of transfer business. Storey-Moore thought Forest chairman Tony Wood had vetoed the move. He had been on holiday and, having already sold Hennessey to Derby, he was not prepared on his return to incur the wrath of supporters by waving another star off down the A52. Storey-Moore made his debut for United against Huddersfield at Old Trafford on 11 March. At the City Ground just 9,872 disgruntled supporters – the lowest crowd for seventeen years – turned up to see Forest beaten 2-0 by Ipswich Town and sent on their way to twenty-first in the table and relegation. Their mood was not improved when an announcer gave out the information that United had taken the lead at Old Trafford 'and the scorer is Ian Storey-Moore'.

There was an amicable ending to the sorry saga. Clough, during his eighteen great years at the City Ground, became a lasting friend of Forest secretary Ken Smales, the man he said had 'whipped Ian Storey-Moore's transfer forms back from me at Derby'. Gillies, though, stayed on in the Second Division for a few months, amid an atmosphere of discontent, before handing in his resignation and finding employment outside the game.

∞

If anyone could dispel the cloud of depression that hung over Trentside, he would have to be a magician, a wizard and a spring-heeled Jack. Step forward Duncan McKenzie, the trickiest of all Trickies with ball-playing wizardry and a leap to startle six-foot centre-halves and clear a parked car for fun – or a bet. 'We all agree, Duncan McKenzie is magic,' chorused the Trent End. 'Is magic … is magic … is magic.'

Though still a schoolboy, McKenzie played for Clee Rovers, a Cleethorpes pub team and soon learned to be nifty on his feet, develop dribbling skills and the ability to accelerate away from tackles. He was spotted by Roly Abrams, a part-time Forest scout, and, after leaving school with ten 'O' levels, joined the club as a ground staff boy, becoming an apprentice and then signing professional on his eighteenth birthday in June, 1968. He was not on the same wavelength as tough trainer Tommy Cavanagh but impressed the players by accepting a dare to hurdle over his car. They were even more amazed when he cleared Joe Baker's Jag. When results dipped and Carey paid the price with his job, former Charlton Athletic defender Bert Johnson came in with Gillies as coach and rejuvenated training.

McKenzie said,

Instead of everybody lining up and running around the pitch Bert had us doing laps two seconds apart … He realized a player at the front did not want to be caught by a player behind, and the player behind him did not want be caught by the next one, and so on. We were pushing ourselves to the limit.

He'd made his debut against Sunderland at Roker Park in September, 1969, replacing Barry Lyons who had been taken ill on the morning of the match. 'I had a few neat touches and tried to do the simple things but I got Henry Newton carried off after playing a hospital ball, which did not go down well with the Forest lads,' he recalled. McKenzie had runs of games in the side but did not hold down a regular place under Gillies and when Dave Mackay became manager he was sent out on loan to Mansfield Town. Mackay saw him banging in the goals at Field Mill and called him back to the City Ground.

McKenzie said,

Dave was a winner but also loved a bit of showboating [...] He'd tell me to trick my way past opponents and wanted me to turn it on for both the team and the fans. There were things I did on the pitch that were quite outrageous and I surprised myself with what I could achieve by sheer effrontery. Dave Mackay was the key manager in getting me to reach my potential as a footballer and I have always been grateful for that. All the lads respected Dave and he inspired them.

A great wing-half with Scotland, Hearts and Spurs, Mackay was a massive signing for Brian Clough's Derby County who swept to promotion from the Second Division before he left the Baseball Ground to become player-manager at Swindon Town. His first match in charge at the City Ground was a 3-2 victory over Millwall before 11,000 supporters on 4 November, 1972. Forest finished the season in fourteenth place and by the time he left almost a year later to take over from the disenchanted Brian Clough at Derby his record was forty Second Division games played, thirteen won, twelve drawn and fifteen lost. At Derby, overcoming discord and a players' revolt in support of Clough, he won the First Division title in 1974/75.

Another Scottish international Allan Brown, who had played against Forest in the 1959 Cup Final and guided Luton to the Fourth Division championship, came to the City Ground after perpetual caretaker manager Bill Anderson had presided over three victories. His first match, at Sunderland on 26 November ended a goalless draw but he was fortunate to find McKenzie in magnificent form and the side looked potential promotion challengers. They were also ready to excite the city with a great run in the FA Cup that included two of the club's most memorable games. It began with first-ever Sunday match at the City Ground, a third round classic cup-tie against Bristol Rovers. Forest came from 2-0 down to win 4-3.

Next up were Manchester City in the fourth round again at the City Ground and on a Sunday. It became known as 'McKenzie's match' and many of the 41,472 fans who saw it say his was the best-ever individual display for Forest. Francis Lee, Colin Bell, Mike Summerbee and Rodney Marsh played for the visitors but McKenzie, up against defenders Mike Doyle and Willie Donachie, stood out. He tore City apart, scoring himself and making two for Ian Bowyer and another for George Lyall in an outstanding 4-1 victory that put him in the media spotlight. The newspaper reports were flattering but what most pleases him is that Forest legend John Robertson still jokes when they are together that Forest won the European Cup twice but supporters still go on about McKenzie against Manchester City in 1974. A McKenzie penalty was enough to see off Portsmouth in the fifth round in front of a City Ground crowd of 38,589 and set up a quarter-final clash with Newcastle United at a packed St James' Park on 6 March. The match was dubbed by the Press 'the battle of the SuperMacs' – McKenzie and United's Malcolm Macdonald being their clubs' leading marksmen.

Second Division Forest were leading 3-1 with about fifteen minutes to go and Newcastle were down to ten men after Pat Howard was sent off for dissent when hundreds of home supporters climbed over the barriers at the Leazes End and invaded the pitch. David Serella, the Reds' young centre-half, was punched in the face by one of the charging fans and was clearly shaken. It was chaotic and referee Gordon Kew ordered the players off for their own safety. They returned after a ten-minute break but the atmosphere remained unpleasant with the linesmen being bombarded with missiles and the noise generated by the Toon Army deafening. Unsurprisingly, the visitors were unnerved and caved-in, conceding three goals including a penalty to make it 4-3 to United at the final whistle. Back in the dressing room the players were even more distraught as they believed the winning goal by Bobby Moncur to have been offside. It should have been as was clearly seen on television coverage.

Forest promptly lodged an objection and the Football Association declared the match void, ordering a replay twelve days' later at Goodison Park, which ended goalless. John Robertson had broken into the side at left-half in the void match and at inside-left in the replay. He was left out for the third leg three days later, his place being taken by none other than Martin O'Neill. Instead of this match being in Nottingham, the FA astonishingly insisted on it again going to Goodison. The Reds were even more aggrieved when a goal by George Lyall from a free-kick was disallowed by Mr Kew for 'ungentlemanly conduct.' Paul Richardson had jumped over the ball to dummy and allow Lyall to strike it. So the tie went to extra time before a Malcolm Macdonald goal settled it. Oddly enough, there had been a close bond of friendship between Newcastle and Forest supporters with travelling United fans regularly calling in at the Forest Sportsmen's Club on Pavilion Road for drinks on the way home after their team had been playing in the midlands.

After their FA Cup exertions, Forest returned to league action at Fulham on the following Saturday when a 2-0 defeat ended their promotion hopes. McKenzie scored in all of the last five Second Division games of which two were won, two lost and one drawn to leave the side seventh in the table. A 3-2 County Cup Final victory over Notts County at the City Ground on 6 May proved to be his last game in the Garibaldi. McKenzie had been Forest's leading scorer with 26 league goals and two in cup-ties. George Lyall was second highest with 11 league and four cup goals. His consistent scoring record – 28 goals in forty-nine matches – attracted top flight attention. Forest committee man Harold Alcock recommended him for international selection and he was called up for England in turn by Sir Alf Ramsey, Joe Mercer and Don Revie and yet never gained a cap. As the only forward on the substitutes' bench against Portugal in Lisbon in April 1974, he looked certain to get on when Malcolm Macdonald pulled a muscle in the first-half. But Ramsey said, 'Sorry Duncan, we're having a bit of a rough ride and I need to shore things up.' He sent on Alan Ball instead to make a five-man midfield and England drew the match 0-0.

∞

During the summer, McKenzie told the Press he was happy to commit to the club and agree a new contract. But he felt 'bitterly let down' by the terms he was offered. 'I rang the manager who bluntly told me to put in a transfer request if I was not happy,' the player wrote in his autobiography. He sought a meeting with chairman Jim Willmer and a date was set but then he was told both the chairman and the manager were on holiday. The next time he arrived for a meeting only to find Allan Brown was playing golf. After a long wait, the chairman arrived to tell him his wage demand could not be met.

'At Forest, I had been happy as Larry and bedded into the team, scoring goals galore. Forest had a great set of lads,' he said. 'There were no prima donnas and the camaraderie was fantastic. But the manner in which club officials treated me was a real kick in the teeth.' Dave Mackay wanted him but there was no chance of Forest selling to Derby. Then Brian Clough, the new manager of Leeds United, came along with a £250,000 bid to take McKenzie to Elland Road and the deal was done. For Forest supporters it was a big let-down, echoing the departure of Ian Storey-Moore two years before.

Manchester United, First Division champions six years earlier, and Forest, the runners-up, found themselves meeting in Division Two at Old Trafford early in the 1974/75 season and the outcome was a 2-2 draw. By the end of September, Forest had won only three times, despite Ian Bowyer scoring in four consecutive games, and mid-table mediocrity seemed the most they could expect. The committee sanctioned a club record £120,000 fee to enable Brown to buy centre-forward Barry Butlin from Luton. He made his debut at Villa Park on 2 October but the Reds were beaten 3-0. Ten days later he scored against Norwich at the City Ground in a 3-1 defeat. That was Butlin's only goal in his first twelve matches. Disaffected supporters were staying away with City Ground gates averaging just above 10,000 until, on 28 December, 25,000 came to the local derby with Notts County, who won 2-0. That was the last straw for the committee and Allan Brown was sacked after thirteen months in the job.

With Bill Anderson once more the acting manager, Forest faced Tottenham Hotspur in the third round of the FA Cup at the City Ground on 4 January. It was a typical cup-tie, end to end stuff, with Martin Chivers putting the First Division side ahead and Dave Jones equalizing in the 68th minute. Butlin had a great chance to win it late on but Spurs' goalkeeper Pat Jennings made the save. The crowd was buzzing not because of the action on the pitch but because the Nottingham Evening Post had revealed that Forest wanted Brian Clough to take over. Could it happen? Forest were thirteenth in Division Two and attendances were falling so dramatic action was needed. But the committee members were divided and outgoing chairman Jim Wilmer was not convinced about the suitability of Clough fearing his perceived acerbic manner particularly with directors. 'We don't want success at any price,' he warned his successor, Brian Appleby QC.

In five seasons Clough had taken Derby County from the depths of the Second Division to the League Championship and then just missed out on a European Cup Final because, he alleged, of Italian deviousness in a 3-1 defeat by Juventus in Turin. When relations with chairman Sam Longson soured, a bitter Clough rather reluctantly accepted an offer from Third Division Brighton but first Forest committee man Stuart Dryden made an unofficial approach. He met Clough and his number two Peter Taylor in Nottingham and urged him contact Forest the next day about the vacancy caused by Mackay's move to Derby. Clough never made the call. Lured to Leeds after Don Revie took the England job, Clough left Taylor behind on the South Coast but his inglorious departure after just forty-four days left him open to a renewed courtship by Forest. Dryden was delegated by the committee to begin negotiations that were soon concluded. Clough was ready. He was appointed on 6 January 1975.

A cartoon in the *Daily Express* showed him walking down the Trent to the City Ground.

22

Rome Wasn't Built in a Day

When schoolboy John McGovern came home with fresh cuts and bruises on his knees and shins, his mum would say to him, 'Don't complain. They're medals you've won.' It gave him the winning mentality that so impressed Brian Clough, then the new manager of Hartlepool United when he started a youth team at the club and included the slight fifteen-year-old who needed to 'stand up straight, shoulders back and get a haircut.' Clough was not to know that the teenager was deeply embarrassed by a badly rounded left shoulder that caused him to run 'with a funny waddle.' It was not until he went for a medical examination at Nottingham Forest that McGovern learned that he had been born with a back muscle missing making him throw his left arm across his body when he ran. The handicap slowed him down but he compensated by having the stamina to run all day. And it did not stop him winning two European Cups, two league championships, one Super Cup, a League Cup and the FA's Charity Shield, a list of honours envied by some of the world's greatest players. One of them, the German international midfielder Gunter Netzer, of Real Madrid fame, saw him play against Cologne in the 1979 European Cup semi-final and commented in the newspapers, 'Who is this McGovern? I've never heard of him yet he ran midfield.'

T-shirts on sale in the club shop have a Clough quote across the chest, 'Rome wasn't built in a day but, then, I wasn't on that particular job.' Rebuilding Nottingham Forest was to be no quick fix either. But the manager knew the people he needed and immediately set about bringing them to the City Ground. He recruited trainer Jimmy Gordon, who had been with him at Derby and Leeds, and tried but initially failed to persuade Peter Taylor to leave Brighton. The key signing, however, was McGovern. He and centre-forward John O'Hare had been with Clough at Derby and were taken by him to Leeds for a combined fee of £150,000. After the manager's sudden departure, both were in limbo at Elland Road and were relieved when Forest paid a total of £60,000 to reunite them with him at the City Ground. McGovern said he would have 'crawled down the M1 on his hands and knees' to Nottingham.

Scotsman O'Hare was born in the Dunbartonshire village of Renton, whose football club he is keen to point out, won football's first world championship. Renton, Dumbarton and the Vale of Leven, all from the football hotbed of Dunbartonshire, were early winners of the Scottish Cup. Renton beat Cambuslang 6-1 in the 1888 final and then won a challenge match against the English Cup-winners West Bromwich Albion 4-1 to determine the 'Champions of the United Kingdom and the World'. The world championship trophy, made of pewter and about a foot high, is displayed in the Scottish Football Museum at Hampden Park.

Clough had won his first game in charge of Forest, the FA Cup third round replay against Spurs at White Hart Lane on 8 January, thanks to a goal by inside-right Neil Martin. The team stayed in London and trained at Bisham Abbey in preparation for the Second Division game against Fulham at Craven Cottage three days' later. Martin's strike partner Barry Butlin scored the only goal. Fulham were also Forest's fourth round opponents and the tie went to three replays before the Londoners triumphed 2-1 in front of a 23,240 crowd at the City Ground on 10 February. McGovern and O'Hare made their debuts at the end of the month and found themselves in a relegation fight. After the league win over Fulham, the Reds went sixteen games before getting another at home to bottom club Sheffield Wednesday thanks to a penalty by George Lyall. Only 14,000 were present. Fewer than 12,000 saw Butlin score twice in the 2-1 defeat of sixth-placed West Bromwich Albion that ended the league season with Forest sixteenth, five points clear of relegation.

On that last day Newcastle United captain Frank Clark was stunned to learn from his manager Joe Harvey that he was finished at St James' Park after thirteen years and more than 400 games with the club he had joined from Crook Town. He was nearly thirty-two and available on a free transfer. Clark, an Inter-Cities Fairs Cup winner in 1969 with a wealth of top flight experience, was already in talks with Doncaster Rovers when, thanks to a tip-off from journalist Doug Weatherall, he came on Clough's radar and was persuaded to swap the Tyne Bridge for Trent Bridge. The summer also saw Ian Bowyer, John Robertson and Martin O'Neill sign new contracts and a recognizable Brian Clough team was taking shape. Viv Anderson and Tony Woodcock took part in a successful tour in West Germany and Bowyer, wearing the number eleven shirt, scored successive hat-tricks against Ballymena and Coleraine in Northern Ireland.

Season ticket prices had gone up from £15 main stand and £7 terraces in 1973/74 to £22 main stand and £10 terraces when Forest opened the 1975–77 campaign with a 2-0 victory over Plymouth Argyle at the City Ground on 16 August. The attendance was just over 13,000. The team lined up: John Middleton, Viv Anderson, Frank Clark, Sammy Chapman, Liam O'Kane, John McGovern, George Lyall, Paul Richardson, John O'Hare,

John Robertson and Ian Bowyer. Terry Curran, a twenty-year-old winger signed from Doncaster Rovers for £60,000 made his debut in the next home league match at the end of the month but a last-minute Les Bradd goal gave Notts County the points.

A serious injury to O'Kane led Clough to approach Manchester City for reserve full-back Colin Barrett, who at first declined a loan move. But Clough wasn't about to give up the chase and spoke to the twenty-three-year-old over the phone. 'You're playing in the reserves and I've got a place in my first team for you', he said. They met outside Leek Town's ground and agreed a loan deal to the end of the season. Barrett played at right-back in the remaining ten league games and his appearances coincided with the season's best run of results. His impressive form encouraged Clough to pay City £30,000 to make the loan permanent. Barrett was to be an important asset over the next two seasons. Martin O'Neill and John Robertson had gained regular places and Forest finished eighth on fourty-six points, three fewer than fifth-placed Notts County.

Word got around during the summer that Jimmy Armfield, Clough's successor at Leeds, was considering letting Duncan McKenzie go to finance a move for Sheffield United midfield playmaker Tony Currie. When Stuart Dryden got a call from Clough inviting him for a drink at Widmerpool Cricket Club, where the manager and McKenzie had both been playing in a testimonial match, the committee man assumed a transfer deal was in the offing. Clough's target it turned out was not the player but Peter Taylor. 'I'm off to Cala Millor to fetch him,' he informed Dryden. He had heard from scout Maurice Edwards, who had turned down an invitation to be assistant manager at Brighton, that failing to gain promotion for the south coast club had been unsettling and Taylor would not be averse to them linking up again but was not willing to make the first approach.

Armfield accepted a £200,000 bid from RSC Anderlecht and McKenzie went off to Belgium. After his debut against the Bayern Munich of Franz Beckenbauer, Gerd Muller and Sepp Maier, one Belgian newspaper reported, 'We thought we'd signed an Englishman but we have ourselves a Brazilian.'

McGovern and O'Hare had noticed a difference in Brian Clough during the past season. 'I know what it is,' McGovern told his team-mate as they travelled from Derby to Nottingham for training. 'I think he's kind of going through the motions.' It was a niggling feeling they shared until Taylor's arrival when, McGovern judged, 'Brian Clough would always be top man yet his change of mood was clearly visible.' Taylor, himself, commented, 'We both knew we were banging our heads against a brick wall on our own. Together we could do any job. There was no point delaying.' Taylor, born in the Meadows, had come home. McGovern recalled, 'With Peter Taylor now on board I knew things would be different. 'It's just a matter of when', I told the rest of the players. 'When what?' one or two asked. 'When we get promoted', I declared. 'Don't you mean if we get promoted?' they said. 'Not if, just when', I confidently replied. The bookies agreed and ranked Forest among the favourites for promotion along with Wolves and Bolton.

Forest returned from a successful pre-season tour in West Germany to play their first competitive games in the Anglo-Scottish Cup. Unbeaten in their qualifying group, which included Notts County, West Bromwich Albion and Bristol City, they went through to the knockout phase of the tournament. Kilmarnock came to the City Ground in the first round and were beaten 2-1. The away leg was drawn 2-2. Ayr United were next up and Forest won the home leg 2-1 with goals by new signings Larry Lloyd, who had joined from Coventry on loan, and Peter Withe, a £44,000 striker from Birmingham City. Gedling schoolboy Stephen Burke, just sixteen years twenty-one days old, came on as substitute to replace Martin O'Neill and become the youngest-ever Red. An England Youth international, it was his only game for Forest but in an eleven-year career he made a total of 156 League appearances and scored fifteen goals, including five in sixty-seven matches for Queen's Park Rangers and eight in fifty-seven outings with Doncaster Rovers.

The second leg at Ayr took place in a torrential downpour with only 3,000 prepared to be drenched. Recalled from a month on loan at Doncaster, twenty-year-old striker Tony Woodcock and Withe were paired for the first time and both scored in a 2-0 win. It was a taste of triumphs to come. Leyton Orient were the opposition in the two-leg final played in the middle of December. A Robertson penalty enabled Forest to draw the London match and a 4-0 home win made the aggregate 5-1. Full-back Colin Barrett, pushed forward to inside-right, scored two goals and McGovern lifted his first piece of silverware as captain of the club.

Having made his senior debut for Forest as an eighteen-year-old at Villa Park in April, 1974, Eastwood-born Woodcock only really established himself in the promotion season. He loved to run at defenders with the ball at his feet, often collecting it from a deep position and darting down one of the flanks. Yet he hated it when Brian Clough played him on the left wing. He plucked up the courage to tackle Clough about it and asked to be played up front. The manager wanted to know why he should make the change. 'Because I'll score goals for you', the player replied. 'Good answer, young man', said Brian.

With his pace and control, Woodcock was difficult to contain and provided a perfect foil for big striker Peter Withe. After the latter's departure for Aston Villa, he linked up equally effectively with Garry Birtles. Ron Greenwood reunited Tony and Peter as an England striking partnership for the 1982 World Cup in Spain. Woodcock was awarded the first of his forty-two England caps against Northern Ireland on 16 May 1978. He scored sixteen goals in full internationals and five in his two England Under-21 appearances. In the promotion season, Withe scored sixteen goals in thirty-three Second Division appearances and Woodcock eleven in thirty. They also scored four and six, respectively, in Cup games.

Lloyd returned to Coventry when his loan period expired at the end of October resisting Clough's efforts to persuade him to sign permanently. Signed from his home town club Bristol Rovers by Bill Shankly as successor at Liverpool to veteran captain and centre-half Ron Yeats, he had won three international caps while at Anfield and played in all fifty-four matches in 1973 when they won the league championship and UEFA Cup. After Shankly's retirement in the summer of 1974, Lloyd left for Coventry, who paid a club record transfer fee of £240,000. Handicapped by a back injury, he did not have a happy time at Highfield Road and his playing career was at its lowest ebb when the Sky Blues tried to sell him to Third Division Walsall for £40,000. The player refused to consider the deal and wasn't keen on dropping a division for a loan move to Forest. The Clough psychology worked, however, when he said, 'Come and see if you like it at Forest. It's not about us having a look at you, it's about you having a look at us.' Back at Coventry, he was still undecided but manager Gordon Milne made it clear he wanted more mobile centre-backs. Forest bid £60,000 and Milne was so keen he was prepared to lose almost £200,000 on the transfer. Clough and, in particular, Taylor, had got the big centre-half they wanted at the heart of their defence. Lloyd was a heavyweight six feet two inches and, perhaps, Taylor recalled Shankly frightening visiting centre-forwards at Anfield by offering to take them on 'a tour around our centre-half' when Ron Yeats was at the height of his powers.

Forest's league progress was interrupted by a third round FA Cup tie with Bristol Rovers that went to a second replay before they went through 6-0 at Villa Park with goals from Woodcock (2), Withe, Bowyer, O'Hare and Anderson. A run of fourteen games without defeat had been ended by Charlton Athletic at the Valley four days earlier. The biggest crowd of the season, home or way, 38,284 saw the fourth round clash with Southampton finish 3-3 at the City Ground. There were 29,401 at The Dell for the replay, which the Saints won 2-1. Successive 2-1 defeats at Wolverhampton and at home to Luton were deflating before Southampton came again to the City Ground, this time in the league, on 16 February. It was looking bleak for Forest when Nick Holmes put the visitors ahead before half-time. Luckily for the Reds during the interval thick fog billowed in from the Trent and two minutes into the second half referee Roy Capey abandoned the game. The Reds won the rearranged match 2-1.

Further bad weather caused more cancellations and blank weekends so the team headed off to Torremolinos for five days. Then came the announcement that George Hardy, who had replaced Sam Longson as chairman of Derby County, had sacked manager Dave Mackay and wanted Clough and Taylor to return to the Baseball Ground. Forest chairman Brian Appleby gave permission for a formal approach and negotiations appeared to go well. A celebratory bottle of champagne was opened. Appleby was said to have arrived at the City Ground on the morning of 21 February and enquired: 'Has he gone yet?' But, overnight, Clough, much to Taylor's dismay, had changed his mind. Clough told the Evening Post at Nottingham that the reason he had remained at the City Ground was loyalty to Stuart Dryden who came in for him after he had been sacked by Leeds. Perhaps, also, he thought the Forest committee would be more malleable than Derby's board of directors, especially as he had wanted Longson and Stuart Webb dismissed. So there was dejection at Derby but relief in Nottingham though there would be more times when Forest fans felt their emotions put through the wringer by Clough's restless opportunism.

A serious knee injury in October had put right-winger Terry Curran out of the side for four months and this forced a tactical change that would prove critical to Forest's success. Robertson had been seen as almost a midfielder really, with Curran an orthodox flanker. Now Robertson advanced further forward on the left and O'Neill adopted the slightly withdrawn role on the right. It was still a lopsided 4-4-2 only with the opposite winger pushed high. Robbo lacked pace except with the ball at his feet when he could outwit and leave straggling more than one defender before crossing accurately. Curran got back into the side briefly and scored the only goal in the victory at Hereford on 2 March. He then made one appearance at centre-forward and three as a substitute.

The match against Hull City, watched by a 15,000 crowd at the City Ground on 12 March, was notable not just for goals by Withe and Woodcock in a 2-0 win but for the debut of 20-year-old local lad Garry Birtles who went on to become Nottingham's best-known carpet fitter and Clough's preferred squash partner as well as the scorer of Forest's first-ever goal in the European Cup. Birtles had been recommended by Maurice Edwards and championed by Taylor, who had admired his ability to wrong-foot a defender by dummying to go one way then dragging the ball back and swivelling away with it. Clough had reservations, favouring another young striker Steve Elliott, and reportedly remarked after first seeing Birtles in action, 'The half-time Bovril was better than he was.' Yet the manager was impressed when after being carried off on a stretcher Birtles returned to the action despite having a huge gash on his shin.

In his autobiography, *My Magic Carpet Ride*, the player wrote:

He must have spotted something in me. Maybe it was just my sheer bravery to come back on to the pitch after getting smashed like that. He was a striker, too. He would have killed to score a goal and even tried to get up and play on when he had his cruciate knee ligament severed playing for Middlesbrough.

In fact, Birtles was used as a midfielder, wearing the number seven shirt, against Hull and found himself facing the tigerish ex-Leeds captain Billy Bremner. It was a position he did not like but had played for the reserves 'to build up my strength and stamina.' Before the match, he travelled to the City Ground in John McGovern's car. McGovern was driving in with John O'Hare from Derby and diverted off the A52 to give him a lift. 'It always stuck with me that our captain would go out of his way to pick up some young kid,' Birtles said. Apparently, he did not play particularly well. Clough said to him after the game, 'If I ever play you in midfield again, tell the chairman to give me the sack.' He had to wait eighteen months for another league chance and to make the number nine shirt his own.

A 2-1 defeat by Notts County, watched by 31,000 at the City Ground, preceded the Hull game, which was followed by a 2-0 loss away to Sheffield United on 19th March that put Forest in seventh place, three points behind their neighbours but with a game in hand. Then came the home game with Southampton, rearranged after the earlier abandonment. Only 12,393 turned up but the Reds, with goals by Woodcock and O'Neill, began a five-match winning run that included a crucial 3-1 defeat of Bolton Wanderers at the City Ground. A drawn game at Meadow Lane did neither Notts nor Forest any favours and it was followed by defeat for the Reds at leaders Chelsea and then to lowly Cardiff City by the only goal after failing to score at home in the league for the first and only time. Frustrated, Clough was furious and demanded better. His team responded, beating Oldham 3-0 at the City Ground, picking up an away point against Bristol Rovers and remaining in the west country to defeat Plymouth Argyle two days' later. This left Forest in the third promotion spot behind Wolves and Chelsea with fifty points from forty-one games, two points ahead of Notts, three more than Bolton and with a vastly superior goal difference. But Notts had a game in hand and Bolton three. 'It's better to have the points,' Clough commented.

The pressure was on the chasing pack but Forest needed to beat Millwall at the City Ground in their final league match of the season on 7 May as defeat could allow Notts, Bolton and Blackpool to leapfrog them. The gate was a surprisingly low 23,529 and the game was as tense as expected. The Reds attacked in waves but the visitors held on until a Robertson cross was headed into his own goal by Jon Moore. Bolton drew and needed five points from their remaining three games to deny Forest the final promotion place. Notts failed to get even a point from their last two fixtures and finished eighth. Clough's message as he and his squad flew off to Mallorca for a post-season holiday was, 'Let Bolton worry'. Their flight left East Midlands airport at 3.00 p.m. just as Bolton were kicking off against Wolves, who were already champions. Kenny Hibbert scored and then had to go in goal after the

Wolves' goalkeeper was injured but his effort proved enough. With a phone call to Nottingham from Palma airport, the Foresters learned they were as good as up because Bolton, thirteen goals behind on goal difference, needed to win by a cricket score to stop them. They drew and finished a point behind.

Colin Barrett recalled, 'It was a week of mayhem in Mallorca. Celebrations, headaches but it was all good fun.' And Ian Bowyer pointed out, 'It wasn't about Bolton. We played forty-two games to get there.' Back in Nottingham fans gathered in the Old Market Square to celebrate.

23

Champions

Forest had scraped into the First Division and were not expected to stay there for more than a season. Pundits had learned little from the exploits of Sir Alf Ramsey's equally unfancied Ipswich side who, in 1962, had become the first in Football League history to win the championship in their initial season in Division One. Ramsey's side began to be taken more seriously after they had thrashed likely title challengers Burnley 6-2 at Portman Road. This was reminiscent of Billy Walker's Reds 7-0 mauling of another highly rated Burnley side in September, 1957, soon after their promotion – especially as both Ipswich and Forest had been beaten at Turf Moor shortly before their victories.

Ramsey did not go on a spending spree to prepare for the First Division but bought only one player, inside-forward Dougie Moran for £12,000 from Falkirk. Clough had complained about lack of support from the Nottingham public but Ipswich had attendances below 15,000. Forest's summer signing was a surprise; £150,000 for Scottish striker Kenny Burns, who came with a fiery reputation from Birmingham. He had just scored twenty goals playing alongside Trevor Francis so eyebrows were raised even higher when it was learned Taylor wanted him as a centre-back. In the first practice match, Clough said to his latest recruit, 'Go and play with the big lad at the back.' And that is how the fearsome, formidable Lloyd-Burns partnership was formed. Taylor saw Burns developing into a Scottish Bobby Moore, just as commanding and more ruthless. Like Colin Todd had been with Roy McFarland at Derby, he proved to be a first-rate defender who was composed and capable with the ball.

Clough and Taylor signed three-year extensions to their original four-year contracts and took the squad off for a pre-season tour in Switzerland, Austria and West Germany, winning all five games with a combined score of 18-4. Not every game proved friendly. In the second match, Austrian champions, Wacker Innsbruck, fired up by a boisterous

7,000 crowd, made some rough-house challenges resulting in Peter Withe receiving an elbow to the face that broke his nose. To add insult to injury, he was sent off for retaliation. Then he was packed off home for treatment and played no further part in the tour. Even so, Forest won 2-0 with goals by Woodcock and Robertson against a side who went on to reach the quarter-finals of the European Cup. The Austrians knocked out FC Basle and Glasgow Celtic before losing on away goals to Borussia Moechengladbach.

Coincidences abound in football and, fittingly, Forest's first match back in Division One was at Goodison Park, where on 3 September 1892, they played for the first time in the Football League and helped Everton open their new ground with a 2-2 draw. It was also where the Reds had played their last top flight game before relegation at the end of the 1971/72 campaign, another draw this time 1-1. There were 38,000 at Goodison on 20 August 1977, when the team nervously awaiting a new season in elevated company was captained by John McGovern, Cloughie's field marshal now restored to his favoured midfield position, and included goalkeeper John Middleton, full-backs Viv Anderson and Frank Clark, centre backs Larry Lloyd and Kenny Burns, Ian Bowyer in midfield, Martin O'Neill and John Robertson on flanks with strikers Peter Withe and Tony Woodcock. Peter Taylor was telling jokes and anecdotes to relax the players when there was a knock on the dressing room door and a surprise guest made his entrance. It was the Liverpool manager Bill Shankly and Clough welcomed him with the request that, 'You give the team talk'. McGovern recalls Shankly telling them to think of the season as 'a marathon, not a sprint'. The bell rang and the team ran out into the August sunshine boosted by the words of Clough, Taylor and the great Shanks.

In the match programme, Everton captain Mike Lyons made a percipient observation regarding prospective title challengers,

> The promoted teams are worth keeping an eye on this time. We will be seeing Nottingham Forest today so there will be first-hand evidence for my hunch that they could be the surprise team of the season.

And the home supporters were shocked when Withe, still recovering from his broken nose, scored with a close-range header from a corner and then Robertson drove in a second off the inside of a post. Centre-forward Jim Pearson pulled one back shortly before half-time perhaps against the run of play but, with thirteen minutes left, O'Neill hammered home a close-range effort to complete the victory. Duncan McKenzie, then Everton's number ten, said he couldn't believe how composed Forest were that afternoon. Clough, however, kept their feet on the ground, even criticizing his captain for trying a couple of shots. 'Give it to someone who can shoot or you're out of the side,' McGovern was told.

The national press, though, gave the Reds effusive praise. The *Sunday People* made McGovern man of the match with a 9/10 performance. *The Sun* chose John Robertson, while the *News of the World* considered Tony Woodcock as the outstanding performer. The *People's* Stan Liversedge wrote that 'Forest marked their return to Division One by playing it coolly, simply brushing the ball from one red-shirted man to another.' The *Daily Mail* said that Clough's players spoke volumes for him on the pitch. The *Daily Mirror* warned that Everton were Woodcock's first victims and he and Forest were going places. Mike Ellis of *The Sun* summed it up, 'It's good to have them back.' Correspondent Harry Durose wrote from Newthorpe to the Forest programme postbag,

Just twenty years ago, Forest won their opening match of the season at the City Ground by beating Preston North End 2-1 to signal a victorious return to the First Division. It was so wonderful, so exciting to see Forest at last in Division One again and winning, too. They were indeed glorious days in Forest's history for, at the end of the next season, the Reds celebrated their great Wembley triumph. So we are back again, hoping for history to repeat itself.

The inveterate Mr Durose turned to darker thoughts; he wrote,

The one big cloud on the horizon, however, is crowd behaviour [...] In the Fifties everyone enjoyed the game but, alas, partisanship has become so intolerant that some matches have battles on the terraces besides the soccer being contested on the pitch. If only we could be mature enough once more to enjoy the game without it being a life or death struggle. But let's be optimistic and look for success to attend all Forest's efforts to make an impact in Division One.

Forest's first home league match was against Bristol City on the 23 August, when the attendance of 21,743 disappointed but may have been due in part to an increase in season ticket prices that some supporters thought excessive. They were £42 for main stand seats and £30 for the East Stand. A young lady from Gedling wrote to the club to say she and her fiancé hoped to marry soon and would not be able to afford £60 to watch football. A Hucknall man also complained that the higher prices might actually reduce revenue for the club. With just eight minutes to go, Peter Withe rose to head home the only goal from a Robertson cross.

Four days later Derby County visited the City Ground for the first time since 1971. Nearly 29,000 fans and ATV's Soccer Special cameras came, too. John Robertson caused panic in the visitors' defence right from the kick-off but the opening goal came from the other flank. Viv Anderson won the ball and sent Martin O'Neill away to force a corner. Tony Woodcock whipped it in with his left foot and when the ball came off Larry Lloyd there was Withe to volley into the top corner despite the close attention of Roy McFarland. Robertson continued to run things in the second half and his long pass enabled Woodcock to race past two Derby defenders and lay off the ball for Withe to score his second. Then, with twelve minutes left, Robertson crowned a virtuoso performance with Forest's third. Television commentator Hugh Johns enthused, 'That was some of the most electrifying football I've seen in a long time.' With just three games gone, Forest were the only team in the division with a 100 per cent record.

Withe scored in his fourth successive game as Forest crushed West Ham United 5-0 in a League Cup tie at the City Ground but the winning run came to an abrupt end at Highbury, where Arsenal won 3-0 and Frank Clark suffered a hamstring injury that kept him out of the side for six months. On the other hand, it allowed Colin Barrett to return to the first team as a converted left-back and he soon made himself at home. What annoyed Clough more than the defeat, however, was indiscipline in the defence where both Lloyd and Burns were involved in off-the-ball incidents that were missed by the referee but punished by club fines. The next game at Molineux was the first Clark had missed for two years but goals by Withe, Bowyer and Woodcock got Forest back on course with a 3-2 defeat of Wolves.

Clough was still not satisfied and in the space of a fortnight signed England goalkeeper Peter Shilton from relegated Stoke for £270,000 and Scotland midfielder 30-year-old Archie Gemmill, an old favourite, from Derby for £20,000 plus John Middleton. Now he and Taylor had got the squad they wanted. And they started to attract better crowds to the City Ground. There were 31,000 for Shilton's debut on 17 September, when Aston Villa were beaten 2-0, and nearly 27,000 saw the Reds go two points clear at the top, never to be dislodged, with a 4-0 drubbing of Ipswich, Withe scoring them all and so becoming the first Forest player to hit four goals in a game since Knocker West in 1907.

The television cameras returned to the City Ground for the visit of second-placed Manchester City on 15 October when 35,572 were also drawn to the banks of the Trent as well as the BBC's *Match of the Day*. Neither the Nottingham nor the nationwide audience were disappointed as the game ebbed and flowed. Brian Kidd struck home a loose ball from a corner kick to give the visitors the lead after twenty-one minutes. Then Robertson twisted and turned past three defenders to set up Woodcock to side-foot the equalizer twelve minutes later. Withe placed the ball under goalkeeper Joe Corrigan for a late winner. There were still observers yet to be convinced by Clough's side. Just a week later after Forest's 2-0 defeat of Queen's Park Rangers in London, former Arsenal goalkeeper Bob Wilson, reporting for *Grandstand* on the BBC, boldly declared, 'Nottingham Forest were lucky to get all the points and although they are now favourites to win the title, I think their bubble will burst.' Clough's response was, 'He's put himself up there to be shot at – and I'm doing the shooting.'

Then the FA upset the applecart. Don Revie had resigned as England manager during the summer and Ron Greenwood had assumed temporary charge. On 5 November Forest were beaten 1-0 by Chelsea at Stamford Bridge but the downer for supporters was the announcement by club chairman Brian Appleby that he had given permission for the FA to approach Brian Clough. The fans pleaded with him to stay. Earlier in the season, Clough had campaigned against foul-mouthed chanting with a poster requesting, 'Gentlemen no swearing please! – Brian.' Now the supporters' response was: 'Brian no leaving please! – The Gentlemen.' Not to be outdone, Clough promptly replied that if they wanted him to stay they should back him. The club sold £3,000-worth of additional season tickets the following week.

In December candidates to take the England job permanently were interviewed and they included Jack Charlton and Dave Sexton as well as Greenwood and Clough. FA secretary Ted Croker, a former Charlton player, wrote, 'Diplomacy is a quality that is required (of an England manager) and that has not figured too highly with Brian Clough.' Greenwood, then general manager of West Ham and seen as the safe option, got the post. Clough reluctantly accepted the role of youth team manager but never took it seriously. Taylor said the highlight of that job was a free day on the beach at Las Palmas after an international youth tournament.

Clough wrote in his final autobiography *Walking on Water*,

What would the national team have been like under Brian Clough [...] It would have been the most relaxed England set-up of all time [...] We would have had a colourful team, playing the type of football the public wants to see, and it would have been winning football as well. The sense of leadership was in my blood and, from somewhere, I had the knack of making players feel good about themselves.

That is a view endorsed by a lifelong friend from another sport, cricket's Geoffrey Boycott, who had known him from days as a young footballer with Sunderland and a young cricketer for Yorkshire, respectively. Boycs wrote in his book *The Corridor of Certainty*, published in 2014,

When I look back and think about all the people I have met during my life, there is one man who has left a lasting impression: Brian Clough. [...] When he retired from playing and became a football manager, I would travel to watch his teams at Derby County and Nottingham Forest, and he, in return, would come to see me bat. I once had a personal glimpse of his man-management skills.

In June 1974, he came to watch me bat against Derbyshire in a championship match at Chesterfield. I was in really good form but early on I pulled Alan Ward straight to the fielder at midwicket, Brian Bolus, and was out for four. I was beside myself with disappointment and, after a little while, Brian came in to see me and I said I had 'ruined the day'. I will never forget what he said to me, 'Look, you see your colleagues outside. They are not sure if they will make a hundred now or ever again. You will get one, if not tomorrow then the week after. You will get plenty because you are that good.' I had just failed and he made me feel ten feet tall. That was his gift, it must have been unbelievable to play for him as he gave players absolute belief in their abilities. I wish he had been my manager as well as a best friend.

With the manager settled again, Forest lost Larry Lloyd to a broken toe in the game at home to his former club, Coventry, and learned that he would be out of action for ten weeks. Former Notts County centre-half David Needham was signed from Queen's Park Rangers for £150,000 as a replacement. He made his debut at Old Trafford on 17 December in what many people saw as the defining performance of Forest's season, the 4-0 drubbing of Manchester United in front of a crowd of 54,374. In their yellow away strip, Forest captured the imagination with flowing, one-touch football that swept a full-strength United away and, as *Match of the Day* commentator Barry Davies remarked, made them 'look pedestrian'. Woodcock's shot was deflected in off the post and the body of defender Brian Greenhoff for an own goal to put Forest in front and he thumped home another in front of the Stretford End before half-time. After the break, Archie Gemmill's non-stop running opened up the United defence for first Robertson and then Woodcock to finish off the game with the home seats emptying. 'They don't play with eleven men', said the bewildered United manager Dave Sexton. 'When they attack, about seven of them come at you and when they are defending, there are about nine of them.'

Paul Fitzpatrick of *The Guardian* wrote,

There has been a widely held feeling that Forest's success so far has been slightly phoney, based on doubtful virtues that would eventually be exposed. But there was nothing false about Forest.

In *The Times*, Tom German enthused,

Robertson and O'Neill gave Manchester a roasting on the flanks while Woodcock and Withe were so shrewdly mobile they fooled the central defenders in so many directions that, by the end, they were as bemused as the man in the middle of some particularly impish game of blind man's bluff.

Forest's quality was emphasized just over a week later when, on Boxing Day, Manchester United beat second-placed Everton 6-2.

The big games were coming thick and fast and on 21 January Arsenal, victors at Highbury at the beginning of September, found themselves on a City Ground pitch that was inches deep in mud. Needham headed in a Woodcock corner after half-an-hour and relentless pressing had the visitors' reeling. Midway through the second-half, the crowd of 35,743 saw one of the goals of the season. Archie Gemmill intercepted a Liam Brady pass just outside the Forest penalty area and played the ball wide to Withe, who took the ball forward as a diagonal run by Woodcock drew central defender Sammy Nelson out of position. Gemmill had not stopped running, ploughing through the mud to slide Withe's cross past goalkeeper Pat Jennings. It was not quite, but almost, as good as Archie's famous World Cup goal for Scotland against the Netherlands in Argentina, which was celebrated in the Ewan McGregor film 'Trainspotting.' The 'Wee man' took the ball into the Dutch penalty area, avoided a lunge by Wim Jansen, went outside Ruud Krol, pushed it between Jan Poortvliet's legs and lobbed it over goalkeeper Jan Jongbloed as he came out. McGregor's character in the movie has just made love and gasps, 'Christ, I haven't felt that good since Archie Gemmill scored against Holland in 1978!' Gemmill's comment on seeing the film was, 'To be fair, I was a bit embarrassed by it.'

Three days later, Forest beat Manchester City 2-1 in front of 38,509 at the City Ground to reach the fifth round of the FA Cup. Then Queen's Park Rangers were knocked out after a second replay. In the League Cup, Forest had beaten West Ham United 5-0, Notts County 4-0, Aston Villa 4-2 and Bury 3-0 to reach a two-leg semi-final with Leeds United. Some 10,000 Reds' fans travelled to Elland Road and saw Peter Withe score twice with John to O'Hare rifling a third in a comfortable 3-1 win. The second leg, with another 38,000 crowd at the City Ground was equally easy, Withe, Bowyer, O'Neill and Woodcock scoring in a 4-2 victory. The biggest problem for Chris Woods, who had made his debut against Notts as a seventeen-year-old standing in for the cup-tied Shilton, was keeping his concentration during long periods when he saw little of the ball. Now the media, much of which had written off Forest's challenge before Christmas, began to discuss prospects of a treble. But the twenty-two-match unbeaten run came to an end with a 2-0 FA Cup quarter-final defeat by West Brom at the Hawthorns.

A week later, on 18 March, Forest made their first Wembley appearance since the 1959 FA Cup Final triumph and the club invited those players to be guests of honour for the League Cup Final against Liverpool. Barrett was out with a stress fracture of the leg and with McGovern struggling with a groin problem and having to be replaced by O'Hare midway through the second half, Forest were under the cosh. Woods, now eighteen years and 124 days but still the youngest goalkeeper ever to play in a Wembley final, showed no nerves and kept the scoreline goalless even after extra time. 'Chris may have been only a kid but he kept us in the game,' John Robertson commented. Clough and Taylor took the squad to Scarborough for a break before the replay at Old Trafford four days' later.

Missing McGovern, Forest brought O'Hare into the starting line-up and Kenny Burns was made captain. They were in their yellow away kit instead of the red they wore at Wembley. Once again Woods was magnificent and was beaten only when Alan Kennedy got the ball in the net but had used his hand. Then Phil Thompson cynically tripped O'Hare who would have been clean through with only goalkeeper Ray Clemence to beat. Under today's laws it would have been a red card offence. Referee Pat Partridge awarded a penalty that Robertson coolly converted. The Liverpool players were furious and television pictures seemed to back up their claim that contact had been made just outside the box. Thompson, however, acknowledged that it had been 'a professional foul'. It was enough to give Forest their first major trophy of the season.

A goalless draw at Coventry secured the First Division championship with four games still to play. A City Ground crowd of 37,625 saw the championship trophy presented after another scoreless match, this time against Birmingham. And the season ended at Anfield with neither the Liverpool nor the Forest defence conceding. In the end of season awards, Kenny Burns was voted Footballer of the Year by the Football Writers' Association, the PFA chose Peter Shilton as their Player of the Year and Tony Woodcock was named Young Player of the Year. Brian Clough, of course, was Manager of the Year. Forest had won twenty-five and lost only three of their forty-two league games. They had scored 69 goals against twenty-four and finished seven points clear of second-placed Liverpool, who had won the European Cup at Wembley. 'Forest will be our biggest threat to retaining it next season,' Bob Paisley, their manager, predicted.

24

Munich

League champions Forest went to Wembley on 12 August 1978, for the traditional season's curtain-raiser against the FA Cup winners for the Charity Shield. Bobby Robson's Ipswich team had beaten Arsenal 1-0 in the Cup Final but they proved no match for the Reds, who swept them aside 5-0. John Robertson had tormented the Ipswich defence all afternoon and deservedly completed the scoring in the last minute. Martin O'Neill scored twice, Larry Lloyd volleyed another and Peter Withe headed what was to prove his last goal for Forest.

The team had the distraction of a four-team tournament in Spain in the week before the opening match of the First Division season and lost Lloyd to a leg injury that kept him out of four league and two League Cup games. Visitors Tottenham Hotspur were welcomed by a 41,223 opening day crowd at the City Ground and included their two new Argentinian signings, Ossie Ardiles and Ricardo Villa. Forest took a first-half lead through Martin O'Neill and Withe hit the bar but Ricky Villa equalized and they had to be content with a point. Steel fences had been erected to prevent fans invading the pitch but, sadly, did not prevent fighting after the game. There had always been a sense that such incidents were not part of the Nottingham football scene.

After the match, news broke of a transfer request by Peter Withe who had not been able to agree a new contract. Newcastle United manager Bill McGarry, who had worked with the player at Wolves in the mid-1970s, made a £250,000 bid that was accepted. The break-up of a prolific Withe-Woodcock partnership was hailed by Clough as 'good business'. The club had made a profit of more than £200,000 with the deal, he pointed out. The problem was that he had only the untried Steve Elliott and Garry Birtles as replacements. Elliott played seven games without scoring before Birtles got his chance. He came into the side in a 2-1 home win over Arsenal on 9 September, when Gary Mills, on as a substitute, became Forest's youngest-ever player in the Football League at sixteen years 302 days. Clough told Birtles he would play against Liverpool in the European Cup the following Wednesday. He hadn't scored but had held the ball up, taken the tackles, felt the pain and shown no fear. That was enough to impress his manager.

Before the draw for the first round, players had hoped for a European adventure with a trip to Spain or Italy and a game against Real Madrid or Juventus. The pairing with Liverpool was a bit of a downer. They'd travelled up the M1 on to the M62 and seen enough of Anfield in the past season and knew they were loathed by the Scousers. Liverpool had been in terrific early form, trouncing Spurs 7-0 on Merseyside, and were seeking a third successive European Cup triumph. Once again Forest's chances were written off by the national press. But the first leg was at the City Ground.

'That September night will remain with me as one of the most amazing of my career,' Birtles recalled. It was a sultry, sunny evening and over 38,000 excited, noisy fans were crammed into the City Ground. And 'here I was in my third professional game contesting the giant trophy coveted from Milan to Madrid and Benifica to Barcelona.' It was about to get even better. The pace of the Forest attacks exposed weaknesses in a Liverpool defence famed for its tactical awareness and organisation. Midway through the first-half, Kenny Burns brought the ball out of defence and chipped it over the head of Graham Souness to Ian Bowyer whose flick-on found Tony Woodcock making a penetrating run and forcing goalkeeper Ray Clemence to come out to meet him. As Clemence closed in on him, he squared the ball for Birtles to tap it home in front of the Trent End with Phil Thompson on his heels. 'One goal won't be enough,' Thompson snarled at the elated Birtles.

With time ticking down, it looked as though this would have to do. Then came Colin Barrett's goal. The full-back charged down an attempted pass by Jimmy Case on the half-way line. The ball fell to Phil Neal and his clearance was blocked by the onrushing Barrett. Rebounding into the Liverpool half, the loose ball was collected by Birtles who evaded Case, skipped past Thompson and crossed to the far post where Woodcock nodded it back across the box to Barrett, who had kept running all the way from the Forest half, and he shrugged off the attentions of Emlyn Hughes to volley home an unstoppable drive. After a split second's stunned silence, the ground erupted for a second time that night. It was arguably the most important goal in Forest's history, enabling the side to go to Anfield with a two-goal cushion without which their European odyssey may never have begun.

'I'd surely have been fined if I hadn't scored,' reflected Barrett. 'I'm told Peter Taylor was going mad in the dugout, wanting to know what I was doing up there and yelling at me to get back. I think it's likely a fine was on its way.' His full-back partner Viv Anderson commented, 'If you analyse it, it was a phenomenal goal from start to finish. Colin broke up an attack on the halfway line and went on a run that ended with him putting the ball in the net from inside the box. Fantastic.' John Robertson, in his autobiography *Super Tramp*, comments, 'It was such a massive goal in our history and without it I often wondered if we would have gone on to achieve the success we did.' Unlucky Barrett suffered a serious knee injury in a home draw with Middlesbrough four days before the second leg that would very soon cut short his playing career. 'It was a tragedy for him and us because there was no doubt he would have been an integral part of our side for years to come,' said Robertson. 'He was playing out of his skin at the time and the gaffer loved him.'

Overtaking Phil Thompson on the way back to the centre circle, Garry Birtles had shouted to him, 'Will 2-0 be enough then?' It was. Even though before the second leg in a poll of the twenty First Division managers only three – John Neal of Middlesbrough, Bristol City's Alan Dicks and Chelsea's Ken Shellito – believed Forest would hold on at Anfield. Clough, who scoffed at talking tactics, nevertheless tweaked things a little. Archie Gemmill was employed on the right flank with responsibility for helping Anderson deal with the forward runs of Liverpool left-back Alan Kennedy and John McGovern was posted in front of Lloyd and Burns as cover for the back four. It worked. Liverpool were stymied. The game was goalless and Forest had a 2-0 winning aggregate. David Lacey in *The Guardian* wrote that Forest played 'precisely the type of tight, containing game with which the European Cup winners of the past two years had frustrated so many opponents away from home.'

Forest were now engaged on four fronts: defending their championship title, retaining the League Cup, and contesting the FA Cup and the European Cup. Peter Taylor made no bones about his priority: victory in Europe. In the League Cup the Reds had been held to a goal-less draw at Oldham but won the replay 4-2. Then, a week after progressing in Europe, Birtles, McGovern, O'Neill, Robertson and Anderson scored as they reached round four with a 5-0 defeat of Oxford United that was watched by only 14,287 at the City Ground. Birtles got a brace and O'Neill again scored as Wolves were beaten 3-1 in the First Division and the crowds returned to Trentside with more than 29,000 fans present. Forest had set a new league record with thirty-five games unbeaten. Bristol City were overcome by the same scoreline at Ashton Gate before the European journey was resumed in Greece.

Forest were paired with AEK Athens with whom they had drawn 1-1 during a pre-season tour. AEK were managed by Ferenc Puskas, the Hungarian international with a legendary left-foot who had starred in the European Cup alongside Alfredo Di Stéfano in the great Real Madrid side. A hostile Athenian crowd greeted Forest at the first leg on 18 October but they were subdued by a John McGovern goal scrambled in with only eleven minutes gone after a quick free-kick from Frank Clark to Robertson led to a cross flicked on by Birtles at the near post. Clark was involved again just before half-time when his well-timed run from deep in the Forest half beat the offside trap freeing him to take Robertson's pass and put Birtles through to finish off the move. AEK played the last seventy minutes with ten men after Uruguayan Milton Viera was sent off for rashly planting a left hook on Burns' jaw. They pulled a goal back from the penalty spot after a foul by Burns, who had been booked and was suspended for the second leg.

Puskas was given a warm welcome from a 38,000 crowd at the City Ground as he took his seat in the directors' box for the second leg on 1 November. Needham came into the Forest side for Burns and John O'Hare replaced the injured McGovern. Lloyd, who had survived a row with Clough after refusing to wear a club blazer in Athens, was made captain and young Mills got a taste of European football when he came on as substitute for the injured Clark. Needham opened the scoring with a diving header from Gemmill's cross after thirteen minutes and it was then all Forest. More good work by Gemmill led to Woodcock heading in a perfect cross from Robertson in the 37th minute and Viv Anderson struck a twenty-five-yarder right-footed into the top corner of the net only two minutes later. Two goals by Birtles in the space of six minutes underlined the Reds' superiority and they ran out 5-1 winners on the night and 7-2 on aggregate. 'I cannot think of any team capable of stopping them,' Puskas commented. 'Are You Crying Liverpool?' sang the Trent End.

Victory at Bolton on 25 November took Forest's unbeaten run in the First Division to a league record forty-two games and Robertson, who scored the only goal, had played in every one of them. Goalkeeper Peter Shilton was the only other player to achieve that. The run was made up of an equal number of wins and draws and the fact that Forest scored just fifty-eight goals in those forty-two matches confirms that Shilton and his defensive colleagues were supreme. It was at Anfield on 9 December that the run came to an end with a 2-0 defeat, Terry McDermott scoring both goals – one of them a penalty. Burns had torn his cartilage in a 3-2 League Cup victory over Everton at Goodison, McGovern was still injured, O'Neill was ruled out and Woodcock missed the game after returning from international duty with a badly gashed ankle. It was a huge win for Liverpool who had not beaten Forest in the six matches they had played since Clough's side gained promotion – two in the First Division, two in the final of the League Cup and two in the first round of the European Cup.

The unbeaten record was previously held by Leeds, who had gone thirty-four games without loss, and Arsene Wenger's 'Invincibles' later surpassed Forest's achievement with Arsenal going forty-nine Premier League games undefeated.

During the international break, Viv Anderson had become the first black player to represent England. He was in the side against Czechoslovakia along with Woodcock and Shilton.

Forest bounced back with a 3-1 League Cup fifth round victory over Brighton at the City Ground and then beat Aston Villa 2-0 in the third round of the FA Cup at Villa Park. January was a good month in cup competitions with the defeat of York City to reach the FA Cup fifth round and a 3-1 aggregate win over Third Division Watford in the two-leg League Cup semi-final. Graham Taylor's emerging side had beaten Newcastle and Manchester United along the way.

There was managerial uncertainty again when Clough was linked with the Sunderland job after the departure of Jimmy Adamson for Leeds. But instead of moving to the north-east, he made transfer history by making Trevor Francis, from Birmingham City, Britain's first £1 million pound player. The previous record fee had been £516,000 paid by West Bromwich Albion to Middlesbrough for David Mills. If Clough was unhappy about having to pay a million, he was equally upset by Francis's obligation to play for American side Detroit Express for a summer season and he stuck the England international in the third team in a Saturday morning game for his Forest debut. It was afterwards found that the player's registration had not been completed and the club had to pay a £250 fine to the Football Association. He was ineligible for the FA and League Cup competitions and could only play in the European Cup if the Reds reached the final.

Arsenal were proving a 'bogey' side for Forest and, with Francis on the sidelines, they went out of the FA Cup to a Frank Stapleton goal at the City Ground on 26 February. He'd scored 4 goals in five games against Forest since their promotion and Arsenal had won three of them. Francis finally made his first team debut in a 1-1 draw at Ipswich on 3 March, when Birtles scored. Four days later, Forest were again in European Cup action at the City Ground against Swiss champions, Grasshoppers, who had put out Real Madrid on away goals in the previous round. Twenty-three-year-old Claudio Sulser, who had scored 9 goals in the previous four European games, was the danger man and he made his presence felt after just ten minutes holding off two challenges to clip the ball past Shilton. McGovern had an effort cleared off the line before Woodcock found Birtles inside the box for the equalizer. In the second-half handball by a defender stopped Birtles running on to another Woodcock flick and Robertson converted the penalty. Two goals in the closing minutes made the scoreline 4-1. First Gemmill stabbed home a cross from the right and then, from a third successive corner, Lloyd met Robertson's centre to score with a header at the near post.

Colin Barrett marked his comeback from injury with a great goal to earn a point at Everton. He lifted the ball over a defender's head, ran past him and crashed a fierce shot into the net. With Viv Anderson injured, Barrett deservedly kept his place at right-back for the League Cup Final against Southampton at Wembley on 17 March and then switched to left-back, replacing Frank Clark, for the second leg of the European

Cup-tie with Grasshoppers in Zurich four days' later. On the eve of the final, Clough and Taylor gathered the players together after dinner at their London hotel for a short team talk in the lounge that became a late-night champagne party.

The League had previously refused Forest permission for both Clough and Taylor to lead the team out at Wembley so without any discussion with officials it was Taylor, resplendent in his blue club blazer who emerged from the tunnel at the head of the procession. There had been snowstorms during the week and although the pitch had been cleared and looked fine on the surface it slowly deteriorated into cloying mud as the game progressed, a situation not helped by the fact that it was still recovering from a recent Horse of the Year show.

Perhaps it was a collective hangover from the night before, but Forest were, in John Robertson's words, 'terrible in the first half.' Southampton's Alan Ball dictated play and David Peach gave them a 16th minute lead. Going in a goal down at half-time, Robertson said Clough greeted them with the warning, 'Right, you lot, don't go blaming this on last night.' And, according to McGovern, he added, 'How dare you underperform with your wives, girlfriends, relations and supporters in the stands.' The manager's instructions for the second half, Woodcock recalled, were simply, 'Get the ball and just pass it to another red shirt.' It was a Jekyll and Hyde performance. 'Without even thinking about it, we found our rhythm and played our natural game.' Now the Reds were rampant. Birtles robbed centre-half Chris Nichol and shot high into the roof of the net for the equaliser. He found the net twice more but each time was denied by controversial offside decisions. Then Barrett won the ball, passed to Woodcock who found Birtles. The irrepressible striker tore through the Southampton defence to put Forest in front. Gemmill's pass put Woodcock in for the third goal. Nick Holmes scored a late consolation goal for Southampton but Forest had won 3-2 to become the first club to retain the League Cup. Clough had another dig at protocol by insisting that he and the Saints' manager Lawrie McMenemy should climb the thirty-nine steps to receive their medals with the players. Not even Alf Ramsey had done that as England World Cup-winning manager.

There was no time for celebrations. Brian Clough took the League Cup home with him and stuck it on the top of the television set while he watched and ate fish and chips. Confidence was sky-high as the Reds flew out to Switzerland for the European Cup third round second leg. Grasshoppers needed to win 3-0, or better. Sulser gave them a 4th minute lead from the penalty spot after Viv Anderson had been harshly adjudged to have committed a foul challenging for a header. Forest secured the tie before half-time when, from close range, O'Neill bundled the ball in from a cross by Birtles. The game ended 1-1 and the Reds qualified with a 5-2 aggregate for the semi-final against Bundesliga champions Cologne, favourites after Liverpool's exit to win the trophy.

Meantime, in the League, Forest had the luxury of a five-star attack featuring, O'Neill, Francis, Birtles, Woodcock and Robertson. They beat Coventry 3-0 and Chelsea 6-0 (O'Neill hitting a hat-trick) at the City Ground before Francis scored his first Forest goal in the last minute at Bolton to save a point. Aston Villa were beaten 4-0 at home and the 'double' was completed over Chelsea with a 3-1 win at Stamford Bridge (Francis scoring in both games) to give the Reds nine out of a possible ten points, scoring seventeen goals and conceding just two, in the three weeks between European engagements.

The first leg of the semi-final was at the City Ground on 11 April and four days earlier John Robertson suffered a terrible blow with the news that his brother, Hughie, had been killed in a car accident. Sensitively, Brian Clough told him to take all the time he needed and left the decision about playing entirely to the player. The rest of his family convinced Robbo that he should play. 'I went into the match with all kinds of different emotions,' Robertson wrote in his book. 'Because of that I had a strange carefree attitude to it all. It was as if football wasn't all that important any more and it took all the pressure of the occasion away from me.'

Cologne had been involved in European competition throughout the 1970s and made good use of their experience. They surprised Forest and 40,804 crowd by taking the game to them and led 2-0 after only 19 minutes with goals by Belgian international winger Roger Van Gool and German star Dieter Muller. Forest fought back and, after Bowyer had struck the bar with a looping shot from eighteen yards, Needham knocked a Robertson cross back across the box for Birtles to head past goalkeeper Harald Schumacher into the top corner of the net. Just before half-time Gemmill ruptured his groin and Clark came on to replace him, taking up the left-back position allowing Bowyer to move forward into midfield. 'Bomber' had a happy knack of scoring important goals and when a Robertson chip was nodded down by Birtles, Bowyer was there to drive home the equalizer with a right-foot shot from sixteen yards. Then Robertson stunned the Germans, the crowd and even himself with a diving header into the net. Forest were ahead until speedy Japanese winger Yasuhiko OKudera came off the bench to squeeze a shot under Shilton for 3-3. 'Forest sunk by Jap sub' screamed a national newspaper headline the next morning.

Once again, Forest's chances were being written off. Even Cologne, with three away goals, were so sure of reaching the final that they printed a club European Cup Final brochure and booked tickets and buses in anticipation of going to Munich. 'This lot are in for the shock of their lives,' said Brian Clough. The first leg had been frantic, end-to-end football. In contrast, the second game, watched by 50,000 fans in the Mungersdorfer Stadium, had the tactical charge of a chess match. Barrett's knee had let him down again and he was in hospital when the team came out in an all-red strip into the concrete bowl on a damp, cold and misty night. Anderson and Burns returned to bolster the defence and Clark was at left-back with Bowyer staying in midfield. With keeping a clean sheet imperative, Forest were content to allow the Germans to push forward and then counter-attack them. It was goalless on the hour and then, in the sixty-fifth minute, Birtles flicked on Robertson's corner at the near post and Bomber, the master goal poacher, stooped to conquer, heading the ball into the roof of the German net.

Forest lost only one of their remaining seven First Division games, going down 1-0 to Wolves at Molineux. Three days after returning from Cologne, they had surrendered the championship title after a goalless draw with new champions Liverpool in front of a 41,898 crowd at the City Ground. Forest finished as runners-up, having lost only three times in the league for the second consecutive season.

Seven days before the European Cup Final, Lloyd, Francis and Robertson scored as the Reds beat Mansfield Town 3-1 to win the County Cup. Only 9,000 fans were at the City Ground to see it. There were 57,500 in the Olympic Stadium, Munich, on 30 May. Malmo, formed in 1910 and the first Swedish club to turn professional, were managed by their second English coach Bobby Houghton, who later had a spell as number two to Dave Bassett at the City Ground. The first had been Roy Hodgson, the eventual England manager. Brian Clough and Peter Taylor went to watch Malmo before the final and took the opportunity have a good look at the cosmopolitan city that, incredibly has 170 nationalities represented in its 300,000 population. Clough also took delight, and a psychological advantage, in beating Houghton at squash.

The Forest manager summed up Malmo as a team that gets results from its defensive strength. 'They place the same importance on clean sheets as we do', he said. 'I think they have mastered the art of keeping things tight at the back and, in Munich, it might be a case of us trying to break them down.' As he predicted, the 1979 European Cup Final was not an adventurous game. Croydon-born Houghton, then only thirty-two and the youngest coach ever to reach the final, was a shrewd tactician who had masterminded victories over Bayern Munich, Inter Milan, Dynamo Kiev and, in the semi-final, stopped a prolific Austria Vienna from scoring over two legs. World Cup midfielder Herbert Prohaska warned, 'Our attackers could hardly get a glimpse of the ball against such a destructive side. Nottingham Forest will find it hard to break them down in Munich.'

Inevitably, it was John Robertson who unlocked the stubborn Malmo defence. 'We tried to mark him man for man but he needed only three or four yards to get the killer cross in,' Houghton reflected. And, inevitably, it was Trevor Francis, in his first-ever European game, who met the ball beyond the far post and headed home the only goal. 'I really thought we could win,' said Houghton. 'But Forest had so many good players in that team. If I had to pick just one for my team it would have to be John Robertson. Then they had Trevor Francis, Tony Woodcock and Garry Birtles. Their centre-backs, Lloyd and Burns, were very strong and, of course, there was Peter Shilton in goal.'

Nottingham remains the smallest city ever to provide European champions. And, remarkably, all eleven of the Malmo players came from the local region – another feat never repeated by any other finalist.

25

Madrid

A £2 million cantilever stand to seat 10,000 was being built at the City Ground as the 1979-80 season got underway and its funding would lead to the 200-member club becoming a limited company in April, 1982. The structure towered over Trentside but only the lower tier was in use when Stoke City came for the first home match on 22 August. The attendance was just over 26,000 and O'Neill scored the only goal.

Frank Clark had told his team-mates after Munich 'it doesn't get any better than this'. And, in fact, the final proved to be his last game as a player. He left Nottingham to become assistant manager at Sunderland. With Barrett still struggling with injury, the need for a left-back was urgent and Forest paid Leeds £500,000 for Frank Gray. Archie Gemmill's was another notable departure. He left to join Birmingham City for £150,000. Peter Taylor said it was too good an offer to refuse for a thirty-two-year-old but Brian Clough later regretted letting the player go – especially after paying £500,000 to Manchester City for another Scottish international Asa Hartford but then offloading him to Everton for £400,000 after only three games, oddly all of them victories. Young goalkeeper Chris Woods, frustrated by lack of opportunity as deputy to Peter Shilton, was allowed to join Queen's Park Rangers for £250,000 and Jim Montgomery, then thirty-five, was signed from Birmingham to replace him. Trevor Francis was tied to his summer contract in the United States with Detroit for the first couple of months.

The season marked the Silver Jubilee of the European Cup with holders Forest and league champions Liverpool representing England. Coincidentally, Oesters Vaxjo, who had succeeded to Malmo's Swedish league crown, were Forest's first European Cup opponents. Two goals in the last half-hour by Ian Bowyer gave the Reds victory in the home leg and a Tony Woodcock equalizer in Sweden assured progress to round two. Much to the surprise of most, Liverpool fell at the first hurdle to Dynamo Tblisi. Forest were First Division leaders when they met Arges

Pitesti in the first leg of the second round at the City Ground. Woodcock and Birtles gave them a two-goal advantage to take to Romania. Pitesti had come from behind to beat AEK Athens in the first round, winning 3-0 at home to overcome a two-goal deficit from the away leg. There was no comeback for them this time though as Bowyer and Birtles scored to give the Reds a 2-1 victory and a 4-1 winning aggregate.

A 5-2 win against Bolton Wanderers in front of a crowd 24,564 on 20 October was Forest's fiftieth successive undefeated league game at the City Ground. Lloyd, Woodcock, Francis, Anderson and Robertson (penalty) were the scorers. Then Francis got both goals in a 2-0 home win against Ipswich but the run came to an end with a shock 1-0 defeat by Alan Mullery's bottom-of-the-table Brighton. Gerry Ryan scored for the Seagulls in the 12th minute and just before half-time goalkeeper Graham Moseley saved a John Robertson penalty. The result sparked a turnaround in fortunes for Albion who were pulling away from the relegation zone by Christmas.

∞

Worse than the result so far as Forest fans were concerned was the news that it was Tony Woodcock's last game for the Reds and he was being transferred to Cologne for £650,000, a bargain for the Germans but the maximum fee allowed under European rules at the time. Woodcock remains one of the few Englishmen to have forged a successful career in Germany, scoring thirty-nine goals in 131 Bundesliga appearances over two spells with Cologne before finishing playing with Fortuna Cologne, where he later took over as manager.

In an interview for the Bundesliga web site in August 2012, he was asked about his record move from Forest to Cologne and answered,

> Players didn't tend to move abroad in those days so it was a massive leap if you did. I wanted to see a new country and learn a new language. The game wasn't better or worse it was just different. In England, I'd been playing two games a week virtually all season whereas I was now playing once a week with a winter break but training harder. I stayed for many years after I stopped playing and I still have friends there today so it stands to reason that I obviously got on very well with the fans in Germany.

After playing in the 1982 World Cup in Spain, Woodcock returned to England to sign for Terry Neill's Arsenal for £500,000. He was the Gunners' top scorer for the following four seasons, his best total being twenty-one in 1983/84. In October that season, he fired five goals against Aston Villa, a post-war record for the club. Tony helped Arsenal reach the semi-finals of both domestic cups in his first season at Highbury and, after the sacking of O'Neill, remained in favour with the new manager Don Howe, who was appointed in December, 1983. He also played his part in a strong start to the 1984/85 season when Arsenal topped the league in the autumn. A serious injury in March 1985, disrupted his career and, with the arrival of George Graham as manager in May 1986, the thirty-year-old Woodcock was told he was surplus to requirements. In all, he had scored 68 goals in 169 matches for the Gunners. He returned to Cologne for £140,000 in July that year and in 1988 joined Fortuna before retiring in 1990 after making 37 appearances and scoring five goals.

∞

A friendly in Cologne on 18 December was agreed by the two clubs as part of the Woodcock transaction and in the Forest side was a surprise replacement. Clough gambled on one of the game's cult characters by recruiting thirty-year-old Stan Bowles from Queen's Park Rangers for £225,000. Bowles made his First Division debut at Old Trafford, where Forest were beaten 3-0, but scored in his first home match, a 2-1 victory over Aston Villa on Boxing Day. He played nineteen First Division games for the Reds, scoring just one more goal. Next to arrive was former Arsenal star Charlie George, who had been on the manager's wanted list for a year but his club, Derby County, had refused to sell him to their East Midlands rivals. Instead George went to Southampton, much to Clough's fury, for £400,000. In January, however, the player came to the City Ground from the Saints on loan with a view to a permanent transfer. The scene was set for the introduction of a brilliant ball-playing inside-forward partnership. In some respects it was reminiscent of Billy Walker's inspired pairing of former London favourites Doug Lishman (Arsenal) and Eddie Baily (ex-Spurs) in the successful 1956/57 campaign for promotion to the First Division except Clough's initiative was doomed to disappoint. Bowles and George had the talent but not the stomach for the challenge. Clough's domineering style offended. They played together only three times yet both left with European Super Cup winners' medals.

A Manchester City apprentice, local boy Bowles showed early signs of a fiery temper when he upset coach Malcolm Allison and, after a series of off-the-field incidents, was released in 1970 with just seventeen first team appearances. In two years he had three different clubs – Bury, Crewe Alexandra and Carlisle United. But his undoubted natural ability caught the eye of QPR and the Londoners bought him in September, 1972, for £112,000 as a replacement for a previous Rangers' folk hero Rodney Marsh, who had been transferred, incidentally, to Manchester City. Bowles had no qualms taking over Marsh's No. 10 shirt. He spent just over seven years at Loftus Road and played a central role in arguably Rangers' greatest ever team, which finished as First Division runners-up in 1975/76 under Dave Sexton.

In 1979 he fell out with new manager Tommy Docherty. The Scot supposedly told Bowles, 'You can trust me, Stan.' To which the player allegedly replied, 'I'd rather trust my chickens with Colonel Sanders.' Docherty made Bowles train with the reserves, though still playing him in the first team, for nearly six months before selling him to Clough. He remains a favourite with the Shepherd's Bush club's fans who, in 2004, voted him Rangers' all-time greatest player.

Bowles missed the home leg of the European Super Cup competition against Barcelona on 30 January, when George scored the winning goal, but played in the second leg five days later when Burns scored after the Spaniards had taken the lead from the penalty spot. Forest might have won but Robertson missed a penalty in the second half after Bowles had been tripped. There was a crowd of 23,807 at the City Ground and 90,000 at Camp Nou. After playing in the City Ground leg of the European Cup third round against Dynamo Berlin, which Forest lost 1-0, Bowles missed the return match apparently because of a fear of flying. Teenager Gary Mills deputized and the Reds won 3-1 with two goals from an outstanding Trevor Francis and a Robertson penalty. Bowles was back in the side when Forest beat Ajax 2-0 in the first semi-final at the City Ground on 9 April but Clough left him out for Mills in the Amsterdam leg, which was won 1-0 by the home side. His Forest career came to a controversial end when he went absent without leave and refused to play in the final against Hamburg in Madrid at the end of May.

Skipper McGovern recalls one occasion when the manager in full flow was interrupted by a cocky Stan who told him, 'No, Boss, you're wrong.' McGovern groaned. He knew what was coming. The player was subjected to a lengthy lecture on his past demeanours, his present weaknesses and how he must improve in the future. It was perhaps this incident that inspired the often-quoted Brian remark, 'We talk about it for twenty minutes and then we decide I was right'. On Clough, Bowles commented, 'He couldn't coach. Him and Peter Taylor just used to walk their dogs down by the Trent, where we trained in the park. Jimmy Gordon, a little Scots fella, he took the training. Cloughie must have had something but I haven't a clue what it was. I never saw it. I liked Peter Taylor. He was a gambler like me. We could relate.'

Charlie George, still idolised by the Arsenal fans, was a key player in the 1970/71 double-winning team, scoring a superb goal in the FA Cup Final victory over Liverpool. He had three decent seasons at the Baseball Ground and memorably scored a hat-trick for Derby against Real Madrid in the European Cup, although the Rams eventually lost the tie 5-6 on aggregate. He must have been a great disappointment to Clough, who admired his swagger and exceptional talent, for he played only four games for Forest – two of them in the Super Cup – and was at the City Ground for less than a month. Bowles and George, for Forest they were the odd couple – moody but sometimes dazzling mavericks.

Forest's inconsistent form was a problem in the League but the cup competitions were a different matter. The Reds began their defence of the League Cup with a 1-1 draw at Blackburn but won the replay 6-1 with Bowyer scoring twice, Robertson also getting two including a penalty, and the other goals coming from Woodcock and Frank Gray. Woodcock hit a hat-trick to knock out Middlesbrough 3-1 at Ayrsome Park but Forest needed a replay to overcome Bristol City. The quarter-final against West Ham finished goalless at Upton Park and still neither side had scored after ninety minutes in the replay but O'Hare, Birtles and O'Neill lifted the spirits of a rain-drenched 25,000 City Ground crowd with extra time goals to set up a two-leg semi-final against Liverpool. Thirty-two thousand at the City Ground on 22 January saw a late John Robertson penalty give Forest a slender lead to take to Anfield. O'Neill, playing up front with Birtles in the absence of Francis, was brought down by goalkeeper Ray Clemence and Robertson put away the penalty. Substitute David Fairclough scored an equalizer in the dying seconds but Forest were through for an unprecedented third successive League Cup Final trip to Wembley.

In the FA Cup the Reds had a comfortable 4-1 third round victory at Elland Road, where Frank Gray scored in the first minute against his former club, but Liverpool returned to the City Ground a week after their League Cup defeat to gain revenge with a 2-0 FA Cup fourth round knockout blow. Francis marked his comeback with a hat-trick in a 4-0 home league win against Manchester City and then scored two more as Tottenham Hotspur were beaten by the same scoreline.

Forest were in fine fettle for Wembley and the League Cup Final against Wolves, who were managed by former Forest player John Barnwell. Both were mid-table in the league but Barnwell had strengthened his team by bringing in former Liverpool and England captain Emlyn Hughes and striker Andy Gray, a £1.5 million record signing from Aston Villa. Forest were without suspended Larry Lloyd who was replaced by David Needham. Clough had led the side out of the Wembley tunnel for the 1978 final against Liverpool, Peter Taylor was given the honour a year later against Southampton and this time trainer Jimmy Gordon was at the head of the team alongside Barnwell. Gordon was as surprised as anyone. He wasn't told of the manager's decision until just before kick-off and didn't have time to change out of his tracksuit. The game is remembered chiefly for its only goal and the collision on the edge of the box as centre-half Needham and goalkeeper Shilton both tried to deal with a long punt from Wolves' right-back Peter Daniel. The ball broke for Gray to tap into an empty net.

With the League Cup route to Europe now closed and Liverpool fighting out the championship with Manchester United, winning the European Cup became of even greater importance not only for the trophy itself but also for competing on the Continent in 1980/81. But at the City Ground on 3 May the Reds suffered a severe blow. The visitors were Crystal Palace, managed by Terry Venables and with Gerry Francis an effective playmaker from midfield. But they were being taken apart by a Forest side playing some of the most attractive attacking football of the season. Trevor Francis, in particular, was on fire. Playing in his favoured central striker role he had scored two goals and was chasing a hat-trick as the Reds led 4-0 with twenty minutes left. Sprinting towards the Palace goal on the heavy pitch, he suddenly pulled up and stumbled clutching his ankle. He had snapped an Achilles tendon and would miss not only the final but would be out for seven or eight months.

Clough and Taylor took the players to Majorca to relax their mood before Madrid. There was no training but McGovern ran three miles each morning and Shilton found a patch of grass on a traffic island in Calla Millor, where Gordon put down two tracksuit tops as goalposts and goalkeeper and trainer set to work. A fitness obsessive, Shilton, as a youngster, hung from a banister at the top of the stairs in his parents' shop with weights attached to his feet trying to add inches to his height. No wonder some later commented that his arms were extraordinarily long.

∞

With Francis injured and Bowles missing, Forest had only one recognised striker, Garry Birtles, so the management pair opted for a five-man midfield bringing in seventeen-year-old Gary Mills initially to partner the front man but then dropping back. As Robertson said, 'It was a case of anyone who was fit would figure.' There were only four instead of the allowed five substitutes on the bench. Forest wore an all-red strip and Hamburg, now firm favourites, wore white. German internationals Manny Kaltz and Felix Magath were Hamburg's defensive stars and England's Kevin Keegan was their main attacking threat though they also had Horst Hrubesch, nicknamed 'The Heading Monster', on the bench. Lloyd and Burns made it their business to unnerve Keegan but the Germans forced Forest on the backfoot for most of the game and Shilton had to be at his magnificent best

McGovern won the ball and began a well-constructed move with a pass to Bowyer. He found O'Neill who drifted infield to send Gray charging at the heart of the Hamburg defence. Mills took over and worked the ball left to Robertson. The winger jinked between two defenders and played a one-two with Birtles before hitting a right-foot shot from the edge of the penalty area and the ball went in off the inside of the post. After twenty minutes, Forest were ahead and now they had to absorb intense Hamburg pressure. Having failed to pass their way through the Reds resolute defence, the Germans sent on Hrubesch and tried to unsettle Burns and Lloyd with 'route one' long-ball tactics. Jack Charlton, sitting alongside Brian Moore in the commentary box, assured his anxious colleague that the defenders were too good for this to work. Clough sent John O'Hare on for young Mills for the last half-hour with instructions to 'calm things down.' Then Gray had to come off injured and was replaced by Bryn Gunn.

Birtles had followed instructions in his lone ranger role and throughout the game repeated to himself the mantra 'hold it and wait for help. Hold it and wait for help.' He had run himself into the ground but might have made it 2-0 in the final minute. One-on-one with Peter Nogly, he nutmegged the defender but, exhausted, stumbled slightly allowing Kaltz to get back and block him. Clough was appreciative. 'I've never seen a lad cover as much ground, willingly and unselfishly, as Birtles did that night,' he said. It was all over. In his excitement Moore told ITV viewers, 'Hamburg are champions of Europe again!' John McGovern was presented with the trophy at the side of the pitch and the Forest players carried it together in a lap of honour while Keegan led away his dejected team-mates. Trevor Francis watched it all on television in a Cannes hotel. He would have like to have been there but the manager wanted him out of the way. 'Everyone was a hero,' Clough commented. 'We had application, tenacity, dedication and pride. We did everything right.'

John McGovern thought this win overshadowed that at Munich, retaining the trophy against a quality side like Hamburg. 'We tackled, blocked, hustled and harried until we dropped,' he said. 'We did drop but only after the final whistle.' Sharing the glory with the players and fans in the Bernabeu stadium and then, back in Nottingham, showing the trophy to thousands more from the top of an open bus made the captain reflect: 'Against all the odds, little old Nottingham Forest had matched and bettered the achievements of some of the giants in European football.' That season Forest had won the European Cup, the European Super Cup, finished fifth in the First Division and reached the final of the League Cup. 'We had probably reached a peak on that magical night in Madrid,' McGovern concluded. 'A massive bonus, which added to the club's respect throughout the world of football, was the conduct of our supporters during the two European campaigns. We won like champions while they had conducted themselves like champions.'

26

Radical and Red

Nottingham in Victorian times was notorious as a radical town. John Beckett, editor of *A Centenary History of Nottingham*, published in 1997, quotes Charles James Fox writing of the 'uncontrollable spirit of riot' pervading elections in the town and Sir Robert Peel thinking it 'a disorderly, radical city.' The Nottingham Journal in 1835 reported that local people travelling away from the town found themselves pitied and frequently asked 'if it was currently quiet'. Nottingham's radicalism was epitomized by the election to Parliament in 1847 of Feargus O'Connor, the only Chartist MP. Reformist rallies on the Forest attracted large numbers. Beckett and his colleague Colin Griffin conclude the history with this comment:

> Travellers at the end of the twentieth century can be sure that wherever they roam across the globe mention of the city's name will bring a response which suggests an association with a mythical medieval renegade by the name of Robin Hood [...] Nottingham has rather more to its past than a folk hero, a castle and a wicked sheriff Although perhaps the same tradition was being kept alive when Brian Clough's Nottingham Forest twice robbed the rich clubs of Europe to bring the European Cup to what at the end of the 1970s was a rather humble city ground.

Many, including former Forest goalkeeper and later chief scout Alan Hill, suggested Clough 'liked to play Robin Hood'. Rick Parry, who as the Premier League's chief executive in 1993 set up an independent inquiry into the transfer fee bungs scandal, claimed he had been told Clough broke FA rules by making unsolicited gifts to staff and players. The Forest manager supported the Labour Party, marched with the miners during the strike of 1982 and once fancied becoming an MP. He persuaded a widow who had been taken into hospice care to stop starving herself and calmed an alcoholic threatening to throw himself off Trent Bridge. There is an unsourced meditation that goes,

> We believe that imagination is stronger than knowledge, that myth is more potent than history, that dreams are more powerful than facts, that hope triumphs over experience, that laughter is the only cure for grief and that love is stronger than death.

Does that, perhaps, sum up the philosophy of Brian?

Sitting on the bench with Brian Clough for the First Division match against Tottenham Hotspur at the City Ground in mid-November, 1980, substitute John McGovern was suddenly asked, 'Do you know what's wrong with Ponte?' The deposed skipper was too stunned to reply. He'd been dropped in favour of Swiss midfielder Raimondo Ponte, a summer signing from Grasshoppers for £180,000. 'I'll tell you', Clough said. 'I bloody signed him, that's what's wrong with him.' Ponte made way for O'Neill but Forest still lost 3-0. The open admission seemed significant to McGovern. Not only was a great team being dismantled, perhaps prematurely, but the management partnership was breaking down. 'Brian was a great manager and Peter was the best judge of a player I have ever known,' McGovern said. Now it seemed Clough no longer trusted Taylor's judgment and neither was he confident of his own.

After a string of friendlies in North America and in Europe, the league season began at Tottenham Hotspur with Ponte and £1.3 million striker Ian Wallace from Coventry City making their First Division debuts for the Reds, who lost 2-0. There had been a dispute on the eve of the match between the players and management over win bonuses. Clough gave them a 'take it or leave it' ultimatum and McGovern, who had tried to get agreement, signed up for the slight increase. 'I didn't think the issue should have been argued so close to the start of the season,' he explained. 'You have to be your own man and stand by your own judgment.' The first home game was won 2-1 against Birmingham City on 20 August, when Brian Clough performed the official opening of the Executive Stand with 26,561 in attendance. O'Neill was sent off.

∞

McGovern's football development owed much to Brian Clough's influence but his strength of character was inspired by his mother's example. He rejected approaches by Clough and Taylor when they wanted him to go with them to Brighton. But he joined Clough at Leeds, where his fortitude was tested to the limit. There was a distinct anti-Clough atmosphere at Elland Road and both he and John O'Hare, who had signed with him from Derby, were ostracised. There was hostility in the stands and, McGovern found, no favours from Revie's old guard on the pitch. Targeted by the boo-boys, he decided to face them and strode into the supporters' lounge after a match. His reception was not pleasant and some beer mats were thrown. It was a bit like a Western film as he made his way to the bar and asked for a half of Guinness. The bartender hesitated and looked nervously round the room but then filled his glass. McGovern took his time over the drink and then left in silence. If nothing else, he had shown he would not be intimidated. Clough stayed at Leeds for only forty-four days. 'I had to stick it out for seven months,' McGovern said. 'By the time Brian asked me to join him at Forest, I'd have gladly walked down the M1.'

Forest's hopes of a European Cup treble were dashed in the first round by unfancied Bulgarian champions CSKA Sofia, who won both legs 1-0. This shock early exit may have influenced Clough and Taylor in their decision to remodel the side. The biggest surprise was that the first to go was Chilwell-born Garry Birtles, a Forest fan since boyhood of whom his team-mate Viv Anderson, another international and local from Clifton, said, 'He could do everything – hold the ball up, turn and run at defenders, score goals. Birtles was the best centre-forward I have ever seen. A fabulous, fabulous footballer.' The next home match after the European Cup-tie was his final appearance before manager Dave Sexton broke the Manchester United transfer record to take him to Old Trafford for £1,250,000. Nearly 30,000 saw the game that was against United, who won 2-1, Wallace scoring the Forest goal.

There were only 12,248 at the City Ground at the end of November when Ian Bowyer scored twice to give the Reds a 2-1 lead against Valencia in the first leg of the European Super Cup. Uruguayan striker Fernando Moreno scored the only goal in the return leg in December to make the aggregate score 2-2 and give the Spanish side the Super Cup on away goals. Having lost out on European glory, Forest could still become World Club Champions if they defeated the leading South Americans Nacional Montevideo of Uruguay. The match took place before a 70,000 crowd in Tokyo on 11 February. Injured skipper McGovern watched frustrated from the sidelines as his team-mates outplayed the opposition but were beaten by a goal from Waldemar Victorino, who was voted man-of-the-match by sponsors Toyota and was rewarded with a brand new car. It turned out to be Larry Lloyd's Forest finale. Three days later he was Wigan Athletic's player-manager and losing 1-0 to Rochdale. Bowyer had moved on a month earlier to Sunderland but came back to the City Ground at the beginning of 1982 for a five-year second spell. Lloyd returned to Nottingham to manage Notts County, then took over the Stage Door pub in the city centre and became an outspoken local radio broadcaster.

Ten days after Lloyd, Martin O'Neill bade farewell to the City Ground. He joined Norwich City for £250,000 later to return to Nottingham with Notts County. It was against Norwich on 28 March that Ponte played his last match for Forest before joining Corsican club SC Bastia. Lloyd's replacement, Norwegian Einar Jan Aas, signed from Bayern Munich, made his debut for the Reds and Trevor Francis, recovered from his lengthy Achilles injury, scored both goals in a 2-1 victory. Aas, a popular and stylish centre-half was limited by injury and in November left to join his home town club Moss.

Forest went out of the League Cup with a 4-1 defeat at Watford but had a good run in the FA Cup. Francis scored twice in a 3-3 third round draw with Bolton at the City Ground and then the only goal in the replay. He continued in prolific form with another winner against Manchester United at the City Ground in round four. Bristol City were beaten 2-1 at home in the fifth round and then Francis was again on target as Forest drew 3-3 with Ipswich in the sixth. Ipswich were 1-0 winners in the replay at Portman Road. The Reds ended the season seventh in the First Division.

In June Frank Gray returned to Leeds United for £300,000 but £1 million centre-forward Justin Fashanu, bought from Norwich, and England Under-21 midfielder Mark Proctor from Middlesbrough for £425,000 made their debuts in the league opener against Southampton at the City Ground on 29 August, when Francis scored twice in a 2-1 win. He played his last game for Forest two days later in a goal-less draw with Manchester United at Old Trafford and was transferred to United's neighbours, Manchester City, for £1,200,000. In early October Kenny Burns departed to Leeds for £400,000.

The 1981/82 season would be the first without European football at the City Ground since 1978. Forest lost at home to Wrexham in the third round of the FA Cup but reached the fifth round of the League Cup before going out 1-0 to Tottenham Hotspur at White Hart Lane. The final league position was twelfth. Willie Young had been signed from Arsenal to replace Lloyd, winger Jurgen Roeber had arrived from Chicago Sting and striker Peter Ward for £400,000 from Brighton but none provided long-term answers. More encouraging was the emergence of youngsters Peter Davenport, Steve Hodge, Colin Walsh, Chris Fairclough, Stuart Gray and Calvin Plummer.

If the Ponte business had given John McGovern some concern about the Clough-Taylor partnership, he had further reason to worry as the season neared its end. With the manager away on a short break with his family, Peter Taylor told McGovern he was on the transfer list with Wallace and Fashanu. Then Brian Clough returned and asked, 'Who told you that? You're going nowhere.' The next day, wrote McGovern in his autobiography, he was summoned to see 'a somewhat agitated' Peter Taylor. 'Look, I told you that you were going and you're going,' the player was told. 'It's over, finished.' The indecision continued with Clough telling him, 'I decide who stays or leaves this club.' Finally, McGovern sat in the manager's office and was informed,

I have had ten enquires regarding the names on our transfer list and, considering Wallace cost over a million and a quarter and Fashanu cost a million, you'll be pleased to hear all the enquiries are about you but I see no reason why you shouldn't play at least twenty games for me next season.

That was not a wholehearted endorsement and when McGovern heard Bolton Wanderers wanted him as their player-manager, he decided to leave.

'At the end of fourteen years there wasn't even a handshake from Brian or Peter,' wrote their captain. 'No sentiment. They paid me my wages. I did my stuff on the field. End of story.' To those supporters who would say to him 'Brian Clough and Peter Taylor loved you' or 'You were Cloughie's blue-eyed boy', McGovern says please replace the word 'loved' with 'respected.' This worked both ways 'for them and me', he adds. 'Every time Brian Clough walked towards me, I didn't know whether he'd shake my hand or bite my head off.' John McGovern's last game for Forest was a friendly in Morocco against the Kuwait national team and it ended as a 1-1 draw. In 2014 he returned to a Kuwaiti-owned Forest as club 'ambassador' – an honour and a job he relished as much as being captain.

Peter Shilton's five seasons at the City Ground also came to a close. With the Reds he had won a League Championship medal, a League Cup winner's medal, two European Cup winner's medals, European Super Cup winner's and loser's medals, a World Club Championship runners-up medal and nineteen England caps. He had reserved probably his greatest individual performance for the 25th European Cup final. Clough's trademark green sweater, usually worn over a red shirt, was inspired by Shilton's number one goalkeeper's top. 'There's only one number one round here,' the manager told him. 'And it's not you.' Shilts won little with his other clubs, who included Leicester, Stoke, Southampton and Derby but he holds a record number of 125 England caps. His replacement at the City Ground was Johannes Franciscus Van Breukelen, known to all on Trentside as Hans, a Dutch international when Brian Clough paid £200,000 for him to FC Utrecht. Six-footer Hans played superbly for Forest between 1982 and 1984 and was immensely popular with the fans before returning to Holland with PSV Eindhoven. Van Breukelen's debut at the City Ground on 4 September coincided with the return of Garry Birtles but there were only 13,709 fans to see a 4-0 victory over Brighton.

All of McGovern's fears for the Clough-Taylor relationship were justified when Peter Taylor said he had 'shot it' and would have to retire. He would not be persuaded to stay but then accepted an offer from Derby County, who were struggling in Division Two, to take charge at the Baseball Ground. As fate would have it, the FA Cup third round paired Clough's

Reds with Taylor's Rams in Derby and it was the second division side who triumphed 2-0 in front of a crowd of 28,494. Forest finished a respectable fifth in the First Division but the only silverware they had to show for the season was the County Cup as Notts were beaten 4-3. In May they played a couple of friendlies in Canada, beating Montreal Manic 4-3 but losing 2-1 to Toronto Blizzard in a televised game.

The zenith of the Clough-Taylor relationship came during the summer when Peter Taylor signed out-of-contract John Robertson for Derby while Brian Clough was away on a charity walk. Clough went to the transfer tribunal with evidence of offers for the player from Luton and Southampton. The tribunal was persuaded to set a transfer fee of £135,000, which was higher than Derby expected and one they could scarcely afford. Robertson's style did not suit the second division, Derby were relegated and Taylor was sacked. Birtles and Davenport scored fifteen goals each as Forest finished third in the First Division. Paul Hart had been signed from Leeds United and the thirty-year-old centre-back formed a solid central defensive partnership with the equally experienced Colin Todd for the first part of the season and young Chris Fairclough from November.

∞

The Reds went out of both the FA Cup and the League Cup in the early stages but had a fine run back in European competition having qualified for the EUFA Cup. Vorwaerts were beaten 2-0 at the City Ground and 1-0 in East Germany in the first round and then PSV Eindhoven were beaten in both legs of the second, Davenport hitting the target in each game. The third round tie with Glasgow Celtic was played in icy conditions in front of a City Ground crowd of over 34,000 and ended goalless. Goals by Hodge and Walsh earned Forest a 2-1 second leg victory watched by nearly 67,000 at Celtic Park. Sturm Graz were the quarter-final opposition and a rare goal from Paul Hart earned Forest a 1-0 win in the home leg. Both sides scored from the penalty spot in the second leg in Austria, Colin Walsh equalizing for Forest with just six minutes of extra time left to ensure a 2-1 aggregate win.

Semi-final opponents were the defending champions Anderlecht, who had beaten Forest 4-2 in Belgium on the pre-season tour. Without the injured Birtles, the Reds were unconvincing in the first leg at the City Ground until the final five minutes when Steve Hodge scored twice, turning in a Gary Mills cross at the far post and then profiting from a fine delivery by Steve Wigley. After making his First Division debut in a 3-0 defeat of Arsenal at the City Ground in October 1982, Wigley gave one of the most dazzling displays of his Forest career in that high-scoring County Cup final in May, 1983. There were only 5,000 fans on Trentside to see it. He had made his reputation as a tricky, ball-playing winger for his home town club Curzon Ashton at Ashton-under-Lyme, where he was spotted and promptly signed by Brian Clough. But, unusually, he was at inside-right when he jinked his way through the Magpies' defence to lay on goals for Viv Anderson, Peter Davenport, Steve Hodge and John Robertson. Both sides were in Division One and, in the league, Notts had beaten Forest 3-2 at Meadow Lane with the Reds winning the return match 2-1. That season, Wigley made only four First Division appearances, all from the substitutes' bench, and played twice in cup-ties. His best season at the City Ground was in 1984/85 when he played thirty-five times in Division One and in nine cup-ties. Steve was a maker rather than a scorer of goals and hit only three in over 100 games for Forest before joining Sheffield United in October 1985.

That was the season Stuart Pearce joined Forest. It seems incredible now but the player who was to become the second of Cloughie's great captains was viewed as the makeweight in a £450,000 summer deal that also brought centre-half Ian Butterworth to Nottingham from Coventry City. Butterworth did not last two years and made only thirty-three appearances. Pearce stayed twelve seasons during which he played 522 games for the club (only Bob McKinlay with 685 and Ian Bowyer 564 have played more), won seventy-six of his seventy-eight England caps and scored 88 of his career total of ninety-nine goals. Pearce and Wigley were Forest team-mates on ten occasions, eight times in the First Division and twice in the League Cup. Wigley returned to the City Ground as assistant academy director to Paul Hart and later joined up as coach with Stuart Pearce when he managed first Manchester City and then the England Under-21 squad. Wigley also had successful spells coaching the young players at Southampton, Bolton Wanderers, Bristol City, Hull and Fulham. The pair teamed up again on Trentside with Stuart as the Forest manager and Steve his assistant at the start of the 2014/15 season.

With a two-goal advantage the Reds eagerly anticipated the away leg in Anderlecht and the strong possibility of taking part in an all-English European final against Tottenham Hotspur, who faced Hajduk Split in the other semi-final. John Robertson confesses in his book that he knew within a week of pre-season training that he had made a terrible mistake in joining Derby. 'I was in a relegation battle and could have been in a side that reached the UEFA Cup semi-final,' he lamented. But the Anderlecht encounter was to prove one of the most controversial games Forest have ever played. It was 1-0 at half-time, a low drive from twenty-five yards by Enzio Scifo putting the home side ahead in the 20th minute. 'We were still confident,' said Paul Hart. 'We'd won every away game in Europe that year and we were used to grinding it out.' Spanish referee Carlos Guruceta awarded Anderlecht a disputed penalty after deciding that full-back Kenny Swain had tripped Kenneth Brylle. Hart said it was a disgrace: 'Ken was two yards from him.' Birtles, sitting on the bench, was equally convinced of the injustice of the decision. 'Kenny was nowhere near the guy,' he wrote in his autobiography. There was 'complete daylight' between them. Erwin Vandenbergh made it 3-0 with two minutes remaining then Forest won a corner and Paul Hart headed the ball powerfully into the net for what seemed to be a vital away goal. The referee disallowed it for an alleged push on a defender. 'We were diddled out of it,' Hart said, 'I never won a medal, ever.' Van Breukelen, who had made a number of fine saves, insisted that Forest had been playing against 'twelve men.'

Anderlecht lost the final to Spurs in a penalty shoot-out. Some years later Birtles, Van Breukelen and Ian Bowyer, on behalf of the players, unsuccessfully sued Anderlecht in the Belgian courts. In 1997 Roger Vanden Stock revealed that his father, Constant, Anderlecht's president at the time of the tie, had paid referee Guruceta £18,000 and the club was punished with a season's ban from UEFA competition. Guruceta could not defend himself. He had been killed in a car crash ten years' before. But he had form in Belgium having sent off two Italians and awarded a controversial penalty to Standard Liege when they beat Napoli 2-1 in the first leg of the 1979/80 EUFA Cup second round. The second leg in Naples ended 1-1. Liege went out in the third round.

Forest ended the season in fine form beating Watford 5-1 at the City Ground, West Ham 2-1 away and Manchester United 2-0 at home. After retaining the County Cup with a 3-0 victory over Mansfield Town, the Reds went on an Australian tour playing matches in Perth, Adelaide, Brisbane and Sydney and losing only one – to Manchester United in Melbourne. The tour party met up with Nottingham's world ice-dance champions Jane Torvill and Christopher Dean when they were in Brisbane. Colin Griffin, discussing in John Beckett's history modern perceptions of Nottingham, credits the ice-dancers and Clough's footballers with projecting a 'glamorous and vibrant' image of the city contrasting sharply with the unflattering picture painted by its most acclaimed twentieth-century writers D. H. Lawrence and Alan Sillitoe.

27

Hillsborough

Intense rivalry, thrilling matches, great goals, controversy and unimaginable tragedy marked clashes between Liverpool and Nottingham Forest during the Clough years. When Labour MP and Celtic season-ticket holder Glaswegian Jim Murphy wrote *The 10 Football Matches That Changed the World* in 2014, he chose to feature two games between the Reds of Merseyside and Nottingham. One kicked off at 4.00 p.m. on 16 August 1992, when a Forest team that included Stuart Pearce, Nigel Clough, Scot Gemmill, Steve Chettle and Ian Woan outplayed Liverpool in the first-ever Premier League broadcast on Sky television. Commentator Martin Tyler welcomed viewers with: 'Good afternoon, everyone. A new league, alterations and amendments to the very laws of the game, even a different button to push on your television set.' Riches generated by Sky's involvement opened up the great divide between Premiership clubs and the rest. Teddy Sheringham scored the only goal with a right-foot drive beyond goalkeeper David James's outstretched left hand high into the net. In sixty-two appearances for Forest, England international marksman Sheringham scored twenty-three goals and this was his last. Before the end of the month he had been transferred to Terry Venables' Spurs for £2.1 million in a deal that later gave rise to 'bungs' allegations.

'Good afternoon. Welcome back,' was the message from Sheffield Wednesday's chairman to the visiting fans from Liverpool and Nottingham in the programme for the abandoned FA Cup semi-final on 18 April 1989 forever known as the Hillsborough Disaster. 'As you look around Hillsborough you will appreciate why it has been regarded for so long as the perfect venue for all kinds of important matches,' the article, unfortunately, continued. His 'welcome back' was because this was the second consecutive semi-final contested by the two clubs at Wednesday's stadium. In 1988 Liverpool had won 2-1, reversing a league scoreline at the City Ground a week earlier. Arrangements for accommodating the two sets of supporters had been identical to those a year later with Forest occupying the Kop end and Liverpool Leppings Lane simply because the police wanted them at the ends of the ground nearest their arrival points.

Inevitably, this match was Murphy's other selection. Also inevitably, the Hillsborough chapter concentrates on the long fight for justice for the ninety-six blameless Liverpool fans who were crushed to death and their families. In the House of Commons in October, 2011, a motion calling for all documents – including cabinet notes and briefings – to be handed to an independent panel set up to review the papers for public release was passed unopposed and with the support of Home Secretary Theresa May. There are many thousands of official documents but the key facts were already known, including that the stadium's safety certificate was out of date. Some 24,000 Liverpool fans had to be funnelled through just twenty-three turnstiles in the north and west sides of the ground. They could not cope before kick-off and when a crush developed outside police ordered an exit gate to be opened to admit hundreds of fans together. Undirected, they tried to get into the central Leppings Lane 'pens', which were already full.

Those at the front of the pens tried to climb out on to the pitch to escape and I have a memory of Bruce Grobbelaar, the Liverpool goalkeeper, gesticulating to persuade police these were not hooligans but potential victims. The game was stopped after only six minutes and the players were sent back to the dressing rooms. It did not restart. I and many others hoped that the season's FA Cup competition would be abandoned but the clubs were ordered to replay the match at Old Trafford, Manchester. Their performance showed the Forest players had no heart for it. Liverpool went through to beat Merseyside neighbours Everton 3-2 at Wembley on 20 May. On 12 September 2012, Prime Minister David Cameron stood up in the Commons to apologize to the nation for the mistakes and deceit that had taken place at the time and over the years since.

There is a side of the story that is unconsidered, unacknowledged, rarely heard: the Forest side. Steve Hodge, in his autobiography *The Man with Maradona's Shirt*, recalled the team coach going down the hill to the stadium on a beautiful spring day. 'When we went out for a warm-up I noticed that their end behind the goal was quiet but our end, the big kop, was packed and really loud.' he wrote. A couple of lads said to him, 'Where are their fans?' The game kicked off and it was end to end. Peter Beardsley hit the bar in the opening seconds and then Forest broke away to win a corner. 'There was some disturbance among their fans behind the goal,' Hodge continued. His mind went back to the pitch invasion at Newcastle in 1974. 'I was half expecting the whole lot would come spilling out on to the pitch. I just thought, "Jeez, we've only just started." Then someone shouted, "There's people dying in there." He was only about fifty feet from the barrier and could hear the screams. Hodge said the FA's Graham Kelly came into the dressing room and told them, 'Whatever happens, the game has to be completed today.' But Brian Clough, having heard people had died, replied, 'Graham, we're going home' and then, turning to his players,' added, 'Lads get changed, we're off.' That was my view, too, and I said to my sons as we sat in the paddock in front of the main stand, 'Let's go, this game won't restart and we should let mum know we're on our way home.'

Author Danny Rhodes followed Forest to Hillsborough that afternoon and he graphically tells what it was like in an outstanding 2014 novel *Fan*. Resembling himself, his hero Finchy is from Grantham. He is a 'home and away' Forest follower who goes to Hillsborough with his mates, a seventeen-year-old full of hope and expectation, believing, like all the rest around him on the kop that this is Forest's season, that they're in the form of their lives. But something is wrong at the Leppings Lane end. Twenty-two days after the horror of Hillsborough, Finchy is at Old Trafford with his mates for the replay. There are gaps on the terracing. Many think the game shouldn't be played. 'You feel it, too, but you go out of duty, out of necessity, out of habit. Because it's in your blood.' The story spans fifteen years. Finchy, now a secondary school teacher in the south, is still haunted by Hillsborough. He cannot settle down, cannot sustain personal relationships, and heads back to Grantham to face his demons.

The Forest team for Sheffield and Manchester was Steve Sutton, Brian Laws, Stuart Pearce, Des Walker, Terry Wilson, Steve Hodge, Tommy Gaynor, Neil Webb, Nigel Clough, Lee Chapman and Garry Parker. According to Chapman, the players did not want to replay the semi-final. 'We thought what's the point?' he said. The whole country away from Trentside demanded an Everton-Liverpool final. 'We were in a no-win situation. We didn't get any counselling or anything and I don't think people realized how it affected the people of Nottingham.' John Aldridge gave Liverpool an early lead but, almost relunctantly, Neil Webb equalized. Aldridge restored his side's lead after the break but then to the disgust of Forest players and supporters alike mockingly celebrated an own goal by ruffling the unfortunate culprit Brian Laws's hair. 'I would have chinned him,' Pearce years later told *Guardian* sports writer and Forest fan Daniel Taylor. It's an incident that also distresses the fictional Finchy in *Fan*.

∞

Five weeks before the disaster a Nottingham man, Brian Ibell, took up the post of assistant general manager at Sheffield Northern General Hospital, which received the injured directly from the match. In a letter written to the *Nottingham Evening Post* just six days after the tragedy, he described how visits from the players of both clubs had lifted beyond belief the spirits of patients, relatives and staff.

Being from Nottingham, meeting my footballing heroes lifted the cloud that had hung over my head and brought smiles to faces that had previously shown none ... My personal highlight was the young Liverpool fan just transferred from intensive care to a general ward who, when I tactfully asked him if he recognized the footballer next to his bed, said: 'Yeah! It's Lee Chapman and he's rubbish.' Lee nearly fell over laughing and was equally stunned when all the Forest lads joined in and agreed with the youngster's observation. I cannot emphasize enough what a good job the Forest lads did. They, obviously, felt somewhat apprehensive to start with meeting Liverpool fans and patients whom they felt may not directly relate to them but, at the end of a visit that spanned many hours, even the likes of Neil Webb and Nigel Clough were in full flow. We can truly be proud of Nottingham Forest Football Club for the joy and happiness they brought to Sheffield in a very traumatic week

Mr Ibell met Prince Charles and Princess Diana but when he asked his son which VIP he would like to meet received the answer, 'Forest goalkeeper Steve Sutton.'

As well as his emotive letter, Mr Ibell forwarded a presentation book of photographs of Forest players at the bedsides of the injured. It is inscribed:

Northern General Hospital, Sheffield. The staff, patients and their relatives wish to express their thanks to the players and officials of Nottingham Forest Football Club for visiting the hospital following the Hillsborough Tragedy on Saturday, 15 April 1989.

The book contains the signatures of 408 hospital personnel involved, including doctors, nurses, physios, X-ray staff, orderlies, caterers, telephonists and porters.

Ten years later Forest and Liverpool set up a junior challenge contest for The Hillsborough Memorial Cup. It was won by a Liverpool under-10 representative side. Arnold Boys brought the trophy to Nottingham in 1999/20 but it was not competed for again. That seems such a shame.

The manner of the FA Cup exit disguised what had been an outstanding season for the Reds. The League Cup and the Simod Cup had been won at Wembley, they were FA Cup semi-finalists and were third in the First Division, for the second successive season, behind Liverpool and champions Arsenal. Forest began the league season with a defeat at Norwich followed by five successive draws before registering a 2-1 victory at Queen's Park Rangers on 8 October after a 6-0 morale-boosting defeat of Chester City in the League Cup first leg. Tommy Gaynor hit a hat-trick in the second leg at Chester, where Forest won 4-0. Lee Chapman, who had been born in Lincoln when his father, Roy, a former Aston Villa star, was with City, joined Forest from Niort, France, for £350,000 in October and for fifteen months was a superb partner for Nigel Clough before moving on to Leeds for £400,000. He made his home debut in an impressive 2-1 defeat of Liverpool and then scored his first goal for the Reds at the end of the month when Newcastle were beaten away 1-0. Coventry and Leicester, after a replay, were dismissed in the League Cup and, in the fifth round, Chapman scored four goals as Queen's Park Rangers were crushed 5-2.

Garry Parker was switched from midfield to the left-wing against Sheffield Wednesday on New Year's Eve and the move coincided with Forest striking a rich vein of form with ten wins in a row including the FA Cup defeats of Ipswich and Leeds. QPR earned a goal-less draw in the league to end the run but a Parker goal at Ashton Gate disposed of Bristol City in the League Cup semi-final and he scored again in the sixth round of the FA Cup to knock out Manchester United. It was the first goal scored by a visiting team at Old Trafford for three and a half months and was a tap-in for Parker after speedy Franz Carr had left Lee Sharpe in his wake and put the ball across the six-yard box.

A tenth successive away win came at the Baseball Ground where Hodge and Chapman scored as Derby went down 2-0 and next Manchester United were beaten by the same scoreline at the City Ground with goals by Pearce and Chapman again. Pearce got another with Clough also scoring as Norwich lost 2-0 on Trentside four days before the League Cup final. The holders, Luton Town, who had beaten Arsenal 3-2 in the 1988 final, were Forest's Wembley opponents. Brian Laws declared himself fit enough to play despite having thirty-six stitches in his hand after an accident at home with a couple of wine glasses. He had been in hospital for forty-eight hours. Clough threw a ball at him and when he caught it said, 'If you can take a throw in, you can play.' There was disquiet in the camp when Lee Glover, viewed as a manager's favourite, was named as substitute instead of Brian Rice, who had played in five games on the way to the final and would now miss out on a £10,000 bonus if Forest won.

More than 76,000 were at a Wembley bathed in early spring sunshine and there was a live television audience of millions. Forest began nervously. Lee Chapman got the ball in the net and that might have settled them but the goal was disallowed for offside. The Reds fell behind after thirty-six minutes when Mick Harford headed in a Danny Wilson cross. At half-time Clough told his players, 'Now my wife's in the stand, so are yours, so are your relations and friends and all those lovely people from Nottingham. So please, go out there and show them what you can really do.' The Reds dominated the second half. Luton goalkeeper Les Sealey upended Steve Hodge as he ran on to a pass from Neil Webb and Nigel Clough equalized from the penalty spot. Webb scored the second himself after Clough had spread the ball wide for Tommy Gaynor, who made a great run and cross for midfielder to flick the ball over the advancing keeper. There was no way back for Luton. Pearce found Gaynor who squared the ball for Clough to stab the ball past Sealey to make it 3-1. Stuart Pearce wore a red and white scarf and a red-trimmed white woolly hat as he led the Forest players up the steps to the royal box to collect the League Cup, the seventh major trophy at club level won by Brian Clough, overtaking the six Don Revie had achieved.

After wins in the league at home to Southampton and away at Middlesbrough, the Reds returned to Wembley for the final of the FA Full Members' Cup, sponsored by Italian sportswear company Simod. Forest had beaten Chelsea 4-1, Ipswich 3-1 and Crystal Palce 3-1 en route and faced Everton, who had eliminated Millwall, Wimbledon and Queen's Park Rangers, in front of a 50,000 crowd. The Blues were desperate for a trophy after a disappointing league campaign and took the lead in the 8th minute with Tony Cottee finishing well after beating two defenders and even getting ahead of Des Walker. Garry Parker equalized from close range after Lee Chapman had flicked on a corner and it became an exciting end-to-end game. Five minutes into the second half, Graeme Sharp lobbed Steve Sutton to restore Everton's lead but a superb individual effort by Parker, who ran sixty yards after receiving the ball from Nigel Clough before driving it past Neville Southall, forced extra time. Forest went in front for the first time two minutes after the restart through Chapman but Cottee put the Toffees back on level terms and the game seemed to be heading for penalties. Then Webb released substitute Franz Carr down the right and his cross was toe-poked home by Chapman to make it 4-3. Forest had become the first side ever to win two Wembley finals in the same season and what a great day out it had been.

Steve Hodge reckoned his decision to return to Trentside had been fully justified. 'In three seasons away I hadn't won anything at Villa or Spurs,' he said. 'Cloughie had proved that he could produce a new young team of high quality and he'd done it without Peter Taylor.' Forest's reserve side won the Central League and their Under-18s won the Midland Youth Cup. Unfortunately, because of another stadium disaster, the new Reds were not allowed to test themselves in Europe. On 29 May 1985, Liverpool met Juventus at Heysel Stadium, Brussels, in the European Cup Final. There was provocation and fighting on the terraces, a wall collapsed and thirty-two Italians, four Belgians, two people from France and one from Northern Ireland died. Not just Liverpool but all English clubs were banned from European competition for five years.

Brian Clough's take on the season was,

> I don't think I have ever been involved with a side who have been applauded so much having won away from home. Supporters have appreciated us, referees are glowing in their praise about our discipline and my fellow managers have been unstinting in their praise for the manner in which we go about our work. We've always tried to play the game in the way it was intended. We don't argue, we don't moan, we don't spoil. We have no negative thought. It's a collector's item if we catch the opposition offside.

28

Second Home Wembley

During Brian Clough's last five seasons – 1988/89 to 1992/93 – Wembley, the national stadium, almost became Nottingham Forest's second home. The Reds played three League Cup finals, winning two of them; won the Simod and Zenith Data Systems (Full Members) Cups and were beaten in the FA Cup Final. The manager had assembled an exciting young squad with home-grown talents like Des Walker, Steve Chettle, Gary Charles, Nigel Clough, Scot Gemmill, Terry Wilson, Steve Sutton and Mark Crossley supplemented by astute signings such as Stuart Pearce, Brian Laws, Franz Carr, Garry Parker, Ian Woan, Gary Crosby, Brian Rice, Nigel Jemson, Roy Keane and the returning Steve Hodge and Neil Webb.

The final payment on the Executive Stand (later renamed the Brian Clough Stand) was made during the summer to add to the optimism on Trentside but Neil Webb opted to join Manchester United for £1.2million. His replacement, John Sheridan, signed from Leeds for £650,000, featured in the pre-season tour in France and in the 3-1 County Cup victory over Notts County but missed the opening league game against Aston Villa at the City Ground, which was drawn 1-1 thanks to a Garry Parker equalizer. Parker switched to the left wing to allow Sheridan to take his place in midfield for the League Cup second round first leg at home to Huddersfield. The newcomer laid on the opening goal for Gary Crosby but the match was drawn 1-1. He wasn't picked again and moved on to Sheffield Wednesday for £500,000. At Huddersfield in the second leg Forest seemed comfortable with goals by Crosby, Clough and Gaynor putting them 3-1 ahead but after conceding twice late on went through only on the away-goals rule.

League form was erratic and again it was the League Cup campaign that would rescue the Reds' season. After a goal-less third round draw at Crystal Palace, Forest romped to a 5-0 victory in the replay. Steve Hodge scored in the first minute, then Nigel Clough caught the goalkeeper going walkabout and Stuart Pearce made it 3-0 after only eighteen minutes.

Pearce forced an own goal before half-time and Hodge completed the scoring after the interval from the full-back's free-kick. Lee Chapman got the only goal seven minutes from the end of the fourth round clash with Everton at the City Ground after an indirect freekick had been awarded against goalkeeper Neville Southall for time-wasting. Aston Villa knocked Forest out of the ZDS Cup and in the third round of the FA Cup substitute Mark Robins got the only goal for Manchester United in the game at the City Ground that famously saved Alex Ferguson from the sack. Terry Wilson had a late equalizer ruled out.

After First Division defeats at Aston Villa and at home to Norwich, Forest dipped into the transfer market to sign Danish-born Icelandic international Thorvaldur Orlyggson for £175,000. He made his debut in a 2-0 home win against Southampton and a shot from him was turned in by Chapman in what turned out to be his last goal and final game for the club before joining Leeds for £400,000. Nineteen-year-old Nigel Jemson was signed for £150,000 from Preston and made his debut at Luton on Boxing Day as Chapman's replacement. Jemson would go on to play an important role in the League Cup run.

A crowd of 30,044, the best of the season at the City Ground, saw Forest go two goals in front through Crosby and Parker against Spurs in the fifth round but Gary Lineker and Steve Sedgeley scored to force a replay. Going back with the Reds to White Hart Lane after his transfer eighteen months before, Steve Hodge scored twice, including the winner, as they triumphed 3-2. Forest gave 'a marvelous display of passing, tackling and finishing' wrote David Lacey in *The Guardian*. 'It was the old Spurs push-and-run set in a modern context and given extra speed and vision.' Nayim had scored first for the home side but Crosby and Clough combined for Hodge to slide in for an equalizer. Then Jemson skipped past Sedgeley to hit a right-footer high into the top corner of the net for a 2-1 half-time lead. Paul Stewart levelled but, within two minutes, Hodge restored Forest's lead and put them in the semi-finals for the second year running. Des Walker, against the club who had not wanted him as a youngster, gave a man-of-the-match performance to deny Lineker a chance. During January Clough signed a more experienced striker, David Currie, from Barnsley for £700,000 but Jemson's form was such that he would make few appearances before being sold in April to Oldham Athletic.

Forest faced Coventry City in the semi-final. Both legs were televised and kicked off at 3.30 p.m. The first at the City Ground was played in driving rain before a crowd of 26,153 on 11 February. Nigel Clough put the Reds ahead with a first-half penalty after Cyrille Regis had handled. With the pitch deteriorating badly, a mistake by Orlygsson let in Steve Livingstone for a seventy-third minute equalizer. Seven minutes later Forest won a free-kick and, from twenty yards out Stuart Pearce smashed in the winner off the underside of the crossbar. Pearce's fearsome free-kicks were as celebrated by supporters as those of Johannes Antonius Bernardus Metgod. 'Johnny' had joined Forest as a twenty-six-year-old Dutch international midfielder from Real Madrid in August, 1984, and soon became a crowd favourite. He scored only fifteen goals in 116 appearances for the Reds but most of them were special and he was a cultured giant towering over midfield. After three seasons as a regular he moved with Chris Fairclough to Tottenham Hotspur, where he made only twelve appearances before rejoining Feyenoord. After 164 games in six years, he retired as a player and became the club's youth director. Metgod came back to England as Portsmouth's coach in 2008 and then joined Nigel Clough at Derby as coach until both were dismissed in 2013.

The weather was equally bad two weeks later when a goalless draw at Highfields Road was enough to see Forest through to Wembley. It also secured a twenty-second Manager of the Month award for Brian Clough, equalling Bob Paisley's record with Liverpool. But League form collapsed and the Reds won only two of their eleven First Division games before the final. They did win the first match at home to Manchester City by a single and controversial goal. City goalkeeper Andy Dibble had the ball in the palm of his hand as he calmly considered his next move. He was too relaxed as he looked downfield and failed to notice Gary Crosby who cheekily nipped in to head the loosely held ball to the ground and tap it into the net.

Second Division Oldham Athletic, who had also reached the semi-final stage of the FA Cup, were Forest's Wembley opponents. It wasn't a great game and was decided by a scrappy goal two minutes into the second half, Jemson forcing home the rebound after his first attempt had been blocked. Forest fans were happy. The League Cup had been retained and they'd had another day out at Wembley. Forest ended the season in ninth place in the First Division after finishing with a flourish. Manchester United's visit three days after the final became a City Ground celebration as Forest scored four goals in the first half-hour to win the game. Garry Parker struck a 20-yard volley for the first, Stuart Pearce slotted a free-kick inside the near post, Nigel Clough had a shot deflected over goalkeeper Jim Leighton and Steve Chettle headed in the rebound after an overhead kick by Tommy Gaynor had come off the bar. The last league match was at Hillsborough where Sheffield Wednesday had to win to survive in the First Division. The Reds were merciless. Stuart Pearce with another of his trademark free-kicks and then after a rampaging run from the back put them two up and Nigel Jemson made it 3-0.

∞

Winger Ian Woan made his debut in the County Cup final against Mansfield Town at Field Mill on 8 May, when Carr with two goals, Parker and Crosby gave the Reds a 4-0 victory and their second trophy.

A few days earlier, the manager had made one of his best-ever signings after being alerted by his Irish scout Noel McCabe to the potential of a nineteen-year-old lad from Cork named Roy Keane. Clough picked him up from Cobh Ramblers for about £50,000.

Forest went on a pre-season tour to Sweden, scoring 21 goals against two in five matches and helping Karlsunds open their new stadium. They then played three matches in Italy without defeat before retaining the County Cup with a 5-0 defeat of Mansfield Town at the City Ground on 22 August. The league season began on Saturday, 25 August, with a 1-1 draw with Queen's Park Rangers thanks to a Jemson penalty and, on the Monday, Forest travelled to Liverpool where it became apparent that Hodge had fallen a victim of flu and was unfit to play at Anfield the next night. Clough took a gamble and got his assistant, Ron Fenton, to bring Keane from Nottingham on the morning of the match. The youngster was helping the kit-man lay out the shirts when he was told to put on the No. 6 because he was playing. Forest lost 2-0 but the Irishman was so impressive he went on to play thirty-five First Division games and make thirteen appearances in Cup competitions that season. Against Southampton in his first home game the City Ground crowd gave him a standing ovation when he was substituted with the Reds leading 3-1. Jemson scored two goals in a minute to become the First Division's top scorer with five goals from four games but this had been the side's only win.

That September Brian Clough signed a three-year contract and, at the end of the month, a Pearce thunderbolt from a free-kick almost forty yards out hit the net at the Stretford End to silence 46,000 Manchester United fans and inflict a first home defeat on their club. The players wore black armbands for the home game with Everton on 7 October after it had been learned that Peter Taylor had died suddenly, aged sixty-two, while on holiday in Majorca. The Reds won decisively 3-1 with Jemson's eighth goal of the season and two from Steve Hodge. Form dipped and when Derby won 2-1 on 24 November it was Forest's first league defeat at the Baseball Ground in a decade. Again it was cup competitions that captured the attention. Keane scored his first goal for the club in a 4-1 League Cup victory at Burnley, who were eliminated 5-1 over two legs. A 2-1 win at Plymouth gave Forest a twenty-two-match unbeaten run in the competition and set up a fourth round clash with Coventry City at Highfield Road.

A Kevin Gallagher hat-trick helped the Sky Blues to a 4-0 lead after only half-an-hour. There seemed no way back but before half-time Nigel Clough scored a hat-trick and eight minutes into the second half Garry Parker drilled an equalizer. A scramble in the 6-yard box led to Steve Livingstone knocking the holders out. After winning 2-1 at home against Newcastle United, Forest went to Barnsley and were beaten by the same scoreline in the ZDS second round leaving them with just the FA Cup to play for. An away tie with Crystal Palace, third in the First Division, was a tough assignment but with Des Walker keeping star striker Ian Wright quiet Forest managed a first clean sheet in ten starts to earn a replay. A freezing cold spell caused two postponements before the teams could meet again. It was again a cold Nottingham evening as Palace led through an Ian Wright goal going into the last fifteen minutes but Terry Wilson's shot went in off defender Richard Shaw to force extra time. Stuart Pearce charged forward and, athletically, volleyed a return ball into the Trent End goal but there was another twist of fortunes as Keane's underhit back-pass made goalkeeper Mark Crossley rush his clearance and John Salako lobbed him from long range for 2-2.

Forest won the draw to host the second replay and the game was scheduled for the following Saturday. This time fog caused a cancellation. The game finally kicked off on Wednesday 28 February when three goals in eleven second half minutes saw the Reds go through. Garry Parker got the crucial first, side-footing home a pass from Hodge, and then he blasted No. 2 with an unstoppable shot that went in off the underside of the bar. Gary Crosby killed off Palace with the third from Terry Wilson's pass.

The fourth round was another tough one with Forest having to travel to Newcastle, who built up a 2-0 lead in the first twelve minutes. In the second half Pearce volleyed home a cross from Keane and, with time pressing, Nigel Clough fired a low shot into the net after Keane and Wilson had combined to put him through. Yet another replay to face but it proved no problem as Hodge, Clough and Parker made it 3-0. Forest were on the road again for the fifth round with another difficult trip, this time to meet Southampton at The Dell. Neil Ruddock put the home side in front with a second-minute goal and the Saints held on for seventy-eight minutes before, in descending fog, a Pearce shot came back off the post, Keane got hold of the rebound and Hodge turned in his cross to equalize and take the tie to the City Ground. The replay began well for the Saints with Rod Wallace pouncing on a headed back-pass by Walker that fell short to give them the lead but a Jemson hat-trick, his first, took Forest to the quarter-finals. For the fourth successive round, Forest were drawn away and on 9 March faced Norwich City on a Carrow Road surface of mud and sand. After withstanding first-half pressure, the Reds gained control and this time no replay was needed as Roy Keane drove in the only goal of the game from the edge of the box.

∞

Three London sides joined Forest in the semi-finals. It was the third time in four years that the penultimate stage of the competition had been reached and, as Tottenham Hotspur met close rivals Arsenal, the Reds went not to Hillsborough, not for a clash with Liverpool, but to Villa

Park where their opponents would be Second Division West Ham United. Speculation in the Press was that 1991 could be Brian Clough's year for the FA Cup glory that had always eluded him. Fate, too, seemed on his side when, after twenty-five inconclusive minutes, referee Keith Hackett showed the red card to Tony Gale for pulling down Gary Crosby. It was the first time a directive to send off the last defender for a professional foul had been applied. Down to ten men, the Hammers were destroyed by Forest's clinical passing on yet another heavy pitch and conceded four second-half goals scored by Crosby, Roy Keane and both raiding full-backs Gary Charles and Stuart Pearce.

Centre-back Steve Chettle said getting to the final for the manager was like lifting 'a monkey off our backs' and, certainly, the side immediately struck a rich seam of goal-scoring form in the league. Chelsea came to Trentside six days after the semi-final and the floodgates opened for Stuart Pearce and Roy Keane to hit two goals each as they were thrashed 7-0. Four days' later Norwich City were given a 5-0 beating. There were birthday celebratory goals for both twenty-one-year-old Lee Glover and twenty-nine-year-old Stuart Pearce. Spurs were held 1-1 in a Cup Final dress rehearsal at White Hart Lane. Then Liverpool were in Nottingham hoping for a victory that would keep them in the running for the First Division title. A 26,000 City Ground crowd saw Crosby shoot as he was brought down by Steve Staunton and the ball hit the back of the net. The referee awarded Forest a penalty instead of a goal. It was calmly converted by Nigel Clough for his fourth goal in four games. Liverpool were given a penalty after the break when Chettle was judged to have fouled Ronnie Rosenthal. It looked a dubious decision and TV replays showed the Forest centre-back had played the ball. Liverpool weren't on level terms for long as Ian Woan chested down a cross and neatly volleyed the winner. 'You're not champions any more!' chanted the Forest fans. The championship would be Arsenal's. The league season ended with a thrilling 4-3 home win against Leeds, for whom former Forester Lee Chapman scored twice to become the top goalscorer with a tally of thirty-one. Parker and Clough got two each for the Reds.

The FA Cup final at Wembley on 18 May was the last game of the season and Forest's sixty-fifth, including ten friendlies. Fourteen league games had been won and twelve lost, earning eighth place. On the day before the final the manager gave his captain his team sheet. Pearce's reaction, he revealed in his autobiography, was that Brian Clough had picked his favourites not the strongest team. Left out were Nigel Jemson, Steve Hodge, Franz Carr and Brian Laws. Jemson, who was in tears when he heard, and Carr didn't even make the substitutes' bench.

Clough wore a rosette proclaiming himself 'the world's greatest grandad' and grabbed Spurs manager Terry Venables by the hand as the squads stepped out of the tunnel together and into the arena. Venables later said Brian had asked to hold his hand because he felt so nervous.

This had been Hodge's impression in the dressing-room. But when the teams were presented to the Princess of Wales before kick-off Clough chatted to her for almost a minute. Later he said he couldn't get Princess Diana out of his mind for the first twenty minutes of the game. That seems incredible since before fifteen minutes had passed a hyped-up Paul Gascoigne had committed what the Forest boss described as 'two despicable fouls'.

Just a couple of minutes after the start, the England star flew into a chest-high tackle on Garry Parker, who went down in a heap. It deserved a red card but referee Roger Milford didn't even produce a yellow when awarding a free-kick. Ten minutes later Gary Charles was the victim of a lunge at the knee. Again Gascoigne escaped punishment apart from giving away another free-kick. Stuart Pearce, though, from twenty-five yards blasted the ball into the top corner of the Tottenham net and turned to the Forest fans with his arms outstretched. It was the captain's sixteenth goal of the season, all from left-back and none from the penalty spot. As Forest celebrated, Gascoigne collapsed in the middle of the field and it became clear that he had hurt himself making the challenge. He was stretchered off and substituted. Clough thought that despite the damage he did to himself Gascoigne should have been red-carded and said that but for the referee 'copping out of his responsibility' the second incident might not have taken place.

Before half-time Forest goalkeeper Mark Crossley brought down Gary Lineker who was attempting to go around him. He then dived to his left to push the Spurs and England striker's penalty away for a corner. Ten minutes into the second-half Paul Allen put Paul Stewart through to equalize with an angled shot past Crossley. It was 1-1 after ninety minutes and while Venables went to encourage his players Clough stayed on the bench, his arms folded. Early in extra-time, the influential Stewart flicked on a Nayam corner from the right and, as Mabbut came charging in on the far post, Des Walker got there first but headed the ball into his own net. It was all over. Forest were like 'the boxer who leaves his hardest punches in the gym', the *Nottingham Evening Post* reported. 'The overwhelming favourites were unrecognisable as the team that had scorched its way through the First Division fixture list over the last month.'

29

Decline and Fall

Four Forest players – Des Walker, Nigel Clough, Gary Charles and Stuart Pearce – went on England's summer tour of Australia, New Zealand and the Far East. Pearce was given the honour of captaining his country for the first time. Back home Brian Clough was pursuing Welsh international striker Dean Saunders but when he decided to join Liverpool instead turned to Millwall's Teddy Sheringham and sealed the deal with a £2 million bid. The newcomer found Forest's training methods of a warm-up and some five-a-sides unusual but went along with his manager's ideas. On a pre-season tour to Sweden he scored five in one game but he would become much more than a stereotypical target man. Clough thought the Reds could mount a reasonable title challenge.

Despite a 4-0 victory against Notts County at Meadow Lane early results were inconsistent. Jemson was signed by Trevor Francis for Sheffield Wednesday for £800,000 and helped them finish third in Division One. Parker joined Aston Villa for £650,000. Forest fell to fourth from bottom by the end of October but victories at home to Coventry and away at Villa were followed by a 5-1 thrashing of Crystal Palace at the City Ground with Sheringham getting a brace. The striker was on the scoresheet with Scot Gemmill and Woan as Arsenal were beaten 3-2 in Nottingham but had a barren spell, failing to get a goal in the next eleven games. He was dropped and Clough sat him on the bench beside him. It was an education, Sheringham acknowledged later. He learned why it was so important for a centre-forward to hold the ball up under pressure rather than trying to flick it on and risk losing possession.

Forest were at their best in cup competitions. Bolton were beaten 4-0 at home and 5-2 away in the two-leg second round of the League Cup and Bristol Rover succumbed 2-0 at the City Ground in the third. It took a replay to dispose of Southampton and another to settle the quarter-final against Crystal Palace but a Sheringham hat-trick in a 5-2 home win took the Reds through to the semi-finals. Wolves, Hereford

United and Bristol City were beaten in the FA Cup but Forest fell to Portsmouth of the Second Division in the sixth round after Crossley dropped a cross from a free-kick to gift the home team the winner.

The first leg of the League Cup semi-final against Tottenham Hotspur was played in driving rain at the City Ground just four days after the quarter-final and Lineker gave the away side the lead from the penalty spot. That award had been disputed and Forest felt they were being robbed when the referee denied them two goals before Sheringham hit the equalizer on the hour. Conditions were no better for the second leg at White Hart Lane and a bomb scare that delayed the kick-off did not improve the mood. An early goal by Lee Glover did, however, until Spurs drew level. A Roy Keane header in front of the Forest support from a Crosby cross took Forest back to Wembley, where Manchester United would provide the opposition. It turned out to be a dull final. Forest missed the injured Pearce and Brian McClair scored the only goal to give United the trophy.

There was Wembley success for the Reds in the ZDS Cup Final, which they had reached with wins over Leeds, Aston Villa and Tranmere Rovers before a two-legged triumph against Leicester in the semi-final. Alan Shearer, Matt Le Tissier and Iain Dowie were in the Southampton line-up for the final but, in front of a 68,000 crowd, Forest went 2-0 ahead through spectacular goals from Scot Gemmill and Kingsley Black. The Saints stormed back to take the game into extra time but Gemmill volleyed the winner past Tim Flowers. Brian Clough had gained a twenty-fifth Manager of the Month award but this was to be his last piece of silverware.

Forest, who again finished eighth in the league, gained a sort of revenge when they dented Manchester United's championship hopes with a 2-1 win at Old Trafford with goals by Woan and Gemmill.

On the 27 May 1992, the First Division clubs who had resigned en masse from the Football League formed the FA Premier League, a limited company administered in an office at Lancaster Gate, then the headquarters of the Football Association. It was viewed by the FA as an opportunity to steal a march over the 104-year-old Football League and by the breakaway clubs as the key to greater television and sponsorship income. Promotion and relegation between the Premier League and the First Division would be unchanged. With the involvement of Sky TV football's elite generated the wealth they dreamed off but to many observers the game lost its soul. And, quite soon, the Football Association lost its influence as in 2007 the FA appellation was dropped and the Premier League became a corporation owned by its twenty member clubs.

Des Walker departed during the summer for Sampdoria, of Genoa, in the Italian Serie A. The England star was never adequately replaced. Both Keane and Nigel Clough were drafted into central defence for spells during the season. Despite the lack of signings, optimism abounded and the *Evening Post* envisaged the prospect of the inaugural Premier League title landing on Trentside. It didn't seem so far-fetched when football's brave new world began with Sky TV cameras and a 20,000 crowd at the City Ground to see Forest humble mighty Liverpool and play like potential champions, especially in a first-half they dominated. A Teddy Sheringham stunner ensured the Merseysiders first opening day defeat for eleven years and another team in red, Manchester United, eventually became the Premiership's first champions – their first title for twenty-five years.

Sheringham played only two more games for Forest before getting his wish to return to London where his young son, Charlie, was living. He joined Tottenham Hotspur for £2.1 million. It was a controversial move on two levels: Forest could ill afford to lose a marksman of his quality – he ended the season as the Premier League's top scorer with twenty-two goals – and the deal was investigated by an independent inquiry into bungs. The case against Clough collapsed for lack of evidence but his assistant, Ron Fenton, was banned from working with an English club again.

At first it appeared the impact of the striker's departure would not be shattering as Gary Bannister, a thirty-two-year-old acquired on a free transfer from West Brom, scored twice on his league debut, a 5-3 defeat at Oldham, after coming on as substitute for Sheringham. He added to his tally at Blackburn Rovers but a 4-1 defeat at Ewood Park was Forest's fifth in a row and left them bottom of the table. 'For the second time in less than a week Forest conceded an early goal, fought their way back to take control of the match and then, in the space of ten crazy second-half minutes, committed defensive suicide,' reported Ian Edwards in the *Evening Post*. Selling their top striker and best central defender was proving destablizing. Chairman Fred Reacher blamed the construction of the Bridgford Road Stand at a cost of £4 million to comply with the post-Hillsborough Taylor Report for lack of spending on players. The stand was opened on 17 October, when nearly 25,000 saw Arsenal win 1-0. Four days later Forest registered their second league win in their twelfth Premiership game when a deflected shot by Kingsley Black saw off Middlesbrough. There were fewer than 18,000 at the City Ground to watch it and Forest remained stuck at the bottom.

Still anchored in the depths, the squad was in need of a boost and at the end of November Clough bought back foraging midfielder Neil Webb from Manchester United for £750,000. He played in the 2-1 home defeat by Southampton, a game notable chiefly for a rare penalty miss by Stuart Pearce saved in the last minute by Tim Flowers. In his second game Webb dictated midfield at Elland Road and prompted Forest to a 4-1 victory against the reigning champions, ending Leeds' thirty-one game unbeaten home record. Roy Keane scored twice with Nigel Clough and Kingsley Black adding the others. 'We thumped them,' Webb recalled. 'And we thought that would be the end of our struggles.' It began to look as though he was right as five wins and two draws were taken from the next ten league games, including a 3-0 thrashing of Chelsea.

For all their problems, the Reds were proving doughty cup fighters. They reached the fifth rounds of both the FA Cup and the League Cup before losing both to Arsenal at Highbury by 2-0 scorelines. It was the FA Cup defeat on 13 February that was to prove disastrous. Webb, who had snapped his right Achillies while with Manchester United, now had trouble with his left and had to be substituted. An operation was found necessary and his season was over. It was also all over for Stuart Pearce, who finished the game but then needed surgery on his groin. Back to back wins against Middlesbrough 2-1 away, with goals by Nigel Clough and Steve Stone on his debut, and Queen's Park Rangers 1-0 at home gave hope briefly but then the Reds won only twice in the last fourteen League games.

∞

On 23 March, two days after his fifty-eighth birthday, Brian Clough was made a Freeman of the City of Nottingham. His decision that month to sign journeyman striker Robert Rosario from Coventry for £400,000 and then to pull out of a £1.75 million deal to take the much fancied Stan Collymore from Southend was enough to convince many Forest fans that the game was up for the club among the elite. They had serenaded him with 'Happy Birthday' at the Leeds game on 21 March and 26,000 hailed him with the chant 'Brian Clough's a football genius' at the City Ground finale against Dave Bassett's Sheffield United, also relegation threatened, on 1 May. United won 2-0, condemning their hosts to the drop, and also won their next two games to ensure their own survival.

At the final whistle Forest fans demonstrated their gratitude to the great man for the good times he brought and the visiting Sheffield fans joined in the acclaim. A distraught young girl approached and presented him with a flower. Taking it from her, he said tenderly, 'Hey, beauty, no tears today please'. To a television reporter who asked 'Brian, can I have a word', he replied, 'Goodbye.'

In an interview with Duncan Hamilton of the *Post*, he admitted that not replacing Sheringham adequately 'was stupid'. He had the money to sign Collymore but, no longer sure about players, 'not the inclination'. Clough also dismissed the prospect of becoming a director or life president of the club. This was not because the club tactlessly precipitated an announcement of his intention to retire at the end of the season but because he did not want to inhibit a successor. Hamilton in his memoir of twenty years with Brian Clough, *Provided You Don't Kiss Me*, recalls Clough saying he tried to line up Archie Gemmill for the vacancy. It was also commonly thought that he had recommended Frank Clark, who was given the job. Judging by comments in *Walking on Water*, Clough's final autobiography, that seems unlikely. He admired the work done by Martin O'Neill like 'a young Clough' at Leicester with John Robertson as his assistant – 'Martin O'Neill and John Robertson, the academic and the scruff, chalk and cheese, just like Peter Taylor and me.' O'Neill turned down an opportunity to replace his mentor. Of Clark, Clough wrote, 'Team management just wasn't in him as far as I could see.'

Family resentment about the abrupt disclosure of Brian Clough's departure led to Nigel Clough leaving Nottingham for Liverpool in June for £2 million. Despite this, they remained on good terms with Chairman Reacher and Christmas cards continued to be exchanged even after Brian Clough's death. Nigel, the 'No. 9', was one of the best Forest centre-forwards, making 412 appearances and scoring 131 goals. He gained 14 senior England caps and played in 15 Under-21 matches. Speed of thought made up for lack of pace, and he soaked up any number of physical challenges from behind as he received and shielded the ball before setting up team-mates. Showing such courage, the fact that he was the manager's mattered little.

Brian Clough said,

> I was secretly chuffed that our Nige signed with Forest [...] I constructed the team around him to get the best out of him and it worked, not only for the team but for individuals within it. Stuart Pearce said to me on one of those occasions when he was accusing me of being too hard on the lad, 'I wouldn't be half the player I am without your Nige in the side – and I play left-back.' Even Teddy Sheringham, with whom I didn't get on that well, told me after that one full season of his, 'I've scored twenty-odd goals this year but without your Nige in the side, I wouldn't have got ten.' Oh yes, the players knew he had talent.

Clough the Younger also played for Manchester City and became first player-manager and then manager of Burton Albion before taking over at Derby. Defeat by Forest in front of 28,000 on Trentside at the end of September 2013, thanks to Jack Hobbs heading in a wicked inswinging corner from the brilliant Andy Reid, led to a sacking that evening that shocked both sets of supporters. Before the weekend was out, a short-lived manager of the Reds, Steve McClaren, had replaced him. Nigel was soon back at work in charge of Sheffield United.

Another Forest favourite to leave during the summer of 1993 was the redoubtable Royston Maurice Keane who cost Manchester United £3.75 million and proved a bargain at that. 'Roy Keane is – and was for me – the genuine article,' Brian Clough wrote in *Walking on Water*. 'I never remember him giving an ounce less than his utmost, his absolute maximum, in a Forest shirt.' Keane 'shone like a beacon through all the gloom' of his manager's last 'desolate season'. He played forty games and scored six goals although 'the way we performed, he had to spend most of his time defending'. Sir Alex Ferguson couldn't have made a better signing at Old Trafford than Keano, Clough declared.

On one occasion after training the manager burst into the dressing room and shouted insults at his players in turn, even Pearce was told 'You've been crap since you got that new contract.' Jemson was told to 'stop rabbiting to refs'. There was a different put-down for each player until, finally, he got to Keane. 'I love you, Irishman,' he said. The affection was mutual. In his latest autiobiography, *The Second Half*, written with award-winning author Roddy Doyle, Keane says he worked under two great managers, Brian Clough and Alex Ferguson, and he puts his Forest manager ahead of the United boss because 'his warmth was genuine'. And, he comments, 'He hit me once, and I thought, "I know why you punched me." I got him – I just got him.' Clough was denied the opportunity to manage at international level. What would he have thought when O'Neill as manager of the Republic of Ireland appointed Keane as his assistant?

David Goldblatt in his social history *The Game of Our Lives*, published in 2014, comments,

> Clough never created an empire in the same way [as Bill Shankly at Liverpool] but winning consecutive European Cups with Nottingham Forest – a club from perhaps England's eighth largest city – was an unrepeatable, demograph-defying achievement. Shankly and Clough were linguistically brilliant. Shankly was more gnomic but sardonic, sharp and funny. Clough, who helped invent the very notion of a television football pundit, was garrulous and could be cruel and arrogant. In the end, they were killed by the same slow horrors that took so many men of their class and generation; Shankly by the pointless empty boredom of life after work, Clough by the bottle.

American academic Harold Bloom credited William Shakespeare with 'The Invention of the Human' through Hamlet's charisma, Falstaff's wit, Henry V's ruthlessness, Prospero's magic and Lear's redemption. Asked to describe Clough's character in one word, one might reply: Shakespearian.

30

Europe Again

Charged with the gigantic task of replacing a living legend and restoring the club to the Premier League, Frank Clark, who had been manager and then managing director of Leyton Orient, began during the summer of 1993 to correct the decisions that Brian Clough possibly got wrong in the relegation season. Nigel Clough, Roy Keane and full-back Gary Charles had left but their departures had given Clark almost £7 million for new signings. He brought in Collymore for more than £2 million and central defender Colin Cooper from Middlesbrough for £1.7 million, both of whom his predecessor had tried to sign but baulked at the fees. Clark also quickly gave Stuart Pearce a new contract.

Des Lyttle came in from Swansea to replace Charles at full-back and Welsh international midfielder David Phillips arrived from Norwich City before the season kicked-off. Just as important, Clark gave a start on the right wing to Steve Stone, who had been signed as a schoolboy in 1987 and took his chance so successfully that he missed only one game all season. Tonsillitis kept Collymore out of the opening First Division match away to his former club, Southend United. It was a televised draw. By the end of September Forest were nineteenth in the table and looking unlikely promotion candidates. Then, in November, Clark made another astute signing: Norwegian international Lars Bohinen from Young Boys of Berne, Switzerland, for £450,000. Bohinen was the midfield inspiration on his debut, a 2-0 victory at West Bromwich, where Collymore got both goals and was equally outstanding. Now the Reds were on song and they moved up to sixth after an unbeaten run of thirteen games.

Notts County put a stop to it at Meadow Lane in the middle of February but the Reds bounced back with only two defeats in their remaining eighteen games to regain Premiership status at first time of asking as runners-up, seven points behind champions Crystal Palace but nine ahead of third-placed Millwall. Promotion was clinched on 30 April at Peterborough, where the Reds fought back from two goals down. Collymore and Pearce, with a brave header, brought them level before the striker belted in a dramatic long-range winner. Stan the Man had contributed 19 goals despite missing no fewer than eighteen matches through illness or injury but it had been a remarkable team effort with Phillips voted Forest's Player of the Season. Pineapple-head centre-forward Jason Lee, signed from Southend for £200,000, came into the side for thirteen of the last fifteen League games only one of which was lost.

Canny Clark had confidence in his squad and made only one new signing in readiness for the Premiership campaign but it was a big one and gave the whole city a buzz. Former Ajaz Amsterdam forward Bryan Roy, a twenty-four-year-old with more than thirty international caps, was playing for Holland in the World Cup Finals in the United States when his £2.9 million record signing from Italian club Foggia was announced. 'There is no doubt about Bryan being a world-class player and the fact that he has agreed to join us is a remarkable coup on our part,' declared the Reds' manager. Roy made an immediate impact driving in the only goal from 25 yards on opening day at Portman Road, Ipswich. Collymore was an absentee but made a scoring return in the next match, a 1-1 draw with Manchester United at the City Ground.

The strike pair led the way as Forest made a great start, going fourteen League and Cup games unbeaten and establishing themselves in second place in the table behind Newcastle United. Collymore had knocked in eight goals and Roy six. After a slump in November, they returned to form with the 4-1 thrashing of Ipswich at the City Ground on 10 December and a week later a 2-1 victory at Old Trafford, where Manchester United had won all nine home games until then without conceding a goal. Collymore put paid to that record with a first-half piledriver and then Pearce got on the scoresheet for the third match running. United's reply came from Eric Cantona.

After a 1-0 defeat by Arsenal at Highbury on 21 February, Forest went unbeaten in their remaining thirteen League games, winning nine of them including the 7-1 hammering of Sheffield Wednesday, managed by Reds' European Cup hero Trevor Francis, at Hillsborough, where Collymore and Roy got a brace each and Pearce, Bohinen and Woan also scored. It took Forest to a third-place finish behind champions Blackburn Rovers and Manchester United, with the bonus of a return to European competition. Collymore scored twenty-five goals in all matches and Roy notched fourteen. Stuart Pearce scored ten from full-back. And, hearteningly, Stone, who had three times recovered from broken legs, was the Forest fans' Player of the Year. He would go on to gain nine caps for England.

∞

Just when it seemed the glory days were returning for the Reds there came a body blow with Stan Collymore, after two amazing seasons in Nottingham, insisting on a move to Liverpool. In return, Forest received a then British transfer record fee of £8.5 million. Powerful striker Kevin Campbell was recruited from Arsenal for £3 million and £2.5 million was spent on Sheffield Wednesday's midfielder Chris Bart-Williams. The third big signing of the summer was twenty-nine-year-old 6 feet 3 inches striker Andrea Silenzi, who cost £1.8 million from Torino and had played alongside Maradona and Gianfranco Zola for Napoli. He was the first Italian international (capped once) to play for an English club but proved a huge and expensive disappointment. He made only seven full appearances and scored twice, in cup-ties against Oxford United and Bradford City, before being released in 1997.

Matt Le Tissier scored a hat-trick for Southampton at The Dell but Bryan Roy struck two for Forest who won the opening day Premiership game 4-3. Bohinen invoked a clause in his contract that allowed him to leave and in October moved to Blackburn Rovers for £700,000. Inevitably, he starred for Rovers at Ewood Park on 18 November when the Reds' twelve-game unbeaten start was ended emphatically with a 7-0 defeat, Bohinen scoring twice and Alan Shearer hitting a hat-trick. Taken with the fine finish to the previous season, Forest had set a Premier League record of twenty-five games without defeat.

Another old boy, Stan Collymore, helped Liverpool with a goal and three assists to pull back from 2-0 down after seventeen minutes to beat his former team 4-2 at Anfield on New Year's Day. A hostile crowd of more than 29,000 awaited him at the City Ground on 23 March when Steve Stone scored the only goal. Collymore, a former favourite and now the target of abuse, was visibly shaken and was withdrawn. There was no revenge for the Reds when Blackburn Rovers came visiting in the middle of April and there was only a Woan goal in reply as five were conceded. At the end of the month Manchester United won 5-0 at Old Trafford and, although Queen's Park Rangers, were beaten 3-0 at home on the final day, Forest ended in ninth place.

The Reds had a notable FA Cup campaign reaching the fifth round after replays against Stoke City and Oxford United. Then when Spurs came to the City Ground on 19 February a blizzard blew up and the match had to be abandoned. Nine days later Ian Woan scored with two blistering free-kicks but the match was again drawn. The replay at White Hart Lane ended 1-1 and went to penalties. Mark Crossley brilliantly saved from three and Forest won the shoot-out 3-1. Former Red Franz Carr got the only goal as Aston Villa won the quarter-final at the City Ground.

Being back in Europe was the highlight of the season. In the first round of the European Cup, Forest faced Malmo, whom they had beaten in the 1979 final. They lost 2-1 in Sweden but at the City Ground a stunning left-footer from Bryan Roy gave them the 1-0 win that took them through.

Stone scored the only goal of a defence-dominated two-leg second round tie against Auxerre and next another French side, Olympique Lyon, suffered a similar fate. Liverpool-born Paul McGregor, who later formed his own pop group, scored the only goal at the City Ground knocking in the rebound after a Pearce penalty had been saved. The away tie was goal-less.

Forest, now the last English team left in European competitions, met star-studded Germans Bayern Munich in the quarter-finals. After another impressive defensive display and with a potentially valuable away goal by Steve Chettle, the Reds returned to the City Ground knowing that a 1-0 home win would be enough to put them in the semis. Having conceded only four goals in seven UEFA Cup matches, optimism was high among the near 29,000 crowd at the City Ground. But the previously reliable defence now let in five in one match with Jurgen Klinsmann getting two. Stone pulled one back for Forest.

With the Trent End rebuilt to seat 7,500, the City Ground, which could now seat the 30,000 minimum EUFA requirement, was chosen to stage three matches, involving Croatia, Portugal and Turkey, for Euro '96, the European Championship. Impressive displays during the competition persuaded Frank Clark to splash £1 million on Croatian international sweeper Nikola Jerkan from Real Oviedo in July. He disappointed and left for Rapid Vienna after just a season and fourteen appearances. Even more expensive was Welsh international striker Dean Saunders, earlier wanted by Brian Clough, who came from Galatasary of Istanbul for £1.5 million during the same month. Both played in the first Premiership match of the 1996/97 season at Coventry, where Kevin Campbell scored a hat-trick in the Reds 3-0 triumph. Unfortunately, troubled by back problems, the striker got only three more league goals all season.

Forest were not to win in the Premiership again until 21 December when 27,000 at the City Ground saw Norwegian international midfielder Alf-Inge Haaland score twice as Arsenal were beaten 2-1. Clark though had resigned after a 4-2 defeat by Liverpool at Anfield a week earlier. It was Forest's sixteenth game without a win, an unwanted Premiership record, and left them trailing by three points at the foot of the table. Frank Clark felt he had no choice but to resign and club chairman Irving Korn asked Stuart Pearce to take over as caretaker-manager. Pearce, still playing for club and country, brought back Nigel Clough on loan from Manchester City and a Boxing Day crowd of 29,000 turned up to see them both in the side against Manchester United. The visitors won 4-0 but Forest had three wins and a draw in their next four league matches. They also beat Ipswich and Newcastle in the FA Cup before going down in the Fifth Round to a 1-0 defeat at Chesterfield on 15 February. Pearce had been named Manager of the Month in January after five successive league and cup wins.

∞

By now Forest were £11 million in debt – not a worrying amount for wealthy Premiership clubs like Manchester United – but a serious concern to seven elected directors who represented 209 £1 shareholders (formerly members) of what was still thought of as a 'club'. Rumours were rife that 'Forest was up for sale' and this was confirmed for one shareholder, Michael Forman, grandson of the great Frank Forman, when a parcel arrived by courier containing a video from entrepreneur Grant Bovey fronted by TV presenter Anthea Turner. Bovey offered to buy each shareholder's £1 share for £10,000. A presentation over lunch at Claridges in London helped to impress the board.

This alerted Nottingham-born publishing executive Philip Soar, a livelong Forest fan. He had formed a bidding group, the Bridgford Consortium, with Irving Scholar, who had floated Tottenham Hotspur on the stock market, and, eventually, Nigel Wray, a property tycoon who owned Saracens rugby clulb. They valued each £1 share at £15,000. But at first the board agreed to recommend a third bid by a consortium led by Sandy Anderson, a former Partick Thistle footballer who had made his fortune at the time of rail privatization. His Nottingham Consortium included Newark-born venture capitalist Nigel Doughty, a Reds' fan from boyhood. Most supporters were also behind Anderson, who would refinance the club but believed shareholders, instead of being paid up front, should only share in its success. But the Nottingham bid failed to get 75 per cent of the shareholders' vote required by the club's articles of association. 'Personal greed' was to blame according to Michael Forman, who supported Anderson's bid. Forest fans were outraged. Despite a short-lived intervention by a group led by American Pulitzer Prize-winning journalist Albert Scardino, shareholders voted on 24 February by 189 votes to seven in favour of the Bridgford Consortium.

The new owners hired Dave Bassett as general manager, Stuart Pearce remained as caretaker but Nigel Clough returned to Manchester City. Saunders scored the only goal against Tottenham at White Hart Lane on 1 March but Forest did not win any of their last eleven Premiership games to finish five points adrift at the foot of the table. Bassett took over as manager on 11 May immediately after a 5-0 defeat at Newcastle whom Pearce then joined on a free transfer. Roy also left, moving to Hertha Berlin.

Bassett's was not at first a popular appointment but he replaced one Dutchman with another, signing Pierre Van Hooijdonk from Glasgow Celtic for a then club record £4.5 million (including £1 million on goals scored) to form with a rejuvenated Kevin Campbell the most prolific strike partnership in the country. Van Hooijdonk scored thirty-four goals and Campbell twenty-third in all competitions and the duo fired Forest as First Division champions back into the Premiership at first attempt. Standing 6 feet 4 inches tall and weighing more than 13 stone, Van Hooijdonk was a formidable figure on the field and had a ferocious free-kick from up to forty yards.

The season's best victory was against Middlesbrough in front of a 25,000 City Ground crowd on 1 March. Both sides had been relegated from the Premiership in the previous season and were battling to return to the top flight. Hooijdonk scored twice and there was a goal each from Campbell and skipper Colin Cooper as Forest won 4-0 to replace their visitors as First Division leaders. Alan Rogers, who took over the left-back spot from Pearce, made the most appearances, fifty-one, Des Lyttle was also a regular in the other full-back position, Jon Olav Hjelde, Steve Chettle and Cooper shared centre-back duties and Steve Stone, Chris Bart-Williams, Andy Johnson and Ian Woan were prominent in midfield.

Forest's 1998/99 Premiership season was a disaster even before it kicked off. Campbell was sold to Turkish side Trabzonspor in July for £2.5 million and Van Hooijdonk went on strike in protest. In August Colin Cooper went to Middlesbrough, who had been promoted as runners-up, for a similar fee. Midfielder Nigel Quashie was signed from Queen's Park Rangers for £2.5 million, Dougie Freedman joined from Wolves for £950,000 and in September Neil Shipperley arrived from Crystal Palace for £1.5 million. But by the time the Dutch striker returned to Trentside in mid-November, the Reds were already among the strugglers and at the turn of the year Bassett was sacked. He was replaced on 11 January by Ron Atkinson, who within a few days paid Southampton £1.1 million for midfielder Carlton Palmer. With just seven wins and thirty points all season, the Reds never looked like beating the drop. They finished at the foot of the table five points behind Blackburn Rovers in nineteenth place having scored only 35 goals from thirty-eight matches and, with 69 conceded, a goal difference of minus thirty-four.

Van Hooijdonk scored only six times all season, including the only goal against Everton at Goodison Park in a rare victory. A week later Manchester United and a 30,000 crowd came to the City Ground but it was a bad day for the Nottingham Reds. David Beckham's passing accuracy destroyed the home defence and Ole Gunnar Solskjaer 'the baby-faced assassin' plundered four goals after coming on as substitute with eighteen minutes to go. It was the superb Beckham though who got the 'man of the match' honour. The win at Goodison Park was the highlight of Atkinson's ill-fated tenure.

31

The Doughty Years

Relegation also led to the break-up of the Bridgford Consortium, which had been no more successful in running the club than the former committee members who had been condescendingly described as 'charming amateurs.' Nigel Wray quit as Forest chairman on 13 April, three days after an away defeat at Derby, and Eric Barnes, chairman of Nottingham-based Experian, one of the world's largest consumer credit information companies, was appointed as his successor. 'I have been a supporter for forty years and think and feel like a fan,' he said on taking office. His aim, he added, was 'to put the Nottingham back into Nottingham Forest'. And the key strategy was to bring in Nigel Doughty.

Born on 10 June 1957, on Hawtonville council estate at Newark, Nigel Doughty first watched Nottingham Forest as a six-year-old going to matches with his father. He left Magnus Church of England School, Newark, after taking O-levels and completed an MBA at Cranfield University School of Management, Bedfordshire, before joining Standard Chartered Bank, with whom he became a founding member of a management buy-out unit. His rise to riches continued when with Richard Hanson he co-founded Doughty Hanson, a private equity firm with global reach.

In July the board of the consortium's Nottingham Forest PLC agreed to an investment of £6 million by Nigel Doughty directly into the company's subsidiary, Nottingham Forest Football Club. Essentially, this meant that he was allowed to invest in the football club without compensationg PLC shareholders, some of whom where Forest fans who had accepted the consortium's invitation to own part of the club they supported. At this stage Irving Scholar had left the board but Philip Soar remained as chief executive. The total debt as at 31 May, 1999, was £5.36 million, including the bond for the Trent End Stand with a capital value of £4.3 million. The stock market flotation had failed to raise anticipated funds but the club was not in financial meltdown as was sometimes suggested.

Doughty appointed Tim Farr and Neil Candeland as his representatives on the football club board and oversaw the appointment of a new manager, David Platt, a highly-regarded England international midfielder who had played for Aston Villa, Arsenal and Italian clubs Bari, Juventus and Sampdoria but, crucially, was without experience of management. Platt's enthusiasm for all things Italian, its language, food and culture, unfortunately got the better of him when in August he brought Moreno Mannini, Salvatore Matrecano and Gianluca Petrachi to Trentside. Full-back Matrecano and winger Petrachi came from Perugia for £1.2 million each and they made fewer than 30 appearances between them. Mannini, a veteran international centre-back who had played with Platt at Sampdoria, struggled with the pace of the English game and played only nine games before announcing his retirement. Trinidadian striker Stern John joined in November from Columbus Crew of the USA for £1.5 million and the tyro manager also spent substantial fees on versatile defender Ricardo Scimeca from Aston Villa and Canadian full-back Jim Brennan from Bristol City.

Striker Ian Wright came in on a two-month loan from Arsenal at the end of August and scored five goals in ten appearances but the expected push for an immediate return to the Premier League was disappearing into mid-table obscurity. A further £300,000 was spent in January for a Forest favourite never-say-die attacker Jack Lester from Doncaster Rovers. Scottish international centre-half Colin Calderwood, who had started his professional career at Mansfield Town, was signed from Spurs in March for £70,000 but made only six appearances because of injury. He played once more in 2000/01 but was forced to retire at the end of that season. Full-back Alan Rogers was joint top scorer with Dougie Freedman on nine goals and Forest ended up fourteenth in the First Division, twenty points behind even a play-off place.

A notable loan signing in April had been that of a young centre-back named John Terry from Chelsea. Terry made five full appearances and one as a substitute and impressed everyone at the City Ground but there was no way the Londoners would sell the player who went on to captain both club and country.

An American who started just fourteen games and made four substitute appearances for Forest during a single season, 2000/01, became such a cult hero at the City Ground that a decade later he was listed seventh on a fans' forum web site themed 500 Reasons to Love Forest. The popularity of Ben Olsen almost made up for the failures of the three Italians. In fact, Ben was here for only three months before a broken ankle ended his loan from DC United of Washington. The injury kept him out of the game for two years and required four surgical operations. But he loved his time on Trentside and, especially the support he got. 'It's really humbling and I can't tell the fans how much that meant to me,' he told me. 'I chose the right club and I had a blast. I was mostly disappointed in that I thought

it was my chance to stay in Europe and play permanently for Forest.'
Ben earned 35 caps, scoring six goals, as a midfielder for the USA and
became the youngest-ever head coach in Major League history when he
took charge of DC United in 2010 at the age of thirty-three. DC United
supporters call themselves 'Olsen's Army.' 'Our fans in Washington have
always been some of the most passionate in Major League Soccer,' Ben
said. With the league expanding – New York City and Orlando City new
franchises – support is growing and becoming more organised. 'I think
people in Europe would be impressed if they came to a MLS game,' he
added. In the opening match of the 2015 Major League season 63,000
saw Orlando City draw 1-1 with New York City in Florida.

The impact of relegation from the Premier League was a big
reduction in revenue, from £17 million to just £9.5 million, lower
gate receipts and television revenues accounting for most of the fall.
To support their new manager, the club had allowed costs to increase
by £1 million to £16.5 million and with additional transfer funds
there had been a £10.5 million loss for the financial year 1999/2000
compared to a £2 million profit the previous year. The losses were
funded by Nigel Doughty's cash investment and by a £5 million
increase in bank borrowing.

With wages rising rapidly and every club desperate to get their hands
on the money pouring into the Premiership, Forest would again gamble
with their finances in 2000/02 but with an improvement only to eleventh
place, they would fall six points short of the play-offs. An increase in
revenue from the ITV Digital television deal helped to reduce cash losses
in the year but heavy investment in the transfer market – most notably
on Ipswich striker David Johnson in January 2001 – saw the club's debts
rise further. Interest payments only had been made on the Trent End bond
over a ten-year period and it remained on the balance sheet at its full
value. The bank overdraft rose to £8.5 million. Crucially the club had
been saddled with a new financial lease relating to funding the Johnson
deal at a capital value of £4.8 million. In just two years the net debt had
more than trebled to £17.9 million.

In the middle of pre-season preparations for 2001/02 David Platt
departed to take charge of England's Under-21 squad. In two seasons
under his management, the club had made total losses on football
operations of £9.34 million and further losses on transfer fees of £6.45
million – £152,000 a week. In a change of direction, Nigel Doughty
turned to academy director and former player Paul Hart who was briefed
to focus on his own young prodigies and bring finances under control. It
started well. Costs were reduced and the first team was rebuilt round
an exciting generation of young players but the high costs of servicing
club debts was taking it toll and disaster was looming with the collapse
of the Football League's ITV Digital deal, which would blow a hole in
the revenue plans of all First Division clubs. The sad thing is that, in

retrospect, this period was arguably the highlight of Nigel Doughty's ownership but the opportunity to build a fulfilling future based on the productive academy was lost in a crisis of confidence.

David Prutton had been the first significant member of Hart's academy to step up to the first team under Platt's management. By the time Hart took the manager's job himself, Prutton was established and there were others beginning to make their way through to join him. Hart ensured that many of them played significant roles in his first season. Prutton and Gareth Williams each made more than forty league starts in midfield while meaningful appearances were contributed by Jermaine Jenas, Andy Reid, Eugen Bopp, Chris Doig and John Thompson. The team finished sixteenth in the First Division but the foundations had been laid for a season to remember.

Financial stability had benefited from the sale of Jenas, after just 33 appearances, to Newcastle United in February for £5 million. By May 2002 the club's net debt was £18.7 million dominated by an overdraft of more than £10million and that expensive Johnson transfer lease. At this point Nigel Doughty made the final moves in his takeover making the overall cost of his purchase of the football club £11 million plus an inherited £5.4 million debt.

For 2002/03 Hart blended the best of Forest's new breed from the academy with a legend from the past: Des Walker returned to the City Ground ten years after leaving for Sampdoria. He was joined at the heart of the defence by Michael Dawson, the youngest of three brothers to represent the club. Marlon Harewood, another home-grown player, combined with David Johnson to score 45 league goals as Forest once again dreamed of a top flight future. When Nottingham-born David Huckerby arrived on loan from Manchester City to score five goals in the last nine league games of the season, including one in a memorable 3-0 victory over Derby in front of nearly 30,000 at the City Ground in March, the stage seemed set.

Play-off rivals Ipswich were beaten in a seven-goal thriller at Portman Road on 5 April. *The Guardian* report was headlined, 'Forest Kids Growing Up Fast'. Sean Ingle wrote,

> You feared for them. You really did, after twenty-six minutes, Forest's pugnacious young gunslingers were suffering and seething: a contentious retaken penalty had already put Ipswich two goals ahead and a rout looked on the cards. And then something remarkable occurred. Forest launched a counter-attack of punkish vigour and verve, scored three goals in six minutes and, after matching Ipswich blow-for-blow in a ferocious second half, clung on for a deserved win.

Marlon Harewood scored twice, including heading home the winner after the home side had equalized on the hour. Despite failing to win any of their next four games, the Reds recovered to claim sixth-place four points in front of the East Anglians.

A crowd of 29,064 watched as third-placed Sheffield United earned a 1-1 draw in the play-off semi-final first leg on Trentside to set up a Bramall Lane tie that at the final whistle had the Blades' manager Neil Warnock raving, 'It must have been fantastic to watch and people will talk about this match for years to come.' Jeremy Cross, reporting for *The Guardian*, wrote,

> Those not in favour of the play-offs should close the page now to avoid the details of an extraordinary contest here last night in which Sheffield United staged a stunning comeback to book a date with Wolves in the final at Cardiff's Millennium Stadium on May 26.
>
> This was a night that will live long in the memory of both clubs and their managers. Nottingham Forest's Paul Hart will be haunted through the summer wondering how his team scored three goals away from home but still finished the losers, sacrificing a two-goal lead with half an hour left. Neil Warnock, on the other hand, was left pinching himself at how his brave side snatched victory from the jaws of defeat.

David Johnson, with his twenty-ninth goal of the season, and Andy Reid scored either side of half-time to put Forest in a commanding position. Goals from Michael Brown and Steve Kabba forced extra time. Then Paul Peschisolido came off the substitutes' bench to put United in front on 112 minutes but even that was not the end. Des Walker, in a devastating repeat of the 1991 FA Cup Final, headed into his own goal only for Robert Page at the other end to turn Jon-Olav Hjelde's cross into his own net. There were five more minutes of almost unbearable tension before it finished 4-3. As the tears told, Forest's moment had gone.

∞

There was a promising start to the 2003/04 season with five wins from the first seven First Division games. Having cleared out thirteen players from the senior squad and replaced them with just a handful of free transfer recruits, Hart was allowed to bring in Welsh international striker Gareth Taylor from Burnley for £500,000 in September but this was offset by the sale for a similar fee of Marlon Harewood to West Ham United. Another six-footer, Marlon King, was signed from Gillingham for £950,000 as Harewood's replacement and made his debut at the beginning of December. But the Reds had failed to record a win in the last fourteen league games and had gone two months without even scoring a goal, when Hart was sacked after a 1-0 home defeat by Coventry City on 7 February.

Former Wimbledon manager Joe Kinnear, who was out of work after being dismissed along with his assistant Mick Harford by new owners of Luton Town, was an unpopular choice as Hart's successor. Forest fans feared that 'route one' tactics would now be employed, forgetting that Kinnear, a Republic of Ireland international, had learned his trade as a young full-back under the managership of Bill Nicholson at Tottenham and had spent ten years with Spurs making 196 appearances. Kinnear changed the system from a 'diamond' midfield to a straight-forward 4-4-2 formation. It worked and Forest lost only twice in the final nineteen Division One games to finish safely in fourteenth place. David Johnson returned from injury after a lengthy absence to score five times in the last four games, a draw with Millwall at the City Ground followed by impressive wins away to Ipswich and West Bromwich Albion and at home against Wigan Athletic. Nigel Doughty said that his only regret was not appointing Kinnear in the first place.

Talk was of mounting a promotion challenge as Forest embarked on a pre-season tour to the United States playing games against DC United of Washington and in Richmond, where the club's sponsors Capital One had their international headquarters. It was an unhappy trip and the players were not impressed by the facilities provided. Disillusion set in as the Reds went nine games before their first league win at the end of September, when West Ham were beaten 2-1 in front of a City Ground crowd of nearly 26,000. After just four wins in the first twenty-three First Division games and following a 3-0 loss at Derby on 11 December, Forest were just two places off the bottom of the table and Kinnear handed in his resignation. His assistant Mick Harford briefly took charge but achieved only a single win in five games. Gary Megson was given the job in early January but was unable to halt the slide and the club slipped into the third tier of English football for the first time in more than half a century. The Reds were the only team ever to win the European Cup and then drop so far down their national leagues.

Michael Dawson and Andy Reid had gone to Tottenham for a combined fee of £8 million but Megson had signed a host of experienced pros, many of whom seemed past their best, and then in January he had spent big again to add some younger, lower league players in Nathan Tyson, Grant Holt, Sammy Clingan and Julian Bennett. Less than a month after this transfer spree he had been replaced by the caretaker duopoly of Frank Barlow and Ian 'Charlie' McParland. Forest were perilously close to the relegation zone but the pair worked a transformation and took that same squad to within two points of the play-offs, losing just once in thirteen games to the end of the season. Megson had been signed as a defensive midfielder by Brian Clough in the summer of 1984 but spent only five months at the City Ground before leaving for Newcastle United without making a single first-team appearance. He lasted just a year as manager.

In the summer Colin Calderwood returned to the City Ground this time as a young up-and-coming manager who had seen some success at Northampton. He reorganized the squad reducing the wage bill by replacing ageing seniors with younger players at Forest's level. With turnover down, the club continued to lose money but the underlying position was much healthier. Football losses in the two years it took Calderwood to deliver promotion back to the Championship – losing to Yeovil in the play-offs in his first season before securing automatic promotion in his second – were the same as a single year under Megson in the same division.

Two Yeovil stars, midfielder Chris Cohen and winger Arron Davies, were signed during the summer of 2007 and former Notts centre-back Kelvin Wilson came from Preston North End for £300,000. Forest started the 2007/08 campaign disappointingly and had to wait to their fifth match before getting a win on 15 September at Port Vale. They lost only twice in the next fourteen games and went top of the league on 22 December after beating Port Vale 2-0 in front of a crowd of 21,407 at the City Ground. The scorers were striker Junior Agogo, who was to finish top marksman with thirteen goals, and a young, promising midfielder named Lewis McGugan.

Away form proved a problem and the Reds found themselves eleven points short of automatic promotion before winning six of their last seven games and clinching second place on a dramatic last day by beating Yeovil 3-2 to give 28,500 fans a City Ground celebration. McGugan, Julian Bennett and Mansfield-born winger Kris Commons, playing his last game before departing on a 'Bosnan' for Derby, were the Forest scorers. Bennett and Commons were selected for the PFA League One team of the year while goalkeeper Paul Smith received the Puma Golden Glove award after achieved a league record twenty-four clean sheets in forty-six games.

Having built a successful First Division squad by picking up lower league talent on lower wages, the wallet was opened again to make a marquee signing in Welsh international striker Robert Earnshaw from Derby for close to £3 million on a three-year deal. French midfielder Guy Moussi came in and Carlisle striker Joe Garner joined for £1.14 million. Grant Holt, Sammy Clingan and Junior Agogo were among those departing.

A run of poor form saw Forest propping up the Championship until their first win in ten games at Crystal Palace at the end of October gave them a lift before going to Pride Park to meet Derby for the first competitive fixture in more than three years and amid media speculation about Calderwood's future. It was an incident-packed encounter with the Rams' Emanuel Villa scoring at both ends, McGugan red-carded and Lee Camp saving a ninety-third minute penalty to deny his former club. Calderwood commented that the save would go down in Forest folklore.

Bottom-of-the-table Doncaster Rovers came to the City Ground on Boxing Day and a 26,500 crowd saw Forest 4-0 behind within an hour and down to ten men after Julian Bennett suffered a career-threatening cruciate ligament injury with all the substitutions made.

The Reds replied with two late goals but, immediately after the game, the board terminated manager Calderwood's contract after two and a half years in charge. Reserve team manager John Pemberton took caretaker charge for the next game and Forest won 3-2 at Norwich to climb out of the relegation zone for the first time in three months.

∞

On New Year's Day Billy Davies was named as Forest manager with David Kelly as his assistant. Pemberton took the team to Manchester City for the third round of the FA Cup on 3rd January and supervised an outstanding performance in front of the television cameras as the Premiership side were beaten 3-0 with goals from Tyson, Earnshaw and Garner. An Earnshaw goal in a 1-1 draw at Pride Park earned the Reds a fourth round replay but Davies' side were beaten 3-2 in front of a 29,000 crowd at the City Ground to go out of the Cup. Loan striker Dexter Blackstock's goal in the penultimate league game gave Forest a vital point at Blackpool and another 29,000 crowd saw goals from Garner, Chambers and Earnshaw, all in the last fifteen minutes, give them a 3-1 home victory against already relegated Southampton to escape the drop, securing nineteenth place just behind rivals Derby. It was a narrow escape but an achievement Davies hailed as the best of his career.

Any thoughts of sustainability that may have existed in the boardroom were cast off and the financial floodgates were opened as Davies invested heavily during the summer of 2009. In came full-back Chris Gunter from Spurs for £1.75 million, Southampton forward David McGoldrick £1 million, midfielder Paul McKenna from Preston £750,000, Paul Anderson, a young winger from Liverpool, for £200,000 along with goalkeeper Lee Camp and Blackstock from Queen's Park Rangers, Joel Lynch of Brighton, and Dele Adebola from Bristol City. Radoslaw Majewski joined on a season-long loan from Polonia Warsaw.

After gaining just two points from their first four games, Forest faced Derby at the City Ground at the end of August seeking to beat the Rams for the first time in seven years. Watched by a crowd of 28,000, they got off to a great start, Majewski firing them in front after only fifty-eight seconds. Blackstock made it 2-0 in the twenty-eighth minute and Tyson got a third three minutes before half-time. The visitors fought back after the interval. Wes Morgan put through his own goal and then Jake Livermore made it 3-2 but the Reds held on for an important victory. Tyson celebrated by parading a corner flag emblazoned with the Forest badge in front of the away fans at the Bridgford End. He claimed he was running towards the home supporters in the Brian Clough Stand but the incident caused the players and staff of both sides to clash. The clubs were charged by the FA with 'failing to control their players'. Forest were fined £25,000, Derby £20,000 and Tyson got a £5,000 fine.

Left-back Nick Shorey joined on loan from Aston Villa in November. Davies wanted more stellar signings in the January transfer window to boost the promotion drive but Doughty was already facing the largest annual loss of his entire ownership and was frustrated by his manager's public criticism. A fourth consecutive 1-0 home victory against Peterborough United on 20 March was enough for Davies to equal Brian Clough's record twelve City Ground wins in a row. The Reds though suffered twelve successive away defeats and lost the final automatic promotion place to West Bromwich but they took the third spot to qualify for the play-offs.

Play-off semi-final opponents were Blackpool, a club with a tiny budget compared to Forest's, who had won home and away in the league and now repeated the feat with a 2-1 victory at Bloomfield Road and 4-3 triumph at the City Ground. Even so, Davies blamed lack of investment in January for the failure of the promotion campaign.

That summer Polonia were paid a £1 million fee for Majewski and exciting young left-back Ryan Bertrand was a short-term loan signing from Chelsea. Forest lost their opening Championship match by the only goal to relegated Burnley at Turf Moor and then had four successive 1-1 draws before Lewis McGugan stole centre stage in his first start of the season hitting a second-half brace as the Reds came from behind to beat Preston 2-1 at Deepdale on 14 September. Jon 'The Beast' Parkin brushed aside Chris Gunter to give the home side the lead three minutes before half-time but Nathan Tyson found McGugan who turned and drove a low left-foot shot that flew into the net from over twenty yards for a sixty-eighth minute equalizer. Now dominating the game, it was no surprise when Forest grabbed the winner in the eighty-first minute. A superb left-wing cross from Chris Cohen was met by midfielder McGugan who smashed an unstoppable shot into the top corner from six yards out.

After a goalless draw at Hull, McGugan was the star of the show again with two more goals as the Reds secured their first home win with a 3-1 success over Brendan Rodgers' Swansea on twenty-fifth September. The midfielder's first came from the penalty spot after Dexter Blackstock had been brought down by goalkeeper Dorus De Vries in the twelfth minute. Good link-up play by Gunter and Cohen created the chance for McGugan to shoot into the roof of the net from twelve yards out early in the second half and then Radoslaw Majewski, who had come on as substitute to replace him, tip-toed past two defenders inside the area to beat De Vries with a low shot with six minutes remaining. A last-minute consolation goal for the Swans did not subdue the celebrating near 20,000 home fans.

McGugan scored his 6th goal in seven games to see off Middlesbrough in front of 22,000 at the City Ground on 19 October with a wicked free-kick and a week later struck a stupendous 35-yard drive on the stroke of half-time to help the Reds gain an impressive 2-0 victory over Ipswich with 22,935 fans on Trentside. Assistant manager David Kelly said the twenty-one-year-old was playing with 'magic in his boots.' Away form was holding back Forest but it was the highly rated midfielder who set them on the way to a notable triumph at Cardiff on 20 November with a twenty-three minute twenty-five-yard strike high into the net. Substitute Blackstock, who had replaced Robert Earnshaw, completed the scoring six minutes from time before succumbing to a serious leg injury that ruled him out for the rest of the season. It was only Forest's second away win of the season and Cardiff's second home defeat. Five days later, on the loan signing deadline, Davies brought in striker Marcus Tudgay from Sheffield Wednesday with a view to a permanent deal and Arsenal's talented youngster Aaron Ramsey until January. They couldn't prevent another away defeat at Leicester.

Because of bad weather Forest played only two games in December but what crackers they turned out to be and both at the City Ground. Tudgay got his first goal for the club as the Reds overran Crystal Palace 3-0 on 18 December. A crowd of 29,490 came to the City Ground on 29 December looking to see the Reds make it thirty consecutive games unbeaten at home. They could not have made a better start. After just two minutes, centre-half Luke Chambers rose above his marker to head Majewski's nicely-flighted right-wing corner past Stephen Bywater in the Derby goal. Then Earnshaw skinned defender Shaun Barker before picking out Marcus Tudgay with a cross the striker met with a header that came off the underside of the bar to cross the line and in first-half added time Tudgay headed home again from a Tyson cross. Pushing forward from the left at every opportunity, Tyson next found Earnshaw with a curling cross hit with the outside of his foot and he turned the ball past Bywater from six yards. Luke Moore had equalized for Derby at 1-1 early in the game and now former Forester Kris Commons made it 4-2, leaving goalkeeper Lee Camp flat-footed with a free-kick fired under the jumping defensive wall. But deep into injury time, Earnshaw emphasized the Reds' superiority with his second and his side's fifth goal. Earnshaw scored again to give Forest a 1-0 victory at Pride Park in January to secure the Reds first double over the Rams, his former club, for twenty-one years.

Hull City ended Forest's eighteen-month unbeaten home run with a Matt Fryatt goal on 5 March and then eleven goals were conceded in three matches against promotion rivals Swansea City, Leeds United and Reading. A brace from David McGoldrick gave them their first win in ten matches and the Reds won their final games against Bristol City, Scunthorpe United and Crystal Palace to claim sixth place and a play-off semi-final against Swansea. The first leg was played at the City Ground, where the visitors went down to ten men early on but still came away with a goal-less draw. Swansea got two goals in quick succession in the first half of the second leg. Earnshaw pulled one back and also struck the post but in stoppage time Lee Camp left his goal to go up for a Forest corner from which the home side broke to make it 3-1.

In the two full seasons that Davies was in charge, Nigel Doughty backed the promotion bid with £24.8 million but when the team once again fell at the play-off semi-final stage the relationship between the two fell apart. Davies demanded even greater investment but Doughty could see his cash investment already standing at £75 million, a third of that handed over in the past two years, bringing him nothing but further grief from all quarters. An irrecoverable rift had opened and it resulted in the manager's departure in June, 2011.

It is possible that the timing of dismissal was driven by the unexpected availability of former England manager Steve McClaren. Having rebuilt his reputation with FC Twente in Holland, McClaren was looking for a return to England but the response of Aston Villa fans to their club's interest led to an embarrassing collapse of that proposed move. Doughty stepped forward and offered him a route back into the English game. It was hailed as an ideal arrangement for both parties but the smiles that were evident at the press conference when the appointment was announced very quickly disappeared. Forest started talking about the constraints of Financial Fair Play while McClaren seemed to be convinced he had been promised substantial transfer funds. Andy Reid returned on a free from Blackpool, midfielder Jonathan Greening was signed for £600,000 from Fulham, striker Matt Derbyshire came from Olympiakos of Athens for an undisclosed fee and West Brom's Ishmael Miller cost £1.2 million. Departures included Adebola, Julian Bennett and Joe Garner. David McGoldrick went on loan to Sheffield Wednesday and Clint Hill was an emergency loan signing from QPR.

McClaren soon seemed to have lost all enthusiasm for the job and at the beginning of October with the club fourth from bottom with 8 points from ten games, he resigned. At the same time, Nigel Doughty announced that he would be stepping down as chairman and took full responsibility for the failure of his manager. Ten days later former player and manager Frank Clark was appointed chairman. He, in turn, brought Steve Cotterill in as manager and between them they endeavoured to reduce the club's costs while retaining its Championship status. With the help of Sean O'Driscoll, appointed as coach later in the season, Forest fought off relegation but the shock death of Nigel Doughty in February 2012 both piled on the turmoil and put the football into perspective. It brought to an end thirteen years of the owner's direct involvement in Forest during which time he spent more than £80 million of his personal fortune chasing an elusive dream of returning to the top flight.

32

The Legacy

Commenting on his resignation in the match programme on 18 October 2011, Doughty said,

> It has been one of the highlights of my life to have chaired the football club I have supported man and boy for almost fifty years. I will not leave the club with a cost-base that will burden it in the next two or three years. Players' contracts signed during my time as chairman will be honoured by me outside the normal cash flows of the club. This will ensure that the club has a breathing space to adapt to a new structure and the Financial Fair Play rules due to be introduced. However, once these current liabilities have run off there will be no more financial support.

Doughty was found dead in the gymnasium at his home in Skillington, Lincolnshire, on 4 February 2012. It was down to Sudden Adult Death Syndrome (SADS). His obituary in *The Guardian* on Tuesday 7 February, was written by Burnley supporter Alistair Campbell, Tony Blair's 'spin doctor'. 'The last time I spoke to him was five days before his death watching Burnley beat his team 2-0,' wrote Campbell. 'He was in Berlin, following the game via the internet. Businessmen round the world were used to Nigel skipping meetings to watch his club.' About his Labour politics, Campbell said, 'Nigel's thinking contributed to the development of arguments about 'responsible capitalism' under Ed Miliband. An assistant treasurer of the Party, Nigel gave it £3.6 million before the last election, and both Tony Blair and Gordon Brown benefited from his advice, ideas and moral support.' His mother, Mercia, had worked as a nurse at Newark hospital and, in her memory, he gave £1 million to help fund a new endoscopy centre and pre-operative assessment unit.

His greatest legacy to Forest was taking ownership and developing for an investment of £2.5 million the international class training ground at Wilford Lane now known as the Nigel Doughty Academy.

Forest had been left in a position of financial uncertainty and had only narrowly avoided relegation to League One. New owners were sought and in July 2012 the Kuwaiti Al Hasawi family reached agreement to purchase the club from the Doughty estate. A holding company was formed with Fawaz Al Hasawi having an 80 per cent and his brother, Abdulaziz Al Hasawi, 20 per cent share.

On 19 July manager Steve Cotterill was sacked and his coach Sean O'Driscoll, who was popular with supporters, was named his successor. Midfielders Adlene Guedioura, who had made a big impact on loan from Wolverhampton Wanderers, and Henri Lansbury of Arsenal were signed for £1 million fees and other recruits included West Bromwich striker Simon Cox and defenders Danny Collins (Stoke City), Greg Halford (Portsmouth) and Dan Harding (Southampton). Sam Hutchinson of Chelsea, Daniel Ayala (Norwich City) and striker Billy Sharp (Southampton) were all signed on season-long loans.

The Reds were firmly among the promotion candidates on Boxing Day with nine wins, nine draws and six defeats when after a 4-2 victory over Leeds United in front of a crowd of 26,670 at the City Ground O'Driscoll was surprisingly dismissed. Former Aston Villa and Birmingham manager Alex McLeish took over the reins the next day. After only one victory and three defeats in six games, he left by mutual agreement on 5 February 2013, paving the way for the regal return of 'King Billy' Davies twenty months after being sacked by Nigel Doughty, who had described him as 'an unreasonable man.' Davies signed a three-and-a-half year deal and took charge of the first match of his second spell on Trentside on 16 February, when there were 24,409 at the City Ground to see the Reds draw 1-1 with Bolton Wanderers.

In a programme note headed 'Kicking off a new chapter', Fawaz, addressing the fans as 'dear friends', said the Davies appointment represented a new start for Forest, adding,

> I've loved Nottingham Forest since I was a young boy and I remember so clearly when the Forest side came over to Kuwait to play [...] the excitement of seeing those great players has always stayed with me. Being chairman of Nottingham Forest is a dream come true.

Between 2010 and 2012, Fawaz had been president of Qadsia SC, one of the largest sporting clubs in Kuwait. His tenure was a successful one, with the club winning two Kuwait Premier League titles and two Emir Cups along with the Federation Cup and the Super Cup. Davies wrote that he had been impressed 'with the enthusiasm, vision and sheer passion to succeed that comes from your chairman Fawaz Al Hasawi'. He added, ominously it turned out, 'I've gone on record many, many times as saying that I have got 'unfinished business' here at the City Ground but I've got 'unfinished relationships' as well.'

Three days later 26,938 on Trentside were thrilled by a Majewski hat-trick as Huddersfield Town were despatched 6-1. Effectively, Forest faced a fifteen-match season under Davies and won six games in a row, including a 2-1 away win at second-placed Hull, to go fifth in the Championship. This form proved unsustainable in the final stretch and defeats at Cardiff and Middlesbrough and on 4 May at home to Leicester left them outside the play-offs in eighth place.

During the summer, forwards Darius Henderson, Jamie Paterson and Djamel Abdoun, midfielder Jamie Mackie, defenders Kelvin Wilson, returning after a successful spell with Glasgow Celtic, Eric Lichaj, Gonzalo Jara and goalkeeper Dorus de Vries were all brought in while Lewis McGugan and David McGoldrick were allowed to leave on free transfers. Centre-back Jack Hobbs was a loan signing from Hull City. The manager's cousin, Jim Price, was employed as an advisor while, controversially, academy coaches and long-serving administrative staff left the club. In September Guedioura was sold to Crystal Palace and young midfielder Nathaniel Chalobah replaced him on loan from Chelsea. January signings included striker Rafik Djebbour, a former Olympiakos team-mate of Abdoun, with defender Danny Fox arriving on loan and midfielder David Vaughan having his loan extended to the end of the season.

Forest had won three of their first four home games and Derby County boasted the same return from their travels when the two fierce rivals faced each other in front of a passionate 28,000 crowd at the City Ground on 28 September. The Reds roused their supporters with fine attacking football as the visitors were restricted to long-range first-half efforts. Majewski turned adroitly and fired a low left-footed shot that was tipped around the post by goalkeeper Lee Grant. Then Eric Lichaj's shot was deflected fractionally over the bar and from the resulting corner by Andy Reid centre-back Jack Hobbs, who had begun his run from the edge of the penalty area, powerfully headed Forest in front. After the break Derby's Richard Keogh was shown a second yellow card after bringing down Chris Cohen. Grant dived low to his right to make an agile save from the penalty kick. So the Brian Clough Trophy, the prize awarded to the winner of the 'derby' match in recognition of the legendary manager of both clubs, came back to the City Ground. For the great man's son, Nigel Clough, who had been in charge of the Rams since January 2009 there was a shock sacking with his team left in fourteenth place in the league table. He had been the longest-serving manager in the Championship. Ironically, he was replaced by Steve McClaren.

Forest went to Derby for the return match on 22 March after a run of six games without a victory and the home side had not scored in four matches but Craig Bryson hit a hat-trick as the Rams secured a record-equalling 5-0 win to revive their promotion hopes. It left Derby third in the Championship as Forest dropped out of the play-off positions to seventh. Bryson's hat-trick was the first for a Derby player in this fixture since the great Steve Bloomer's treble in a victory by the same scoreline in 1898. This time a 'derby' defeat did for a Forest manager. Davies departed two days' later. Fawaz thanked supporters for their 'sensational' backing at Derby and announced that 'with immediate effect any bans imposed on members of the media are lifted.' He promised that the local and national press would have regular access to whoever was appointed as the new manager. Academy chief Gary Brazil was put in temporary charge of the first team and John McGovern was given an influential role as club 'ambassador.' Forest finished eleventh in the Championship.

At the beginning of April the chairman announced that Stuart Pearce had signed a two-year contract and would take over as manager from 1 July. 'Stuart is a Nottingham Forest legend who embodies the passion, fight and desire our supporters expect of this famous football club,' Fawaz said. Pearce commented,

> I was fortunate enough to have six years at Manchester City as both a coach and manager. I also spent six years working with England's Under-21s. I've got good experience at managerial level and I've spent all my time since the age of forty working towards a day like this. I wouldn't have felt fulfilled in my management career if I didn't take the opportunity to walk back through the doors of this great club.

Before officially taking charge, Pearce brought together all members of staff from cleaners to first-teamers and called for unity and a sense of purpose within the club. He appointed former England Under-21 coaches Steve Wigley, Brian Eastick and Tim Flowers to his staff and emphasized the importance of the academy under Gary Brazil. There would be no separation.

Summer signings included striker Matty Fryatt from Hull City, Birmingham winger Chris Burke, stylish former England Under-21 defender Michael Mancienne from Hamburg and formerly from the same club German midfielder Robert Tesche. Goalkeeper Karl Darlow and centre-back Jamaal Lascelles became Newcastle United players but remained at the City Ground on season loans. With the cash from this transfer deal, Peterborough's highly rated young striker Britt Assombalonga and powerful forward Michail Antonio of Sheffield Wednesday were brought in three days before the opening day clash with Blackpool. A crowd of 28,000 on Trentside saw Antonio and Burke score in a 2-0 home win.

Forest began the season brightly and were Championship leaders with a 100 per cent home record when Derby County came to a City Ground packed with more than 30,000 fans on Sunday 14 September. In the tenth minute, rival supporters united were with applause in tribute to former manager Brian Clough, marking the tenth anniversary of his death. Britt

Assombalonga's shot on the turn gave the Reds a seventy-second minute lead, which lasted just eight minutes before Derby full-back Ryan Shotton scrambled the ball over the line to equalize. The visitors played eight minutes of stoppage time with ten men after Jake Buxton was shown a second yellow card for a crude challenge on Chris Burke but held on for a point. The biggest blow for Forest was the loss of skipper Chris Cohen after only fifteen minutes with a knee injury that put him out of action for the remainder of the season. Playmaker Andy Reid also went off after being injured and he, too, became a long-term casualty. Commanding centre-back Jack Hobbs then missed the next nineteen games.

The Reds' unbeaten run came to an end at Tottenham with a 3-1 defeat by Spurs in the Capital One Cup at White Hart Lane on 24 September and the first league loss was by 2-1 at Cardiff in the middle of October. Unsettled by injuries to key players, Forest had won just twice in twenty games in all competitions, including a third round FA Cup exit at Division One Rochdale, when the under-pressure Pearce and his team headed down Brian Clough Way, the A52, on Saturday 17 January to face their greatest rivals Derby County, then the Championship leaders, in a mid-day match televised by Sky. The intense rivalry of the two clubs has its roots as deep in history as the 1898 FA Cup Final, when the unfavoured Reds beat the Rams 3-1. It has been the nemesis of six managers since 2003: John Gregory (Derby), Joe Kinnear (Forest), Steve McClaren (Forest), Alex McLeish (Forest), Nigel Clough (Derby) and Billy Davies (Forest). Pearce was greeted at the iPro Stadium with chants of 'You're getting sacked in the morning' from home fans. But Pearce had spoken with Fawaz the day before and been buoyed by the owner's support. And the Forest fans had been behind him throughout, notably in the defeat by Sheffield Wednesday at the City Ground a week earlier when the crowd almost to a man had 'stood up for Stuart' and applauded him. Now they responded with, 'Stuart Pearce, he's one of our own.'

It did not begin well for Forest. After a quarter of an hour, from a corner the ball had glanced off Henri Lansbury's head into his own goal. What made this worse was that it came shortly after they had been denied a clear penalty when Michail Antonio had been wrestled to the ground by Derby centre-back Jake Buxton. The Reds shrugged aside the injustice and stayed strong to take control after the break. With fifteen minutes remaining, a Ben Osborn free-kick was knocked down to Assombalonga and the striker pounced for the equalizer. Pearce threw his arms aloft in his technical area and punched the air twice. Forest looked the likeliest to grab the winner. And they did. In style. In injury time. Robert Tesche played the ball into the path of Osborn and the youngster rounded off a penetrating run with a majestically struck winner that had his manager racing on to the pitch and jumping for joy. Osborn, a twenty-year-old graduate of the Forest academy, was named Sky TV's 'man of the match' and deservedly so.

As a consequence of past profligacy, Forest now found themselves penalized by a transfer embargo under the Financial Fair Play regulations intended to rein back the super rich clubs but, in practice, more severely restricting the operations of those of medium size. And hopes that the victory at Derby would spark a revival in fortunes were soon dashed. A midweek defeat at Fulham was followed on the last day of January with a 1-0 humbling by relegation battlers Millwall at the City Ground. It proved to be the last straw for owner and chairman Fawaz Al Hasawi and after a meeting between the two the next day Stuart Pearce left the club and another former Red Dougie Freedman became the seventh Forest manager since the summer of 2012.

With Pearce went the coaches he had appointed. Freedman named Lennie Lawrence, who had been with him at Palace and Bolton, as assistant manager. The sixty-seven-year-old had never played in the Football League but managed over 1,000 games beginning at Plymouth in 1978 and including time at Charlton Athletic, Middlesbrough, Bradford City, Luton Town, Grimsby and Cardiff City.

The chairman described relieving Pearce of his duties as 'the hardest footballing decision I have ever made.' Pearce had won ten, draw ten and lost twelve of his games in charge. Freedman, a forty-year-old Glaswegian, represented Scotland at schoolboy, Under-21 and senior levels. He joined Forest in 1998, and scored 23 goals in sixty-one starts and twenty-three substitute appearances. His other clubs were Barnet, Crystal Palace (two spells), Leeds (on loan) and Southend United, scoring a total of 160 goals in 524 league appearances. Freedman went back to Palace in March 2010 as assistant manager to Paul Hart with John Pemberton as first team coach. He was appointed manager in January 2011 and guided the Eagles away from the relegation zone. In October 2012 he was appointed manager of Bolton Wanderers, and led them from twentieth to seventh place in the Championship, missing out on the play-offs on the final day of the season. He left Bolton by mutual consent two years later.

∞

'You're not famous any more.' Even this taunt by visiting fans at the City Ground has just about died out. Forest, according to them, no longer rate that level of derision. Yet the club's achievements are not forgotten. They are still remembered throughout Europe. Jorg Jakob, editor-in-chief of Germany's leading football magazine *Kicker* proved as much in March 2013 with a special edition featuring the world's greatest clubs. Three pages were devoted to Forest. The article was illustrated with pictures of Clough and Taylor enjoying success together, John Robertson scoring the winning goal against Hamburg in the 1980 European Cup Final in Madrid, action shots of Tony Woodcock and Martin O'Neill, and portraits of Viv Anderson, Kenny Burns, Peter Shilton and, a later hero, Stuart Pearce. Forest's 'tree and river' badge was prominent on a poster insert highlighting the forty best clubs alongside the emblems of Real Madrid, Bayern Munich, Manchester United, Barcelona, Benfica, AC Milan, Penarol, FC Santos, Boca Juniors, Inter Milan, Juventus, Liverpool and Chelsea et al.

Manager Brian Clough was hailed as a genius but his players still feel they never got the recognition they deserved. On a scale of one to ten defender Kenny Burns gives his old boss a rating of nine. 'Cloughie, good as he was, the team was better – ten out of ten,' he insists.

Kenny and his team-mates might applaud the action Doug Freedman took when he was appointed Bolton's manager. Clough, at Derby, had ripped down pictures of past stars like Raich Carter, Peter Doherty, Sammy Crooks and Jack Stamps saying history begins now. Freedman took the opposite view. He drew on the past to inspire the present generation. He removed images of the current squad on display and replaced them with those of stars of the 40s, the 50s and the FA Cup finals. 'I only want pictures up when you've done something here,' he told his players. It was an idea he picked up on a visit to AC Milan. 'They only had pictures of players who had won European Cups on the wall,' he said. 'If you've lifted the European Cup, you go on the wall. I want the players to know the history of the club because that's building the spirit.'

Clough, Peter Taylor and the extraordinary players who made up their two European Cup-winning squads raised the level of expectation among subsequent owners and supporters alike to heights their successors would find unattainable. In terms of financial turnover, Forest are as much a mid-table Championship club off the pitch as they are on it.

A more realistic model than the exceptional, probably unrepeatable, Clough era is that provided in the late '40s and '50s by the impressive stewardship of the great Billy Walker. Clough bought a Second Division club a return ticket to the pinnacle of European success. Walker's Forest climbed from the Third Division South to the First Division and an FA Cup triumph, when that competition was regarded supreme in England, and on his retirement he left behind a club established in the top flight. What's more, he achieved this on a cash-strapped footing with home-grown players of the calibre of Bobby McKinlay, Tommy Wilson, Geoff Vowden and 'Flip' Le Flem supplemented by a handful of bargain buys including the likes of Jeff Whitefoot, Jim Barrett, Stewart Imlach and Billy Gray.

On bringing young players to the club, Freedman said he told parents their sons would be in an environment that offered them the best chance to become footballers and one that embraced education. 'We are not going to buy our way to the Premier League,' he said. 'We have to develop players and allow them to flourish. If I don't have a long-term objective then I'm not doing my job. I have to get the place ready for success.'

The restrictions of Financial Fair Play may help Forest to redevelop 'the Walker Way' with the emphasis on academy graduates.

Doug Freedman was introduced to the media as Forest's new manager at a low-key press conference at the City Ground on Tuesday 3 February. Without the owner who was in Kuwait on business, he was supported by John McGovern. Asked why Freedman had got the job, an uncomfortable-looking McGovern replied perhaps hastily that 'well, he was available.' Unruffled, the new manager came across well. He was open, confident, smiling and composed. At Crystal Palace he had to cope with a spell in administration. With Bolton his challenge was to address tens of millions of pounds worth of debt and cutting back the squad. A transfer embargo held no fears. Fawaz Al Hasawi had kept his word not to sell players and had rejected big bids for Henri Lansbury and Michail Antonio over the weekend. 'I told him that I would bring to the job passion, energy and enthusiasm,' Freedman said. He got off to a good start with a 3-2 victory at Brighton that left the Reds thirteen points from the play-off positions and ten from the drop zone.

Four days later a first home win under Freedman was marred by a serious knee injury to £5.5 million record signing and top scorer Assombalonga suffered just as he was in the act of shooting sixty-seven minutes into the match against Wigan. He had already scored his 15th goal of the season in the 3-0 victory making him one of the Championship's leading marksmen after twenty-nine matches. Surgery was successful but the twenty-two-year-old was ruled out for twelve months. It was also learned that Reid would miss the rest of the season.

Despite these setbacks, Freedman's Forest won eight, drew one and lost only two of his first eleven games in charge lifting them well clear of the relegation zone and to the fringe of the play-off places. A 2-1 defeat by promotion-chasing Wolves in front of a 27,000 crowd at the City Ground on Good Friday put the Reds out of the running. Promotion favourites Derby faltered in the home straight too and also failed to make the play-offs, ending eighth. Forest had taken four points out of six from them. Going up as champions were Bournemouth. Forest had beaten them home and away. Notts County, needing a win to stay in Division One, were 1-0 ahead at Gillingham when, with only minutes of the campaign to go, they conceded three goals and so descended to the League's lowest tier.

Undaunted by his depleted squad finishing fourteenth, the Forest manager talked about building a club fit to challenge for a top-six finish with a squad made up of talented young players such as Ben Osborn and Tyler Walker built around the likes of Michail Antonio, who had terrified opposition defenders with his strength and pace, and Henri Lansbury. Because of the transfer embargo it would also be about acquiring well-chosen loan players. Tyler, the eighteen-year-old son of Forest legend Des, scored his first senior goal in a 2-2 draw away to promotion hopefuls

Brentford on Easter Monday. 'He's an exciting prospect who can play for the club for a very long time and make the striker's role his own in the very near future,' said Freedman. 'All I'm going to do is polish him up and, with the environment I will create, I will make him into a very good player.' The manager brought in Leon Hunter, a thirty-three-year-old highly regarded player recruitment specialist from Stevenage. He was given the job title 'football co-ordinator' and briefed to operate at senior level. Gary Brazil would continue to look after all aspects of the academy.

Perhaps, almost by accident, in Freedman, with his respect for history and support of the academy, Fawaz had finally found the right manager for Forest. But the new man knew the score, 'This is a grand club of great expectations and limited patience,' he told the *Daily Mail*.

A Tree by a River

Football is a game of tomorrows.
Sir Geoff Hurst, 1966 Word Cup Final hat-trick hero

It's not about the name on the back of the shirt, it's about the badge on the front.
David Beckham

Nottingham is known the world over for the legend of Robin Hood but the city has many more strings to its bow. It's the unofficial capital of the East Midlands region with more than 640,000 residents in its conurbation. Had England's bid to stage the 2018 FIFA World Cup been successful, it is probable that Forest would have built a new stadium at the end of a River Trent walkway and linked to the city by a new bridge crossing near the National Water Sports Centre. The stadium would also have become the permanent home for the Women's FA Cup – a Wembley for Women. It would have staged FIFA World Cup matches in 2018 and the Women's World Cup in 2019. The England bid failed and at the end of 2010 FIFA announced that the finals would be in Russia. Nigel Doughty's dream faded and it was possibly then that his disenchantment began.

The majority of fans were not impressed by the prospect of a move to Gamston or to another suggested site near Clifton. Most wanted Forest to stay at the City Ground or if a new ground was the only option then somewhere nearer the city centre such as Eastside. Wherever or whatever is decided in the future, in its 150th anniversary year the club returned to its birthplace and spiritual home at Nottingham's second largest public park the Forest recreation ground located in the heart of the city. There Nottingham Forest in the Community, working in partnership with the City Council, has built and now operates a £1.8 million football and sports complex. It has full-size floodlit 3G (Third Generation Artificial Turf) and Astro turf pitches and a two-storey pavilion with reception, meeting and changing rooms.

As well as being a safe place for youngsters, the complex hosts a new Nottingham Forest Development Centre that will support the club's recruitment of talented young players and will provide a home for Nottingham Forest Ladies' Football Club. It is also used by local football teams, schools, colleges and universities. Appropriately in view of the shinney-playing founders, the facilities are available to hockey clubs like the Sikh Union.

It is twenty-five years since the first football in the community programme was launched at Nottingham Forest and in 2008 Graham Moran crossed the Trent after sixteen years with Notts County to become Forest's community director. Two years later Nottingham Forest in the Community became a registered charitable trust and Graham, Nottingham born and bred, was appointed its chief executive. It now has a staff of more than twenty and, commented Graham,

> We are especially proud of the fact that we have built up a community department that has grown so quickly and that is now so diverse in terms of it staff and the work it delivers. Our focus on education, training and employment of young people has been very rewarding with the satisfying progression of participants becoming volunteers and then finding full-time employment.

The Champions education centre was opened at the City Ground in 2012 and provides a high quality learning resource for the community and for Forest's young elite academy footballers. 'Over the years we have developed excellent working relationships with more than 100 primary and secondary schools in the city and county,' Graham said. 'Raising Aspirations' is a school programme designed to inform primary children about their learning and work options, think positively about their futures, set goals and work hard to achieve them. The 'Forest Factor' is national curriculum-based and 'Forest Factor Extra' includes football specific techniques and skills aimed at all genders and ability levels. There is also a BTEC Level 3 diploma in sport for sixteen to eighteen year olds interested in jobs within the sport and leisure industry. In one of the Forest in the Community's biggest projects, some five hundred young people completed the government-sponsored National Citizenship Service in 2014. They planned, resourced and delivered a wide range of social action projects benefiting the community including renovating homeless shelters and building a sensory garden for the blind.

Nottingham Forest in the Community is also developing its work overseas. African Adventures, with Forest star Andy Reid an ambassador, helps local people to work as community volunteers in Ghana with roles ranging from teaching in schools, working with under-privileged children to football coaching. A partnership with the College of Charleston, one of America's oldest academic institutions, has seen one of Forest in the Community's most successful projects, *Kicks*, delivered to deprived football mad Hispanic neighbourhoods in that city, where the first shot in the American Civil War was fired, along with Forest soccer schools across South Carolina. Charleston college students first came over to Nottingham in 2012 as part of their study abroad programme.

'Forest means so much to the community. That's why we do the work we do,' Graham said.

Nottingham won a three-way final with Manchester and Portsmouth to become in 2015 Sport England's first City of Football. As well as the title, the city received £1.6 million of National Lottery funding to transform football participation and become a test-bed for developing new ways of encouraging more people to play the game, especially fourteen to twenty-five-year-olds, women and girls, and those from black and minority ethnic backgrounds. The lessons learned will be shared so that the whole country can benefit. Phil Smith of Sport England praised the city's 'exciting and inventive' response to the challenge. 'Nottingham was simply the best,' he said. 'It was a terrific bid.'

Said Graham. 'With these key developments coming to fruition, it's certainly an exciting time for everybody at Nottingham Forest in the Community.'

∞

The Happy Forester was the first badge to appear on the Garibaldi red shirt. It was worn by the team that won the Third Division South title in 1950/51 with more victories (thirty) than in any other season in the club's history, scoring a record number of goals (110) and gaining more points (seventy) than ever before or since – equivalent to 100 under the present three points for a win system instead of the two points awarded at the time. Only forty goals were conceded – a difference of seventy, bettered only four times in the history of the Football League. The head and shoulders drawing of the Forester, with a feather in his hat, was adapted from a title-piece illustration on the Football Post's front pages. It was in green on a white background.

The shirts were plain red by the time Forest won promotion to the First Division in 1956/57 and then manager Billy Walker and vice-president Bill Pryor got their heads together to design a new badge. They settled on the Nottingham coat of arms with the lettering NFFC replacing the castle at the top of the city crest. It was worn on the shirts of the FA Cup winning team in 1959.

In March 1973 the club invited supporters to submit ideas for a new badge and a competition was launched with the Nottingham Evening Post. A prize of £25 was offered by Forest with the newspaper giving a £25 sports voucher for the best entry in an Under-18 section. On the closing date at the end of the month, 587 designs had been received from adults and 268 by juniors. One came from former star centre-forward Wally Ardron. His entry featured Nottingham lace and a Raleigh bicycle. The city was known for producing both, he reasoned, and anyway he had ridden a bike to training every day. Well it was an original idea. The winning design was by Mr. David Lewis, a lecturer in graphic art at Trent Polytechnic (now Nottingham Trent University).

The thousand-year-old Major Oak in Sherwood Forest was crowned England's Tree of the Year in 2015. The tree's branches spanning a 92-foot area are now propped up by steel poles. It was beaten to the European title by a 150-year-old oak that stands in the middle of a village football pitch in Estonia, and which, villagers claim, defied Stalin's tractors. Dylan Pugh's poem 'The Major Oak', written for a Newark and Sherwood District Council millennium poetry project and printed on Nottinghamshire library bookmarks, ends with these lines,

> And, though the heavy branches may hang low
> With memory of younger, greener years,
> Beneath the Forest sward its roots still grow,
> And carry all of Trentside's hopes and fears.

Aiming for simplicity and an emotive identity, Mr Lewis produced an iconic stylised image of a tree by a river. The crest can be printed red on white or white on red over the name Forest in capitals except for the lower case letter 'e' to add individuality to the word. After more than forty years, this strong official copyrighted badge is loved by supporters as the most appropriate symbol possible of their club and its unique history, representing both the Forest, its spiritual home, and the Trent by the banks of which its famous ground stands. The tree has long been associated with life, family, growth and strength. The river, too, is throughout the world recognised as a source of life, recreation, power and progress. May all these qualities be forever Forest's.

Bibliography

Arlott, John, *Concerning Soccer* (1952)

Anderson, Viv with Lynton Guest, *First Among Unequals* (2010)

John Ballard and Paul Suff, *The Dictionary of Football* (1999)

John Beckett (editor), *A Centenary History of Nottingham* (1997)

Garry Birtles, *My Magic Carpet Ride* (2010)

Melvyn Bragg, *12 Books That Changed The World* (2006)

Andreas Campomar, *iGolazo!* (2014)

B.O. Corbett (editor), *Annals of The Corinthian Football Club* (1906)

Marshall Cavendish (publisher), *The Book of Football* (weekly parts, six volumes, 1971/72)

Alfred Gibson and William Pickford, *Association Football and the Men Who Made* It (four volumes, 1906)

Brian Clough with John Sadler, *Walking On Water* (2002)

David Goldblatt, *The Game Of Our Lives* (2014)

Duncan Hamilton, *Provided You Don't Kiss Me* (2007)

Steve Hodge, *The Man With Maradona's Shirt* (2010)

Gary Imlach, *My Father And Other Working-Class Heroes* (2006)

N.L. Jackson, *Association Football* (1899)

Roy Keane, with Roddy Doyle *The Second Half* (2014)

Sheila Mason, *Nottingham Lace 1760s-1950s* (1994, revised 2010)

John McGovern, *From Bo'ness to the Bernabeu* (2012)

Duncan McKenzie with David Saffer, *The Last Fancy Dan* (2009)

David McVay, *Forest's Cult Heroes* (2007)

Jim Murphy, *The 10 Football Matches That Changed The World* (2014)

J.B. Priestley, *Delight* (1949), *English Journey* (1934), *The Good Companions* (1929)

Danny Rhodes, *Fan* (2014)

John Robertson with John Lawson, *Super Tramp* (2011)

Daniel Taylor, *Deep into the Forest* (2005)

A.J. Turner (editor), *Forest, The Hundred Years Story* (1965)

Ken Smales, *Forest, the first 125 years* the official statistical record (1991)
Billy Walker, *Soccer in the Blood* (1960)
Jonathan Wilson, *Nobody Ever Says Thank You* (2011)
Percy M. Young, *A History of British Football* (1968)

Newspapers and Periodicals

The Nottingham Post, The Daily Telegraph, The Times, The Guardian, Daily Mail, The Blizzard, When Saturday Comes, World Soccer, Kicker (Germany)

Acknowledgements

I am not alone among recent historians writing about Nottingham Forest Football Club in owing a debt of gratitude to its former secretary Ken Smales, who died aged eighty-seven in March, 2015, for his invaluable statistical history first published in 1991. From an anonymous Victorian writer I learned that the early Foresters played football together long before the club was formally established in 1865 and that the nineteenth-century Reds were even then known as 'The Trickies'. Others whose work has been helpful include the late Arthur Turner, Rob Jovanovic and Philip Soar.

Thanks also to John McGovern, Chris Key and all at Nottingham Forest, to Nick Clifford and the Lymbery family, Mike Forman and the Forman family, and to Jenna Whittle and Phillip Clement at Amberley Publishing. Special thanks to my wife, Barbara, for her patience and support.